Timberline, U.S.A.

*High-Country Encounters from
California to Maine*

Timberline, U.S.A.

High-Country Encounters from California to Maine

Donald Mace Williams

UTAH STATE UNIVERSITY PRESS
Logan, Utah
2003

Utah State University Press
Logan, Utah 84322-7800

Typography by Ian Hatch
Maps by Brent Castillo
Chapter heading illustration from photo of the trail to South Arapaho Peak
  by Randy Abbott

Manufactured in the United States of America
Printed on acid-free paper

Library of Congress Cataloging-in-Publication Data

Williams, Donald Mace.
  Timberline, U.S.A. : high-country encounters from California to Maine
  / Donald Mace Williams.
      p. cm.
Includes bibliographical references (p.   ).
  ISBN 0-87421-571-4 (pbk. : alk. paper)
  1. United States—Description and travel. 2. United States—History, Local.
  3. Mountains—United States. 4. Timberline—United States. 5. Mountain
life—United States. 6. Williams, Donald Mace—Travel—United States.
  7. Hiking—United States. I. Title.

  E169.04.W545 2003
  917.3'0943—dc22
                                        2003017640

To Bob

CONTENTS

PREFACE

My main hope in writing this book, I suppose, was to show what it is about the treeless parts of high mountains that awes, attracts, and frightens me and millions of other hikers. Also, I wanted to see how, in each of the major ranges of the lower forty-eight states that get above timberline—the Rockies, the Sierra Nevada, the Cascades, and the northern Appalachians—the high country is different from that of the other three ranges. For both those purposes, I hiked.

People were another part of my research. When I met other hikers, I asked them to tell me about themselves and why they were up there. But I couldn't keep them and me standing on the trail talking for too long when we all had to be somewhere else before dark. If they seemed especially interesting—as many of them did, mountain hikers by and large being a thoughtful as well as adventurous lot—I phoned them later to get their stories in detail.

In spare time from my job in the low country, I read about high altitude and its effects. I interviewed some of the scientists who specialize in those effects, often finding that they were explorers and adventurers as well as scientists. And I looked up accounts of people who, as far back as Colonial days, hiked and climbed, sometimes with grim results, in the same mountains I had hiked in. I found myself writing nearly as much about people as about mountains, though always with the high country at the centers of their stories.

I have often envied people who live in the mountains and can climb to timberline whenever they like. My jobs have usually been a long way from mountains. Still, as a child of the Depression I doubted that I would be happy living where every time I looked out the window I would feel on vacation. What would I have done to earn such a life? But I felt only moderate guilt as I took my research hikes, knowing that I had to get back to my newspaper job in Kansas when I had used up my vacation time. Those hikes were in the summers of 1991 and 1992, when I was in my early sixties, and as I set out I wondered whether hiking at high altitudes would still exhilarate me as it had in my youth. The answer, I found, took some examination to get at. Here and there in this book I have reflected on the results.

With whatever modifications, exhilaration still comes upon me in the mountains, as I am often reminded because now that I have retired and moved to the Texas Panhandle, only four hours from the wonderful Sangre de Cristo Range in New Mexico, I hike above timberline whenever I can. The effort does grow, year by year, but as it does, the guilt diminishes.

Many thanks to those who, on or off the trail, talked with me for this book and are mentioned in it. For help of other kinds, I am especially grateful to Guy Boulton, who offered me not only his keen perceptions as a reader of the manuscript but also a bit of observation without which the book would not exist, and to Susan Raihofer. Thanks also to Richard Phelan, to my son, Andrew M. Williams, and to my wife, Nell, for valuable suggestions and, in the last instance, patience.

Canyon, Texas
March 2003

PART I

The Rocky Mountains

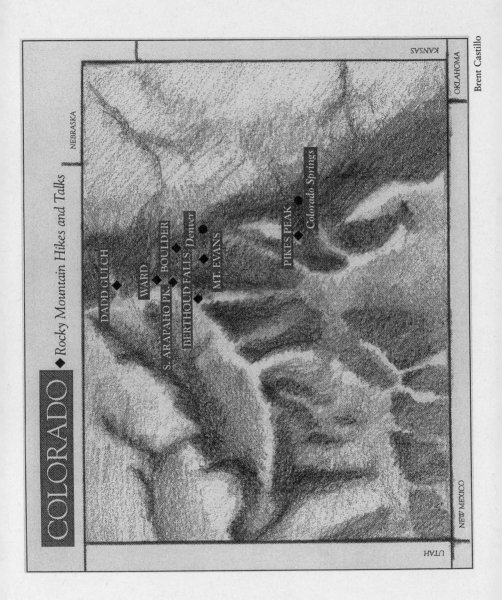

COLORADO ◆ Rocky Mountain Hikes and Talks

DADD GULCH

WARD

S. ARAPAHO PK.

BOULDER

BERTHOUD FALLS

Denver

MT. EVANS

PIKES PEAK

Colorado Springs

NEBRASKA

KANSAS

OKLAHOMA

NEW MEXICO

UTAH

Brent Castillo

CHAPTER ONE

Timberline, the level on a mountain at which summers become too cold for trees to grow, has fascinated me since I was a child. At first it was because the name resounded with adventure, especially as uttered by my older brother, Bob, whose awe of the wilderness infected me early. Later, when I lived in Denver in my midteens, hiking above timberline on weekends and sometimes studying the alpine displays in the Denver Museum of Nature & Science, I came to appreciate also the strangeness of timberline, the separateness from the land where most people lived. Foothills, I learned, become mountains when they attain timberline, and from there up, the country has its own climate.

A different climate means a different world. Flowers above timberline grow practically on the ground instead of on long stems like some of their low-country cousins. Animals that don't exist in the low country perch on rocks and yip at hikers. The air is so thin that a mile looks like across the street, and so lacking in atmospheric pressure, at least in the central and southern Rockies and the High Sierra, that you can dip a finger into boiling water. (Timberline is lower in the Cascades and northern Rockies and lower still in the northern Appalachians; the boiling-water trick is not a good idea in those places.) You can actually feel the thinness of the air—you move more lightly than you do at home in Boston or San Francisco or Dallas or, in my case, Wichita. Most of all, timberline has the charm of danger— its weather being capricious and violent—and of exclusiveness, at least when it has to be attained on foot and with effort.

I had not experienced timberline for a few years when, on a damp July day, starting a vacation, I pulled into Denver after the long westward drive across the Kansas and Colorado plains. Having anticipated a view that would arouse pleasant memories, I found myself disappointed. I should have known that would happen. The Front Range of the Rockies, as seen from Denver, doesn't often look as clear and dominant to a visitor as it does to someone who has been in that vicinity awhile. Though the peaks rise nine thousand feet above town, they're also fifty miles away. If you live in Denver, especially if you sometimes go up high and walk a few miles so that you get the size of the country into your bones, you learn to interpret the view. You convert apparent inches to yards, translate gullies into gorges, and remember that what looks like grass is probably head-high willow scrub. Living somewhere else for a year or two strips away the interpretative faculty along with your adjustment to altitude, and when you go back, your eye has to learn to multiply all over again. My eye was rusty. I saw a distant line of sky-colored mountains melting into a clabbery buildup of clouds. It was uninspiring, but I had been up there enough to hope that sunshine and reeducation would bring back the old excitement.

This was the start of a string of trips I planned to make to timberline and above in the four major ranges of the contiguous states. I had hiked above timberline in each of the ranges, all the way from forty years to two or three years before, and I wanted to see if in my early sixties I still had a thrill in me that high places could pull out. For that matter, I wanted to see if I could still get up to high places. Wichita is five hundred miles from Denver and four thousand feet lower, and though I tried to keep in shape by walking a lot and by doing laps on the back stairs at the newspaper where I worked, I knew that nothing gets you in shape for hiking in the mountains like hiking in the mountains. A dozen times or more, I had tried to live close to mountains, but I always came around to the same fact: jobs grow best in low, flat places. If I had taken an inferior job to be near mountains, I would have felt like a ski bum. Now, with vacation time to use up, I was starting a brief, fully hedged dropout from the Protestant ethic, which also seems to grow best a long way below timberline.

I checked into a motel in Lakewood and phoned Paul Fretwell, a young Briton who had just flown in. He was staying in Boulder, and he planned to climb South Arapaho Peak, where, fourteen months before, he and two friends from England had been caught in a frightful early-summer blizzard. As the only survivor of the experience, Paul had come back for his first look at the peak since that time, and during our phone conversation he invited me to go with him as soon as the weather permitted. While I waited for the weather, I drove to the Western History Department of the Denver Public Library to do some reading. I parked at Thirteenth and Bannock and walked the couple of blocks to the library. I was disappointed in the air. When I lived in Denver, it had buoyed me onto my toes as I walked, but now, because of the rain, it lay over me inertly like Long Island or Arkansas air. At least it was cool air, a nice change from the hundred-degree days in Wichita. But I had been disappointed so far in Denver's failure to look or feel like its old self. Maybe it was because I was not my old self. Maybe it was because Denver had changed. The suburbs had tripled in size and gracelessness since my college days there in the late 1940s.

Even in those days, Bob and I had looked on Denver mainly as an obstacle between us and the mountains. We didn't have a car, but buses and streetcars took us close enough to the mountains to permit weekend hikes. Usually we stuck to the foothills. But if we could make it up through the ponderosa pines, the Douglas fir and aspen belt, and finally the stands of symmetrical Engelmann spruce or boring lodge-pole pines to some little summit just above timberline, we felt that we had accomplished something, and we ran down the hills to the interurban line in Golden and rode home satisfied. Timberline gave us a chance to show our power. Sitting on a rock on the tundra and looking down, out, and up to towns and aspen groves and distant snow-fields, we felt as if we had planted flags on all we could see. We would have become timberline addicts if we had had the time and money.

Timberline fixes are more or less readily available to millions of addicts and potential addicts in the lower forty-eight states. The main ranges with timberlines are the Sierra Nevada (California), the Cascades (Oregon, Washington, and northern California), the Rockies (New Mexico, Colorado, Wyoming, Montana, Utah, and Idaho), and the northern Appalachians (Maine, New Hampshire, Vermont, and New York). The Olympics of Washington and the Wallowas of eastern Oregon are tall enough and have extensive enough spreads of tundra or semitundra—covering forty peaks in the Wallowas, according to Stephen F. Arno's *Timberline: Mountain and Arctic Forest Frontiers*—to qualify as main ranges by many standards, though not in comparison to their nearest neighbors; I was sorry not to be able to include them in my plans, but I had only so much vacation time. In northern

Arizona, the San Francisco Peaks stick up out of the trees, as
Charleston Peak in southern Nevada and several mountains and small
ranges farther north in the state also do, where there are trees for them
to stick out of. The range most strongly challenging the requirement
that real mountains must be above timberline is the Great Smokies in
Tennessee. The Smokies do have their own climate, as the wide belts of
spruce and balsam fir toward their summits reveal. Still, they lack a
crown of tundra to look distinctive from miles away and to give hikers a view with no trees in the way. That view probably has as much
as anything to do with making us feel that until we outclimb the trees,
we are not really up.

A climber's break through the tree line is sometimes also a break
into a furious wind. At timberline the atmosphere kicks free of its evergreen hobbles. When you step out of the trees into the stands of knee-
high to head-high krummholz—the "crooked wood" that survives in
dwarf form above the limit of full-sized trees—the wind is likely to
ambush you as if you had walked into a swift-running river of air. That
can be exhilarating, whether it happens at 4,500 feet on the slopes of
Mount Washington in New Hampshire or at 12,000 feet on Wheeler
Peak in New Mexico. It can also be dangerous; that is part of the exhilaration; the skies above any of our timberlines can produce storms as
sudden and devastating as the one that hit Paul Fretwell's party. The
top of Mount Washington, 6,288 feet above sea level, is the windiest
spot in the world, or such of the world as has anemometers; the wind
has reached 231 miles an hour there, and it averages 35 year-round.
On Pikes Peak in Colorado, nearly eight thousand feet higher than
Mount Washington, the midwinter wind blows at an average of
twenty-seven miles an hour. Running air reacts to obstacles or the lack
of them as running horses do: it goes slower or faster. On bare ground
it rips along; Teflon plains would be intolerably windy. But air clings
to air; if something drags at its lower layers, those hold back the layers above them. On alpine tundra, the impediments to wind consist
only of pebbles and rocks, grass, miniature flowers, and the peaks and
ridges themselves, with miles of open space between.

Apart from its velocity, the air at high altitude feels different
because it *is* different. With less atmospheric pressure to force its mol-
ecules together, it is literally thinner than low-country air. It resists you
less. The thinness and lightness change the way of life up high.

Homemakers use high-altitude recipes or learn to adapt low-altitude ones; when we moved to Denver from Fort Worth in the 1960s, my wife put less baking powder and soda in her biscuits to keep them from rising three inches and then flopping, and she found she couldn't cheat on soaking pinto beans overnight before cooking them: water boils at only 202 degrees Fahrenheit in Denver. (And at 194 degrees in Leadville, at a little over 10,000 feet, and at 187 on top of Pikes Peak.) Filling stations sell eighty-five-octane gasoline in Denver; it works as well there in most cars as eighty-seven-octane does in Wichita. At Leadville a still lower octane would be fine, if it were available. But midwestern drivers who fill up in Colorado may hear tap dancers in their engines when they start home across the plains.

At 5,000 feet, standard tennis balls bounce like Superballs; at 10,000 feet, like super Superballs. Balls designed for altitude don't entirely make up the difference; players in Denver adopt a serve-and-volley game, avoiding backcourt action. "You can't keep it on the court," a tennis-playing friend says. "It just keeps sailing." As the Colorado Rockies and their guest opponents know, altitude is good for home-run hitters and fast-ball pitchers but bad for curve-ballers. It encourages world-record high jumps, long jumps, and hundred-meter dashes, but it cuts time from mile races because after a lap or so, oxygen starvation cancels out the ease of slipping through the thin air. Users of hang gliders have to run farther and faster on takeoff to make up for the feebler lift. Clarinetists have to scrape their reeds thin, and they find that, though the tone responds quickly to the breath, it lacks depth. The effects of altitude on people's insides provide material for ceaseless study: in the summer, there are always scientists on top of Colorado mountains testing the blood chemistry of people on stationary bicycles so they can learn more about the body's adjustments and maladjustments to lack of oxygen.

When I was in my teens and living in Denver, I never got mountain sickness on a hike, and neither did my brother, who is four and a half years older. It wasn't because we were young; boys in and near their teens are more, not less, susceptible to the illnesses of altitude than older men, or so the high-altitude physiologists say. And we not only hiked far above timberline, which in the Front Range of the Rockies begins at 11,000 feet or higher; we slept there, too. That is the worst thing you can do. The breathing mechanism of a person unaccustomed to thin air gets confused during sleep, gulping air awhile and then lying passive long enough to frighten listeners. The next morning the hiker wakes up wearier than before, his brain and muscles oxygen hungry, his blood sludgy with the additional red cells it has manufactured to carry oxygen. To circulate the thickened blood, the heart has to work harder.

Blood thickening is such a problem among old people who have spent their lives in Leadville, Colorado, the highest incorporated city in the United States, and have finally developed the breathing difficulties and fatigue of chronic mountain sickness that they regularly have to get bled. The blood banks in Leadville, it is said, never run short. Most elderly Leadville residents who smoke or who have inhaled too much rock dust in the mines come down with chronic mountain sickness. When that happens, their doctor tells them to move somewhere lower, like Denver. Move down from the mountains? Most longtime Leadville residents would rather die. They stay, and they go on oxygen, eventually twenty-four hours a day. From the figures I got from Dr. John Perna, the Lake County health officer, Leadville houses must be full of old folks pulling oxygen tanks from room to room on wheels. Mostly their lung capacity was already reduced by tobacco or silicosis, and the additional hardship of the thin air has finally become too much for them. Only about one-in-ten residents with no other lung or heart problems gets chronic mountain sickness, Dr. Perna said. Of the smokers and the former mine workers with damaged lungs, two out of three do.

I talked on the phone once with Henry Bentert, a seventy-six-year-old man, born and raised in Leadville, who smoked for many years and had worked outdoors at the Climax Molybdenum Mine, twenty-four miles north of Leadville, where the wind blew waste material at him off the tailing pond. Carrying a fifty-pound pack, he used to hike all over the alpine tundra to hunt and fish. At seventy he collapsed on a hike. When I interviewed him, he was in the extended-care unit at St. Vincent's Hospital in Leadville. He had tried going down to Denver to live, he said; he didn't like it. If he could be sure he would feel a lot better in Denver, I said, would he consider staying there? "If I was maybe forty years old, I might consider it," he said. "But I've had enough. What's a year or two?"

I asked him what it was about the high country that made him want to stay there, regardless. "Well, it's my home," he said. Sure, I said, but what else? "I love the mountains," he said. Expressing sentiment was clearly hard for him. After a moment he said, "And I like this view I have, where I can see Mount Elbert and Mount Massive." His accent was northern blue collar. I imagined him sitting up in bed, lanky and angular, blue eyed and with a couple of days' growth of beard. I told him I didn't blame him for staying. "My apartments always faced the mountains, too," he said. Another patient at St. Vincent's, Dorothea Schroeder, had been on oxygen day and night for ten years. She was eighty-one. She and both her parents were born in Leadville. Once she went to Chicago to live. She stayed six months. "I really missed the mountains," she told me. I was glad to know that she, like Bentert, had a room with a view.

In Leadville a room has a view if it has a window. I saw the town for the first time on a three-day summer weekend. When I arrived, it was late afternoon and, for the moment, cloudy. At that altitude, any weather is likely to be momentary. I walked across the motel parking lot to get my boots out of the car and saw a dark cloud bank to the south with what I took to be puffs of white cloud pushing through like hernias. Then I found a faint outline in the haze above the flecks and realized that they were not cloud but snow. The outline was Mount Elbert, the highest mountain in the state, as I was told later by the high-school girl at the counter. Everybody in Leadville seems to know the names of at least that peak and Mount Massive, the second highest in the state. Elbert tapers to an elegant peak, more pretty than magnificent. But Massive, to its north and west, blocks off enough sky to be a range of its own; I couldn't decide which of the heaps above its complex of slopes, bowls, cliffs, and snowfields was the top.

I stood by my car, searching the peaks. A few drops of cold rain fell on my shoulders while sunlight thrust between the cloud bank and the tops of the mountains and streamed over me. I got the boots out of the trunk, turned back toward the motel, and stopped dead. A brilliant rainbow hung over Leadville, one end vividly purpling the old buildings of the business section. It lasted maybe two minutes. I watched it dissolve, then finished unpacking, drove a quarter mile in sunshine to a Mexican restaurant for supper, and emerged at the last instant of sundown. A sheaf of peach-colored rays shot like arrows around the end of a black cloud bank, tinting everything they touched—as striking a display as the rainbow had been. I drove back to the motel and stepped out of the car. All was gray. The sun had set, and Mount Massive with its snowfields seemed to have jumped into the edge of town. It looked far more distinct than it had a minute earlier when the sun was setting behind it. Odd. I went to bed. The rain was beating heavily against my window.

That experience of the changeability of high-altitude weather came to mind as I passed that showery day in Denver. I couldn't work Leadville into my six days of vacation, plus two weekends, on this trip, but if the rain pulled back, I intended to go to higher places yet, among mountains almost as grand as Elbert and Massive. All I had seen of the mountains that day was the treeless hogbacks around Golden. With clouds shutting off the mountains, I had trouble re-creating them in my mind and imagining myself among them. I was afraid that when I was finally there, all would seem bland, like Denver on that day. (What I was really afraid of was evidence that I had started a slide through the blahs of age.)

After I finished at the library, I drove back to my motel in Lakewood and called Paul Fretwell again for final instructions, which it was his prerogative to give. Eight o'clock the next morning, he said, at the Buckingham Campground. I packed a thermal blanket, a wool muffler, extra wool socks, and United States Geological Survey topographical maps into my red daypack before I went to bed. The motions stirred only a little of the old anticipation.

After reading newspaper stories the previous year about Paul's experience, I had written him at Lancaster University in England and asked for as many details of the fatal hike as he was willing to give me. He replied in a long letter on both sides of punched notebook paper, saying at the end, "It has been good to go through it all again." His experience in the Rockies shows the ferocity of timberline weather. With his friends, David Paddon and Katherine Choules, both of whom, like him, were members of the hiking club at Lancaster University, Paul set out at 4:30 A.M. on June 1, 1990, to hike from the trailhead at Buckingham Campground to the summits of North and South Arapaho Peaks. They had arrived at the campground only at midnight and had slept in the old brown Toyota station wagon they had borrowed from their hosts in Boulder. For breakfast they heated a can of chow mein on a camp stove.

So far they may sound like college kids out for a lark. No: they were experienced, well-equipped mountaineers. Paul had climbed all over the mountains of the Lake Country, Scotland, and Wales, though his still stronger interest was in caving. He and Katherine had, in fact, just returned from a caving trip to New Mexico. They were friends, not sweethearts. She and David were twenty-one; Paul was still nineteen. He was tall and slender, quiet, and funny—I learned about him in phone talks during the subsequent year with his hostess in Boulder, Joan Frisch. He had acquired a nickname when someone had misunderstood his name on the phone and addressed a letter to him as Mr. Footleg. He could draw and even sew; he made himself a fleece mountain suit in blue, green, yellow, and red with "Footleg" down each leg. His friend Dave was similarly tall and slender and even quieter, a regular at the Tuesday night meetings of the Presbyterian youth group of the University of Colorado during the year when he and Paul were students there. Katy was a violinist and had spent time camping on a glacier in Chile and building a bridge over a crevasse in connection with some kind of help-your-neighbor organization.

The first of June seemed a good time for them to climb the icy slopes in the Indian Peaks Wilderness Area, northwest of Denver, but even so, they needed to get to the steep part before the sun had softened and destabilized the snow. They started their hike in darkness and deep snow. The climb with ice axes and crampons up a pitch called North Star II took longer than they had expected because the chow mein or something had made Dave sick. He vomited twice and felt better. But it was a quarter after four in the afternoon when they reached the top of the north peak, 13,502 feet above sea level and about two thousand feet above timberline. On the summit, they tied Dave's Union Jack flag to a ski pole, took photographs, and set off across the ridge to South Arapaho Peak. The ridge, about six-tenths of a mile long, is fairly narrow; it made Katy "a little unnerved," Paul said, and he helped her. The weather had been fine all day, and although Paul saw some storm clouds in the distance, the wind was blowing them away from the climbers. Nonetheless, Paul said,

we had just finished the difficult part of the ridge when suddenly the weather changed from sun to complete white-out. The wind started gusting and we hurried to complete the ridge and get down into the valley. Suddenly I felt my back being stung by hailstones. I then realized that this was impossible as I had a big

pack on. It was electricity in the air. I could feel it crackling
behind my ears, and when my ice axe which was in my hand
was close to the rock it hummed. I yelled to the others, who
could also now feel it and we ran blind down off the side of the
ridge to get to a safe level, and then lay down hoping that we
would not get hit by lightning. We heard thunder and found it
was safe to get up again. The wind was howling now and we
had hardly gone any way before the electricity built up again.
We lay down again until it passed, then found a rock overhang
which was a little sheltered from the storm. I am now aware
that such shelters are extremely dangerous in thunder storms
because the lightning striking the rock tends to spark across the
gap at the mouth of such shelters, and we were in that spark
gap. We lay there for a while and twice within five minutes the
lightning struck some rocks about 15 feet from us. I saw a
bright orange streak and heard a loud explosion, along with a
pungent smell of burnt rock and ozone.

The lightning stopped, though the snow kept falling hard. During
the half-hour wait in the shelter, the hikers put on the thermal suits they
had packed. They crawled back to the ridge and then from rock to rock,
feeling their way, unable to see the difference between the snowy ground
they were covering and Arapaho Glacier, several hundred feet below.
After a while they found they were on top of South Arapaho Peak,
13,397 feet. "The only reason we knew we were there," Paul wrote, "is
that we found a metal plaque explaining all the other mountains you
should be able to see." They started down, guessing at the way and trying to avoid gullies because the deep snow in them might slide. The
steepness of the rocky slope forced them into one anyway, and Paul led
Katy with a ski pole; the wind was blowing up the gully at a hundred
miles an hour, by Paul's estimate, and had practically blinded her. The
two young men, having ski goggles, could see a little.

When the gully became too steep to manage, they traversed to a
parallel one, which also turned sharply steeper. Unable to climb out
and frightened because Katy was showing signs of hypothermia, they
lay on their stomachs, heads uphill, and slid, braking with their ice
axes. They quickly lost control. Paul's axe was torn away by the violence of the descent. He felt himself falling, then slid again, bounced off

rocks, and stopped. When he got up, his knee bruised, he saw nothing of his friends and could not rouse them with his shouts. After a while he saw a light below and managed to get to it without falling. The other two had landed together. Katy "seemed a little delirious," and

> Dave was badly injured. He lay there groaning and had blood and ice around his face. He was not responding to me. It was obvious that he would not make it and I tried to get Katy into her climbing harness so that I could tie her and the packs to a rock . . . I went to check on Dave and found he had slipped off into the darkness. That was the last time we saw him.

Paul tried to help Katy down the slope but lost her and slid again, out of control, a long way. "I put my arms over my head to protect it and tried to get my feet below me so I could use my heels as brakes. Several times my heels suddenly dug in and I found myself tumbling, hitting the ground again with a thud. I remember hitting rocks with my back and it jarring me to the extent that I saw sparks across my vision." But except for bruises, he wasn't hurt. He anchored himself to a rock to keep from sliding again and called for Katy. After a quarter of an hour, she answered; she had somehow made her way down to him. The grade had lessened by then. He went on down, leading her by the hand and constantly talking to her. Whenever he stopped, she said, "Don't leave me"—she could neither see nor feel him. The danger had concentrated Paul's powers of analysis and decision. "This," he said, "proved very useful for survival, but made it difficult to comfort Katy. She was getting more and more delirious from hypothermia and began saying things like 'I'm dying, aren't I.'"

They came to a boulder field, and when they had made their way through the worst part of it, Katy crawled into the shelter of a large boulder. "She said she wanted to carry on, but when I tried to get her to move she would not. Then she would say she wanted to carry on again and it went on like this. I tried to shelter her and eventually she lost consciousness." Shivering violently, Paul slept, woke with the wind howling, and slept again, over and over. At 4:30 A.M., it was growing light. He looked at Katy. She was dead. Paul threw out all but the essential contents of his pack and hiked the three miles to the station wagon in three hours through a constant ground blizzard, on one stretch repeatedly breaking through snow-covered ice into water up to his thighs. He shoved the deep snow off the car and drove in a daze to the Frisches' house in Boulder. No one was home. He went in, phoned the sheriff's office and the Rocky Mountain Rescue Group, and spent the rest of the morning directing searchers by phone to the two bodies. In Boulder, thirty miles from the Arapaho Peaks and eight thousand feet lower, it had rained a trace—that was all.

Paul signed his letter Footleg, with his proper name in parentheses and with small ink drawings of a foot and a hairy shank, separated to form a rebus. When I talked to him on the phone from the motel, he sounded detached but not somber. I was eager to meet him.

The computerized motel phone burbled at me at 5:30 A.M. on Sunday. I sat up and put on hiking clothes, the wool inner socks soft and warm and immediately conforming to my feet; nothing else feels as good as wool. I drank canned tomato juice and ate oatmeal cookies from home and one of the half-dozen ripe bananas I had also brought, which had thoroughly smelled up the room. I had put a couple of bananas into my pack, too, along with more cookies, some peanut-butter cheese crackers from the market down the street, tomato juice in small cans, and some pocket-size boxes of raisins. Except for the pop-top cans and the bananas, which I had never taken on a hike before, the trail food was like that of my teens.

The understanding with Paul was that if the weather was bad, we would stay low and look at the flowers in the subalpine meadows. It was sprinkling as I drove to Golden and west up Clear Creek Canyon, but although the foothills blocked my view of the mountains, the sky above where they should be looked encouragingly light. I was prepared to enjoy the drive in any case; part of the pleasure of timberline is getting there, and I have loved the eastern foothills of the Rockies for many years. At first the hills along U.S. Highway 6 were bare for a long way up, but as the road climbed, the evergreen stands at the top began dropping farther down the slopes. Soon they were funneling into the arroyos, following them down for the hint of moisture in them and then pooling up in clumps at the bottom, along the creek. The trees constituted the lower fringe of the belt of mostly ponderosa-pine timber that tells people escaping the Eastern Slope cities, "Now you're on the way up."

It was still early; my car was one of the few on the road. When I rounded a bend, I saw a mule deer buck and doe standing at the right side of the pavement. They sprang up the rocky slope as I approached. In Black Hawk, a restored mining town with fish-scale houses and an old hotel, one house had a donkey in a pen at the back, looking old enough to be a link across the years of decay between the mining days and the tourist boom. The sun had come out, shining between clouds. The road wound and wound. Suddenly I saw a peak above timberline with a spot of snow on it, the first real mountain of the trip. Then, around another bend, the whole central part of the Front Range appeared—red-gray rocks and patches of snow with wisps of tawny cloud behind the summits. I singled out a long, nearly level ridge well above timberline. As Russell Hayes, a professor and mountaineer, had reminded me the year before, there is a special exhilaration in walking on flat ground above timberline. Looking up, I caught myself taking a deep breath in anticipation of being there.

CHAPTER TWO

From Eldora, altitude 8,700 feet, it took me eighteen minutes to drive the five miles along the gouged, rocky road that led to the trailhead. I fretted about being late, but the silver Honda with a MEEOW license plate that Paul had described wasn't among the dozen cars in the parking lot. It came along after a few minutes, and I met my day's companions: Joan Frisch, who was in her fifties, with short blond hair and an immediately apparent vitality; Megan Chanter, Paul's pixieish girlfriend, also from Lancaster University; and Paul, as described: very tall, very slender. He had a fragile chin and a look of anachronistic innocence. We slipped on our packs and started up the trail. The altitude at the campground was 10,121 feet; I felt winded immediately and noticed that Joan, too, was breathing hard. Not the youngsters. She and I talked in phrases chopped up by breaths, they in regular sentences. What they were saying, though, wasn't always evident to me. Megan finally had to spell "Hair-uh-ford," the city she was from. "Oh," I said, "like the cattle"; did they have whiteface cattle there? "We've go' all sorts of colors of ca'-ul," she said. Delightful. Later, when I told her and Paul that I had an interview scheduled with a ski bum, it occurred to me that the term might mean "ski arse" to them.

The trail paralleled the North Fork of Middle Boulder Creek, which we could hear rushing several hundred feet below. The going was easy at this stage of the climb and day. Below us and across on the far slope, the valley was covered with a dense stand of Engelmann spruce, each tree slender and tapered—an ideal, beautiful forest. Flowers grew from knee to waist high all around us. It had been a good flower year, Joan told me, and we were hitting it at its peak. We saw purple delphinium, its blossoms hanging like bells; big bright sunflowers with

16

vertical disks, fresher than the sunflowers that grew wild all over Kansas; columbines, pale blue and creamy white, both showy and delicate, like pretty girls' party skirts; paintbrush; fireweed; dozens of others, more than I could describe, much less identify. When you looked upslope into a stand of flowers, they seemed head high. Everybody, including me, exclaimed over the display, and yet I felt a shade disappointed. When I was in my teens, living in the foothills near Colorado Springs, I saw flowers so thick on one southwest-facing slope that a daddy longlegs could have crossed the field on a catwalk of petals. So it seemed in my memory.

As we climbed, a long white cascade came into view across the valley—falling, Joan said, out of Diamond Lake. We could hear it. "'And the wild cataract leaps in glory,'" I said. (No response. Who reads Tennyson these days?) We were in the Indian Peaks Wilderness Area, established only thirteen years before. It covers 70,894 acres and suffers 110,000 visitors a year, all of them on foot or horse since no vehicles are allowed, not even leg-powered mountain bikes. Of course, foot traffic also harms the wilderness. Forty years ago not many of us worried about what our boots were doing to nature. But forty years ago not many people hiked. That was part of the pleasure.

Paul volunteered that when he had come up here the previous year, at the start of June, the snow was so deep it was hard to find the trail. I had held off, planning to broach the subject of his experience only later and with gentle questions. I needn't have. "Paul," Joan said as we looked upslope to steep terrain, "was this the snow chute you came down?" "I'm pretty sure it is," he said. "Yeah. Yeah, that is the one." He was looking at the place where he had nearly died, but he might have been talking about the route of some everyday hike. He showed us a streak of snow on the west face of North Arapaho Peak. That was his party's route to the top. "We thoroughly enjoyed it," he said. One reason he had survived the storm that hit later, he thought, was that he had eaten a lot of high-energy food, which had fueled his violent shivering during the night next to the boulder. Katy had been unable to eat by then. Paul thought also that psychology had been part of survival— that Katy's mental state had as much to do with her death as her physical condition.

It was a pleasure to observe the young people together. Megan could not have been taller than five feet, one. She had red-blond hair, blue eyes, and a skin that flared instantly to red in the high-altitude gusts and subsided just as quickly to white in the lulls. She seemed self-deprecating in all things. Like Paul, she had a camera with her, but it was one, she made clear, that does it all for you. (His was a complicated-looking Nikon, and he had brought more than one lens.) She was an English and music-history major at Lancaster; she had chosen music history, she said, because it didn't require much performing. Her English had a lilt like Norwegian; when she and Paul kidded, the lilt kept breaking into laughter. They kidded all the time. She grabbed his pack strap from behind, trying to catch a ride; he stopped and pretended to push her out in front of him where she would have to supply her own power; they laughed. When we got higher, something impelled him to shove her into a patch of limber-pine krummholz. She shrieked obligingly. Sometimes they held hands. He would say something, and she would aim a play slap at him, or as near him as she could reach.

When we came to the boulder where Katy died, at the foot of a rock slide, Paul said, answering a question from Joan, "We stumbled getting through, because we didn't want to try to climb over the rocks." Half a minute later, he and Megan were talking lightly about the trail. Then Megan was giggling about something Paul had done or said. Their amorous horseplay seemed to me like new life springing up from soil where death had been. But how innocent they seemed, like teenagers of the 1930s. By design, a time or two, Joan and I kept walking when they stopped by the trail. After a very few moments, they would pass us again. I had a notion that our considerateness had been wasted.

An hour and a half after leaving the trailhead, we found ourselves in the krummholz. Breaking out of the timber, it struck me, was not sudden, not a release. One thing dulling the moment was that a timberlinelike wind had sprung up before we left the trees. Clouds had materialized, too. I put on my windbreaker. From the Fourth of July Mine, 11,240 feet above sea level and long abandoned, the teeth of the high ridges on the way to the Arapaho peaks looked as rugged as the Prealpi Venete in northeastern Italy. At the mine, the trail turned into the slope to the right, crossed a creek bordered by miniature willows, then cut to the right again and sliced across the contours amid boulders and meadows. Crossing the krummholz line into tundra, I felt a mild pleasure—far short, it seemed to me, of the old exhilaration. The trail became a rocky streambed, two feet wide, with a trickle down the middle. Cushiony tundra grass and flowers grew right up to the sides.

Paul walked with me awhile , and we talked about mountains in the British Isles. He had climbed Ben Nevis in Scotland, the highest of the lot. No trees in those mountains, he said, and only a few in the valleys: "Megan was remarking on how many trees there are here." But the trees were a good distance below us now. We stopped to watch a pika—or coney, as some of us call it. The size of a half-grown cottontail rabbit, it was hunched beside a boulder of its own color. Its rounded leprechaun ears were set into the sides of its head.

We walked on an hour or so and stopped for lunch, sitting on rocks. My two bananas had ripened a week's worth on our three-hour climb. They were a gooey mess. I shook up a can of tomato juice and popped the top. It spewed like Coca-Cola, splattering red froth onto the leg of my khaki pants. At that altitude, about 12,400 feet, I should have been prepared. Though I took care not to shake the next can, it still made a puff like truck brakes when I opened it. The altitude was affecting Megan, too. She said she felt yucky, but after lunch she got up and climbed cheerfully with the rest of us.

We approached the saddle above Arapaho Glacier not long afterward. Climbing teaches perspective, even philosophy: across the canyon, peaks that dominate the terrain at the start become, in a couple of hours, only nubs, barely recognizable in a new landscape. We were well above Diamond Lake and its cascading outlet now and could see its small indigo feeder lakes in still higher cirques. A jumble of snow-pitted mountains—the Sawatch range—was just coming into sight. Around us, close by, the neat yellow blossoms of the alpine buttercups had shrunk to thumbnail size. I watched unsuccessfully for forget-me-nots, the bluest and among the tiniest of the alpine flowers.

From the saddle we looked steeply down at the glacier. It stretched maybe a half mile across its cirque. Patches of bare rock stuck out of it here and there. The lake at its foot had the usual turquoise tint—the effect of the silt that the glacier ground out of the rocks in its constant descent. Megan and I saw a disc of light scudding across the glacier ("glass-i-er," she and Paul pronounced it) as if someone far above were panning a magnifying glass. After a few moments, something—we didn't know what—produced the same effect on the lake, a flitting spot of intensely bright turquoise on the turquoise.

Beyond and below the glacier, a watershed with several good-sized lakes spread out, the lakes dark blue and deep enough to sit firmly in their hollows. It was inviting country, but forbidden. A metal sign in the saddle, between us and the view, said: "City of Boulder. No fishing, no hunting, no trespassing." Having worked to attain this altitude, I thought perversely that it would be nice to be down there, hiking alongside pretty water in the sheltered bowls.

We soon hit the steepest part of the climb. Because of my workouts on the stairs, I managed easily enough when I could lift my knees and pick my way between boulders. But I found that my breath ran out in a hurry when I had to use my hands to help. Still, when I stopped to gasp after a tough stretch, my pulse was only 150, appreciably slower than after a workout on the stairs, nearly twelve thousand feet lower. Why? Because I wasn't lifting my weight as fast for as long as I could have in Wichita. According to the formula of a 3 percent loss of working capacity every thousand feet from the 5,000-foot level upward, if my office stairs had materialized on South Arapaho Peak I could have done only 76 percent of my usual workout. No; 76 percent of my *utmost* Wichita workout; as Dr. Charles S. Houston observes in an article in *Hypoxia: Man at Altitude*, altitude does not necessarily cut far into the capacity to do sustained work at less than an all-out pace. And who, barring athletes, ever goes all out? Nonetheless, the altitude cut into the capacity that I was willing to tap.

Joan, who had been back only a week from a trip to Florida and needed more time for reacclimation, felt it, too. I used to suppose that adjustment to altitude was partly cardiopulmonary know-how—that once you had acquired it, you hung onto some part of it. No such thing, most physiologists say: after a few days at sea level you have to regain it as if you had always lived down low. (But Houston says it seems reasonable to him that the body may remember how to acclimatize well and fast.)

Paul loafed along, staying a little ahead of us. At a grassy spur, I stopped to look at the glacier again and called him over. The slope directly beneath us was steep enough that I stayed safely back from the edge. "This pitch here," I said, "is this the kind of thing you were going down?" I meant on the night of the storm, when he and the others had slipped over the dropoff. "It was a bit that was steeper than this," he said. I guessed that the slope beneath us, at the top of the glacier, was

60 percent, but Paul said no, more like 50. "They always look steeper than they are," he said. But what would happen if one of us fell onto the glacier? "You wouldn't stop before you got down to the bottom," he said. That was six hundred feet below, judging by my USGS contour map (the Monarch Lake quadrangle). We could see, across the way and only a little above us now, the craggy ridge that Paul and his friends had crossed from North to South Arapaho Peak. He said the reason they had crawled most of the distance, aside from the bad visibility, was that they were afraid the wind would blow them over the edge if they tried to walk.

The young heal quickly. Whenever I asked Paul about his experience of the year before, he not only answered readily but elaborated. There weren't slabs where he slid, he said, but separate rocks. After hitting his back on one and seeing colored spots from the impact, I said, he must have been sore for days. No, he said; the thermal gear apparently padded him; nothing bothered him afterward but his bruised knee and a slight cut on one leg. When he landed, he said, "I had the physical sensation of being jarred, but the force was spread over a large area." While we talked, Megan came up, asked Paul where the ridge between the peaks was, and wandered a hundred feet to the side to get a better view of it. He sneaked up behind her and lifted her by the waist. She made a noise of mock dismay—or possibly, considering the way she felt, real dismay. I had a touch of what she had. The pulse in the back of my head sounded like stereo drums from a basement apartment, and I could taste the tomato juice again.

Two young men passed us as we clambered. We heard them yelling in exhilaration on the summit a little later, the wind and rocky resonances giving their voices a wild sound, like baritone marmots. Two young women had passed us, too. When we made it to the top, they were looking at the view, which took in Longs Peak to the north, or the part below where it vanished in clouds, and long stretches of the Continental Divide to the south and west. One of them, Katrina Junge, a Californian, said she and her friend had been camping at Lake Dorothy, which we could see in its saucer-shaped bowl and meadow across the Arapaho Pass trail to our west, well above timberline. I had never before seen two women backpackers alone together, such was my strangeness to the new world order. Katrina Junge stood smiling in the wind, her head thrown back with Valkyrie pleasure. I felt pretty good, nothing more. Maybe my youthful delights in the high country had actually come after the fact, in the retrospect of each climb.

In another Colorado range, 116 years earlier, an often-exuberant young man had made similar reflections. He was Franklin Rhoda, a topographer who helped map the San Juan Range for the U.S. Geological Survey. On a grueling climb of Mount Sneffels, he and his partner stopped briefly to pick their route, looking over a craggy alpine landscape that he describes at length in his report. But, he says,

> we did not remain on the pass long enough to think half that I have written, for it has always been a maxim with us that every minute saved in the morning brings us back to camp so much earlier in the evening, and we can never tell how long a climb is going to take us. We find sufficient time while climbing to observe the scenery around us in a very general way, but the romance of our work is not fully appreciated by us till we reach civilization, where we can find leisure to think over what we have seen. (480)

That is honest, and how different from the accounts of, say, John Muir, who portrays himself, hiking the Sierra alone, as in a constant high from an unfailing store of sublimity.

On the same expedition, Rhoda experienced an electrical storm that must have carried as much voltage as the one Paul Fretwell survived, though it was not accompanied by snow or extreme cold. Taking readings with surveyors' instruments on top of a mountain nearly 14,000 feet high, he and another topographer noticed a tickling at the roots of their hair, the electricity coming from a cloud several miles from them. Then a frying sound started, soon becoming "highly monotonous and disagreeable." The cloud moved quickly toward them, spreading to cover much of the horizon, and the sounds and sensations of charged air increased. They kept on working. As the electrical charge grew stronger, "the instrument on the tripod began to click like a telegraph-machine when it is made to work rapidly; at the same time we noticed that the pencils in our fingers made a similar but finer sound whenever we let them lie back so as to touch the flesh of the hand between the thumb and forefinger." The effects would intensify until lightning struck some neighboring peak, draining the power from the air. Then a new charge would build up.

When the cloud reached the two men, "the sharp points of the hundreds of stones about us each emitted a continuous sound, while the instrument outsang everything else." The effect was as if wind were plucking at the rocks; but the air was still. The humming of the instrument grew so loud that both men crawled quickly downslope. After lightning had hit again, some distance away, Rhoda's companion "made a sudden dash for the instrument, on his hands and knees, seized the legs of the tripod, and flinging the instrument over his shoulder dashed back. Although this occupied only a few seconds, the tension was so great that he received a strong electric shock, accompanied by a pain as if a sharp-pointed instrument had pierced his shoulder, where the tripod came in contact with it." They walked down fast, and after a moment lightning struck the summit thirty feet above them. "We had only just missed it," Rhoda says, "and felt thankful for our narrow escape."

I have never experienced such effects, though once, on top of a foothill, I heard the air crackle and felt my hair rising. But I have rarely been high in the Rockies in the summer without hearing thunder during the day. We heard it now and then from the top of South Arapaho Peak. Mostly the weather had been pleasant, though the temperature rose and fell so markedly with the frequent sudden alterations of sun and cloud that the other three changed many times from shirtsleeves to jackets and back. I wore a wool sweater and my new windbreaker nearly the whole time, not bothering to change. We started down. I found three vivid forget-me-nots, the blossoms scarcely wider than the head of a match, the color as concentrated as if the flowers were little pulsars whose intensity was expressed in blueness instead of gravity. Joan walked over to look, but not Megan, though she was no more than forty feet down an easy slope and had been eager to see forget-me-nots. Drink a lot of water, I told her. Water, because of its effect on the body's chemistry, is one of the main preventives of mountain sickness.

We had considered whether to cross the ridge to North Arapaho Peak. Though the clouds looked fairly threatening and I could imagine our getting caught in something miserable, possibly perilous, I had

declined to make the decision that my age would probably have entitled me to make. Nobody ever articulated a decision, in fact, but when
the time came, we picked our way down instead of heading across.
Shortly Joan remarked how far down it looked to the trail we had
taken, near the Fourth of July Mine. "Yes," Paul said, "and I fell
nearly all the way." He could see the route his party should have chosen; if they had gone a few hundred yards farther, they would have
made it down safely. As he talked, the sun disappeared again and,
instantly, something peppered my hat and jacket. Bits of ice bounced
off me in sideward arcs. Close by, the sleet came down in slanting
stripes; a few hundred yards downslope, it billowed like ground fog.
It fell for three or four minutes, covering the ground, then abruptly
quit. The sun shone again. We unzipped our jackets and stopped to
look and rest.

All day I had been aware that this hike, though pleasant and in
more than one way illuminating, had lacked a moment to set aside
and keep—one which, if it were in a Shakespearean play, would be
written in iambic pentameter rather than conversational prose and
would have a rhymed couplet at the end. When the moment came, it
came like so many of those set speeches: without notice. The sun
shone warmly. The temperature after the spate of sleet must have
jumped to sixty-five degrees. There was very little wind. I clipped on
the dark plastic covers for my glasses, which I had stuck into a pocket
on the way up because the wind kept blowing them off, and walked
ahead of the party along a gently descending stretch of green tundra.
I rounded a shoulder of the ridge that shut me off from the others and
from such stirrings of breeze as remained. The air there was silent and
so light that I practically floated. A strange serenity closed around me.
I felt free of time and all other constraints, a part of the weather and
the landscape. The sensation arose partly from the solitude, I'm
sure—the brief separation from the other three. It may have needed
the stillness, too. When I remembered previous experiences of the
same kind from many years before, it seemed to me that they had also
occurred when I was alone and in sheltered places. They had certainly
occurred. I realized from the first moment of this one that they were
what, more than anything else, had drawn me to the high country in
my youth. Somehow I had almost forgotten—had thought of meatier
sensations and, failing to reexperience them to a satisfying degree, had

supposed that my ability to feel was at fault. More likely it was just that I seldom found myself alone above timberline in a pocket where my surroundings could do their work. This time the feeling must have lasted no more than two or three minutes. When the wind picked up and the others came into earshot, it was over.

Joan exclaimed at something she saw downslope. It was a man coming our way, bypassing the trails and cutting across the tundra at a terrific pace.

"He's jogging!" Joan said. "Twelve thousand feet up, and he's jogging up the mountain!"

"Must be altitude sickness," Paul said.

The jogger had on a green parka. When he was still a quarter mile away, he yodeled, "Odle-aydee-hoo," a soft, clear sound. Exhibitionism, I thought; the guy is dramatizing the self-as-mountaineer, like a dude riding a rented nag and singing, "Git along, little dogies." At least he had something to show off; the sound was so well projected that he might have been in a room with us. In a remarkably short time, the man was standing in front of us. He was my age, probably, with a World-War-I-fighter-pilot mustache and a vaguely British accent. He seemed not the least out of breath. "Nobody else up here?" he asked. He said he was looking for his son, Chris: "He had a big square backpack and a lacrosse stick, so you couldn't miss him." We hadn't seen such a person, but I told him that if his son was over on North Arapaho, we wouldn't necessarily have seen him—we hadn't gone there. He nodded and headed on up, not jogging now but walking very fast. We were standing near the saddle of the Boulder Watershed sign, at the foot of the pitch that rose steeply several hundred feet to the summit. In a very few minutes, we saw the man again, running straight down the slope. How could he have made the summit so fast? He yodeled as he ran, laying the sound right against our ears. An astonishing performance. I assume he found his son back in camp, waiting. At least I read nothing in the papers afterward about a lost hiker.

The descent, as usual, took more out of me than the climb. It made my feet and ankles and shanks ache, and I blamed the rocky trail in the creekbed. I missed the days when you never worried about delicate vegetation but struck out over the springy tundra or cut across the switchbacks. In some quarters, these days, that's considered vandalism. It kills plants that will not be replaced in the harsh environment for decades,

even centuries, we are told. Still, a biologist who lived in a cabin at
11,740 feet in the Colorado Rockies for longer than four months,
studying plants and animals, mentioned "the amazing resilience of these
alpine plants," whose thick, narrow leaves protect them from damage
by hail and graupel. Having read that observation in his book, *Above
Timberline: A Wildlife Biologist's Rocky Mountain Journal,* I phoned
the author, Dwight Smith, in Fort Collins. What, I asked, did he think
of the strictures against walking on the fragile vegetation of alpine tun-
dras? Was the environmentalists' concern possibly exaggerated?

"Well, I think so," Smith said. "Like many of these things, I think
people go overboard. I certainly do not enjoy the alpine by staying off
of it." He said he walked over the tundra every day of his sojourn,
"and it doesn't cause me any concern at all." He said that "if it's exaggerated, continued, people walking in the same paths, it can certainly
create damage." He went on, "But I do know people that talk about
stepping very carefully from rock to rock and not stepping on the
plants—well, my interpretation of that is in remote areas, where there's
not a great deal of use, that that's silly. Certainly an elk or a bighorn
sheep or a mountain goat or a deer—it's much more damaging when
they step on it with their sharp, cutting hooves than you are with soft-
soled hiking boots." After fire or logging, Smith says in his book, damaged vegetation up high does take a long time to recover because of the
harsh environment. But he says today's abuses are much less than those
of the three peak decades of exploitation, starting in 1880.

Smith is a long way from being a tundra-gouging philistine. He
bitterly resents the excesses of mining companies, reclamation proj-
ects, resort developments, and the like (see, for instance, pages
173–77). His pithy contempt for what he considers excessive or sen-
timental environmentalism is more than matched by his scorn of new-
style backpackers who cut live trees for wood, smoke marijuana, and
leave obscene messages in guest registers of remote cabins. His contempt has, in fact, quite a generous catholicity to it. Still, when he
directs it toward the flower avoiders, it makes me ponder. Though I
catch myself more and more deferring to today's scruples, I can't help
being drawn at the same time toward the possibility that the old heed-
less ways can still be defended.

After the yodeler, our only other encounter on the way down was
with a marmot. He did not emerge or arrive but appeared, as they do,

and he stayed so close to the trail that we could tell he hoped to be fed. I tried him with a gob of the overripe banana from my pack. He put his whiskered nose against it, sniffed, and backed away, decidedly uninterested. We watched him snip off American bistort plants at the bottoms of the stems—each with a pufflike blossom on top, a little like a dandelion gone to seed but in the shape of a truncated cone. He chewed the bottom of one stem, dropped it, and snipped another. When I lured him over again with three raisins on my fingertips, he tried to take one, scraping my finger lightly with a sharp incisor, then backed off and refused to come near us anymore but lay on his belly thirty feet away, nibbling listlessly at flowers. The tourist trade that day may have kept him above ground overtime; normally he would have come out only for a couple of hours in the morning and again in the late afternoon till sunset.

Habits of the yellow-bellied marmot—the species usually seen in the Colorado Rockies—and the three other kinds of American marmots, including the woodchuck of New England lore, are recorded in *Wild Mammals of North America: Biology, Management, and Economics,* edited by Joseph A. Chapman and George A. Feldhamer. Marmots hibernate, living off their own fat in tunnels they have padded with grass. They dig marvelously; they have great claws. Yellow-bellied marmots construct at least three entrances to their burrows, and they spot a couple of auxiliary burrows around their feeding grounds for shelter when it's too far to scramble home. Golden eagles, hawks, coyotes, cougars, grizzly bears, and possibly bobcats eat young marmots but seldom grown ones, which, though the yellow-bellied species grows only to about ten pounds, fight fiercely when they have to; a woodchuck is supposed to have whipped a pack of dogs.

When they see people, marmots warn each other with a sharp whistle. It is a characteristic sound in boulder fields near and above timberline in the West. If you stop and look carefully when you hear it, you can usually find the marmot. Farther down the trail, Joan and I, who had paired off for a while, heard a PEET! so sharp it startled us. A big black marmot was perched thirty or forty feet downslope on a rock with a somewhat smaller, tan companion in front of him. In a minute we saw two still smaller ones behind those. They all posed for us like sea otters, the big presumed male frozen in profile at 60 percent of upright, his presumed mate more nearly recumbent, the two immature ones at their own angles between down and up. Burrowing rodents have charm when topside and reacting to people.

A party again, the four of us stopped for a closer look at what Paul said had to be the cliff where he and his friends had fallen. It was several hundred feet above us up a steep, steep slope. I guessed that the cliff was thirty feet high, but the others guessed twice that. Thirty feet is three stories; people die when they fall that far. But Paul said the runout was so steep that the impact was spread down the slope. After we moved on, he and Megan strode a long way ahead and sat on a rock, facing the boulder where he and Katy had huddled. He looked pensive, it struck me as Joan and I drew closer, and in fact he had not joked or horseplayed with Megan on the way down as he had earlier. I thought he must be considering whether to walk over for a closer look. But shortly after Joan and I passed them, they got up and followed us. It was like Paul to avoid doing anything that might break his control, and I imagine he felt, on the other hand, that it would be unfitting to walk over to the boulder and look at the fatal bed without apparent emotion.

At the Frisches' house that night after dinner—I jump ahead because the rest of the hike was uneventful and, for me, wearying—I asked him if he hadn't found it depressing to return. "No, I didn't, actually," he said; it had been good to see the country in pleasant circumstances. "I hadn't a clue as to whether it would upset me or not," he said, "but after a year, it sort of—memories faded." The next day he and Megan would set out in the Frisches' second car—the same Toyota wagon he had cleared of snow and driven down to Boulder the year before. They would hike and climb all over western North America. I kept thinking that if I had been in Paul's place, I would never have climbed again. But of course, I couldn't know.

CHAPTER THREE

In a research center on top of Pikes Peak, 14,110 feet above sea level, in a building that reminded me of Headquarters, Company A, I waited for Dr. John Reeves to come out of the bathroom. It was a tense, rushed scene. Doctors bent over instruments and in the voices of movie howitzer officers fixing coordinates against a charging enemy called out numbers to technicians, who entered them on pads with ballpoint pens. I caught a couple of the doctors flicking their eyes at me, an outsider, but none had time to nod, much less speak. Several men and women occupied themselves with a bare young man, a towel wrapped around his middle, into whose mouth a woman was jamming a thick black-plastic tube. He made a sour face around it. Two electrodes were taped to his chest. I stood in the doorway of the bunkroom amid unmade army bunks with olive-drab frames. Next to one bunk was a Monark 818 exercise bicycle. Packs and hiking boots lay about.

This was the site of an experiment, coordinated by the University of Colorado, in which Reeves and others would test and probe eleven young men whose homes were at sea level in California, feeding them a measured diet of bread, peanut butter, and an all-nutritious drink for three weeks. "They give us things that do not vary at all, which means that they are exactly tasteless," a young man named Mark from the Bay Area told me later. The scientists also required their subjects to ride exercise bicycles. That was what the blond, bearded young man I watched while I waited for Reeves was doing. Breathing through the large-bore tube in his mouth, he pushed the pedals down slowly; it must have taken much effort.

In another part of the room, barely visible from where I was, another cluster of experimenters stood around a second captive. I didn't want to edge into the room far enough to see what they were doing to him. On an erector-set stack of shelves close to me, laden with electronic gauges and wires, a taped-up piece of paper bore in grease pencil the notation "Borg" and then numbers, one through ten, with explanations alongside them ranging from "nothing at all" through "very slight," "slight," "moderate," "hard," and "very hard." Seven, eight, and nine were blank. The line next to ten said "maximal." Another penciled sign, on a yellow sheet of paper taped to the refrigerator in my corner of the bunkroom, said, "Fecal buckets in freezer in laboratory—for a better environment. Love, Gail."

Reeves, tall and thin and about my age, with a lined face like mine, came out of the room that had the restroom in it. He did not look happy when I told him who I was, though he had sent word to me at the motel in Denver that I could come up and talk with him, not saying what day. Sunday would have been much better, he said. (This was Monday. The day before, I had climbed South Arapaho Peak.) "But we can talk," he said. That was good, because he was the only high-altitude physiologist I could find that week, and I wanted to get some questions answered. We went outside and sat on adjoining rocks in the sun, close to the level place where six or eight of the young men had just broken up a volleyball game. One player sprawled on his back on the ground, a knee up, arms behind his head, resting. It was warm and not especially windy. Having anticipated neither such a day nor an outdoor interview, I had neglected to put on lotion to protect me from high-altitude sunburn, and I tried to keep the backs of my hands in my own shadow as I bent over, taking notes.

Mainly I was curious about the effects of high altitude on people who go there or who have always lived there. That, of course, is what Reeves was on the peak to learn more about. But the top of Pikes Peak is high only by some standards. I gather that high-altitude physiologists for a long time tended to dismiss the paltry teens of thousands—the Rockies, the Sierra Nevada, Mount Rainier, the Alps—and to do their studies in the twenties—the Andes and the Himalayas. So science knows a comparative lot about what happens inside Everest climbers and not so much about what happens inside people who go up for a weekend above Boulder or Fresno, much less Boston. Some of the things that happen to Everest climbers, who spend days or weeks in base camps 20,000 feet and more above sea level, would dismay your cardiologist if he observed them in you. On top of Everest, the oxygen level in the blood drops to about a tenth that at sea level, and oxygen pressure in arterial blood in the lungs falls so low that a pulmonary specialist at sea level would take the reading to mean that the patient was near death from a lung disease. The shortage makes organs sluggish or otherwise dysfunctional. The intestines become less absorptive than normal; the body's capacity to extract nutrients from food lessens. Climbers lose from one to three pounds a week, some of it in muscle, even if they eat a lot; people returning from Everest expeditions have skinny arms and legs. Memory and coordination may suffer, and not just in the presence of altitude; a year after an Everest climb monitored by Dr. John B. West, most of the participants had yet to get back full finger-tapping ability, though their short-term memory had returned. "Some physicians liken living at high altitude to having some kind of chronic, grumbling disease," West says; "nothing is really working as well as it should." He tells about the climb and his experiments in *Everest: The Testing Place*.

Never mind Everest. I wanted to know whether, extreme altitude being extremely bad for people, moderate altitude was moderately bad for them. Well, Reeves said, the number of old people decreases in Colorado as you go higher; those with heart and lung disease have left for lower altitudes. Not all have, as I knew from my talks with the man and woman in the hospital at Leadville. But I didn't take time to discuss that or anything else with Reeves. I was intimidated by the scientific tension all around me. So I simply fired questions, scribbled as fast as I could, and hoped my tape recorder was working. Reeves added this about life in the Rockies: "We don't think that the moderate altitude of nine thousand feet is harmful to people who are healthy." (Around us the young men from sea level were back at their volleyball game. They shouted and laughed as they played.)

Leadville is a thousand feet above the altitude he called moderate; I asked if Leadville natives showed adaptations to the altitude. Probably a larger lung volume, he said: "We're not one hundred percent sure of that for the Leadville natives, but other populations show that." Animals show it, too; Reeves told me that beagle puppies, moved to Leadville when very young, developed large lungs. Another question: I had read in the diary of Herbert A. Ford, a mine manager who spent a couple of years in Leadville in the early 1880s, that "this is the worst place for colds on the face of the earth." Was that right? Reeves said he didn't know about colds at Leadville, but the body's immune system was not as effective at high altitude as at sea level: "Wounds heal slowly. Infections are more in-do-lent." (For my benefit, he spoke the word like a pronouncer at a spelling bee.)

Why, I asked, still hurrying, are some people exhilarated by high altitude? I had read the words of one Professor Roget of Geneva, who said,

> I am at my best, most playful and light-hearted at an altitude. As if by magic my corns disappear, any rheumatic pains vanish, gouty twinges pass away, any lumbago or sciatic neuralgia contracted at home lessens its hold perceptibly day by day. No sooner do I return to the level of civilization than my feet drag, my corns call for the knife, all the symptoms reappear that bespeak an organism placed at a physiological disadvantage.

That seemed to belie what Reeves had told me about the immune system; but Roget was not talking about altitudes like that of our interview-on-the-rocks, or even like that of Leadville. "I am a 6,000-feet man," he concluded. (He is quoted in a 1932 article by Dr. James J. Waring in *Journal of the Outdoor Life.*) Reeves's answer about high-altitude exhilaration was that high altitude and alcohol are synergistic: "The headache of altitude sickness is an awful lot like a hangover. And we say at altitude that one drink does the work of two. And there seems to be something about the two that is analogous. But we don't know what it is." He said yes, he thought altitude exhilarated him. He didn't show it, but I'm sure I didn't, either. We were under our separate kinds of pressure.

Also, he said, and his voice grew louder and higher pitched as if we were now getting to the interesting part, "the sympathetic nervous system gets turned on." It sets up a kind of high, he said. We talked a minute or two longer. Then a woman came out of the research building and walked toward us, fast. She looked even tenser than the standard for that group on that day. Reeves broke off.

REEVES: Yes, Gail.

GAIL: Well, John, we're coming to a . . . a little complaint. Nobody let Tyson eat. He hasn't eaten all day. And that won't do.

VOLLEYBALL PLAYER (overhearing): He's ridin' the bike.

GAIL (yelling across to him): That's true.

PLAYER: That's what happened to me when I did my vee-oh-two max; I didn't do my max till 1:30, and I hadn't eaten all day.

GAIL: We *can't do that* . . .

PLAYER: I know.

GAIL (to Reeves, scolding): I mean, that's why I've set lunch at noon and said the VO_2 maxes cannot happen until after two, because these guys have to have a chance to *eat*.

REEVES: Yes, of course they do. Well, I wasn't aware of it. I wasn't aware of it.

(Gail and the player talk during this, repeating things they have said about Tyson and about not getting enough to eat.)

GAIL: Well, I mean—it's not fair to him.

REEVES: Of course not.

GAIL: Because he's not—he's not going to be able to perform in this batch.

REEVES: Well, he'll be able to perform, but it's not right that he didn't have lunch, that's for sure.

(She says something about finishing with the blood volume. All three are talking.)

REEVES (very quietly): Well, we finished—the blood volumes were finished by twelve-thirty.

GAIL (she is quieter now, too): Well then, why didn't he eat?

REEVES: I have no idea. (louder and more decisively) Tyson bears some responsibility in this.

GAIL: Well, right, right. But I mean, there must have been something going on if he didn't eat.

REEVES: I, I, I don't know. I don't know what it is.

(She turns and strides back into the building.)

I asked Reeves what Gail's last name was. Butterfield, he said; she was a Ph.D. nutritionist. I assume she was the author of the fecal-bucket note.

REEVES (to me): Anyway, I don't have a lot more time because . . . (unintelligible on the tape because I, similarly tense, keep saying, "Oh, yeah. OK; OK.") things going on. But the sympathetic

nervous system contributes—or prevents the symptoms of altitude sickness, whether it alters the fuel which the body uses for
exercise, whether it alters the cardiovascular responses to exercise in terms of cardiac output and blood flow . . . , whether it
alters the brain function and visual function. So, I mean, it's a
huge study.

He got up and walked quickly back to the research building. In the
doorway, his face civil and harried, he stopped to answer a last question before returning to the quiet refuge of science.

I talked with some of the volleyball players, who had broken off
their game again—partly, I think, to observe the scene between the
nutritionist and the doctor. The players said no, the experiment had-
n't been so tough, though the scientists sometimes made them work
hard, either at riding the exercise bicycle or playing volleyball. The
usual bike ride wasn't all out; that—the VO_2 max—happened only
twice during the stay.

> I: What do you do in your leisure time?
> PLAYER: Read, play board games and cards.
> I: You can't have a beer, though?
> PLAYER: No, not at all. (chuckles from the others)

I told about an experiment I had just concluded in the parking lot
next to them. With a six-pack of Coors, a package of plastic glasses,
a wooden ruler, and a stopwatch as my scientific instruments, I had
determined that the head on beer climbs much higher on top of Pikes
Peak than in Manitou Springs, seventy-seven hundred feet below,
where I had conducted the first part of the experiment earlier in the
day. Also, the head dissipates sooner. (Oddly, this seems to be a virgin
field for research. Even the Coors people in Golden professed to know
nothing about such effects.) One of the players asked, hopefully, what
I had done with the beer I had used in the test. I had to tell him I had
poured it out. I refrained from mentioning how wonderfully tempting,
in that dry air, the feel of the cold beer through the thin aluminum can
had been: *I* could look forward to enjoying one of the science-surplus
beers that evening in the motel.

I asked the young men if they were continually getting stuck with
needles; they calculated that it had already happened at least twenty
times. (Earlier in their stay, one of them had told a *Rocky Mountain*

News reporter, Joseph B. Verrengia, about the scientists' probing deep into thighs for muscle samples: "The worst thing about the biopsy is that your thigh muscles cramp around the tube like a charley horse." The observation was credited to "Tyson Vaughan, 21"—the Tyson of the missed lunch, I assume.) One of the players told me he was a medical student. Another, a dietitian, planned to apply to a medical school. The third, Mark, told me, "I'm unemployed—this is my job." The young men were paid two thousand dollars, plus transportation and all the peanut butter, bread, and nutritious drink one could desire. "Not too terrible," I said. *"Pretty terrible,"* a player said.

Only one of the group around me was married. "It's missing that, too," one told me. I said I was sure that wasn't allowed, any more than beer was. No, not allowed, one said, laughing. "Or available," I said. "No, not available," he agreed. Another said, "You don't miss something, you know, till it's gone." I speculated that up here they might be disappointed anyway, since performance seems to be lessened at high altitude. "Probably the performance would be impeded," a player said, "but not the desire." I told them I had read that the Spanish settlers of the Andes had to go to lower altitudes to conceive children. "Why?" one asked. "Because of the air? Because I don't care if I ran out of air, I'd keep on going." They stirred and arose from their rocks, getting ready to leave. "We need to take our pills," one said.

I walked over to the summit house, which was full of souvenirs and picture postcards and of tourists who had driven their cars up or ridden the steep cog railroad from Manitou Springs. Bill Carle, a member of the family that owns the summit house, told me he had lived up there eight months of the year for seventeen years. (In midwinter on the summit, the average temperature is two degrees.) "I'm the fourth generation of my family up here doing this," he said. "We started in ninety-six, my family, and the carriage road started in eighteen eighty-nine. So we weren't too far behind the first personalized stuff up here. But they'd been running burros up through the eighteen-seventies and the eighteen-eighties." Why had he stayed in that business? Tradition, he said: "It's like a family farm, is how I characterize it. It's just something that your family's got so much into, and you're going to carry on because it's what you are; it's your identity."

Carle, a slender man of thirty-six with inchoate dark whiskers showing just at the surface of his delicately rounded chin, stood at the end of a counter while we talked. He seemed very serious, not smiling when I wisecracked. Down the counter from us, his employees hurried to serve fountain drinks to tourists. He said he and his wife had met up there; she worked in the summit house seven years. He had thirty employees, he told me; they worked ten-hour days, slept in bunks, and got two nights and one day off a week. When they first came up, he said, they had a couple of rough nights. Usually that was all: "Once every other year there will be somebody that comes up that does not acclimate." Such people went back down after a week, he said. Carle had also run the store on top of Mount Evans, west of Denver, until it burned in 1979. That was the mountain he loved, he said: Evans, not Pikes. "It's greener," he said, "and there's more animals." On Evans he had seen mountain goats and bighorn sheep, ravens, pikas, marmots, shrews, mice, and weasels.

It was true about the absence of greenery on Pikes. Though the view was splendid down the notch to Manitou Springs, across Colorado Springs, and far beyond, over the ridges of the Black Forest and across cloud-shadowed plains that never disappeared but merged with the sky a hundred miles away and more, and though the foothills of the peak made up a whole landscape of rich forests, each a more-or-less separate domain set apart by its own craggy ridges, the peak itself lacked charm. From my car window on the way up, I had seen only sparse patches of tundra flowers, and instead of mats of juicy greenery between them, there was bare, reddish, rocky soil. That red makes magnificent effects from a distance, especially at sunrise.

People who live in Colorado Springs, as I did my last year of high school and again when I was twenty and edited a starving weekly paper on the west side of town, keep their bearings and their perspective by The Peak. They say you never see it the same way twice, and it's true that because it reaches high and spreads over a great expanse of itself and its foothills from north to south, it presents every opportunity for both the occurrence and the display of changing weather. And it is so close to town that you have to walk only a few feet along Tejon Street or Nevada Avenue to make The Peak shift into a new relationship with Cameron Cone on the south and Mount Manitou on the north. I suppose that residents of Innsbruck may feel the same mixture of subjectedness and solicitude concerning their civic heights as Springs people do concerning theirs, but the competition of cities elsewhere in the world has to be scarce. Still, it was as Carle said. Up close, The Peak has feet of clay.

I didn't much want to go stand by the cog road at the summit and look at the view. I was getting a headache. It must be because I had driven up, not climbed, and so had not had time to adjust, I told myself. Nonetheless, I walked over and stood amid the other tourists—fathers holding small children; pairs of thirtyish women with sunburns up to the hems of their shorts. Cameron Cone, which I had once climbed with my high-school friend Clare Gregg, looked big even from above. I remembered his mocking the tourists who looked west from town on a day when clouds hid the peak but left Cameron Cone visible. "Oh, I didn't know Pikes Peak was *that* big," they would say. At 10,707 feet, the cone is below timberline, but its slabs of summit rock reflect the light like snowfields. I stood looking at the green foothills, with the red earth showing here and there between trees. Beyond, the redder formations of Garden of the Gods jutted up prominently, but the Kissing Camels seemed, from where I stood, not to be kissing; nothing endures. A filmy shower like dark nylons was falling between the summit and Manitou Springs. Clouds, suspended above me, dangled fringes hundreds of feet below me. Enough. I yielded to my headache and walked to my car. On the way, I noticed parked cars with license plates from Wisconsin, Minnesota, Nebraska, Louisiana, Texas, New Mexico, and New York. Only six were from Colorado.

At 9,500 feet on the road down, amid a fine aspen grove, my head felt much better. At Cascade, at the foot of the highway, where the foothills were covered with symmetrical Douglas firs and red-barked ponderosa pines, I felt fine, and I thought, "This is the part of the mountains I really love." Later, though, as I turned onto Interstate 25 going north from Colorado Springs, I looked to the left, and there was The Peak, partly covered by clouds but—and this was as great a thrill as if I had never seen the mountain before—with the north part of the summit and the long north slopes unexpectedly emerging, looking higher than anything rooted in the earth could possibly be. The grand old Peak after all; the real country.

* * * * *

What a night. The two men in the next room, behind an onionskin wall, yelled drunkenly at each other and kept me awake for hours. But I finally went to sleep, and at 7:40, when I woke up, I felt fine. I wasn't even sore from the Arapaho climb of two days before, except for a little tightness around the Achilles tendons.

I was going back to the Indian Peaks Wilderness Area and taking my fly rod. On my USGS map I had picked out Upper Diamond Lake, which seemed to be eight hundred feet higher than Diamond Lake— a gentle walk, to judge by the amount of white showing between the brown forty-foot contour lines. I had an interview set up that evening at the foot of Berthoud Pass, but I figured I could fish a couple of hours and get back to my car in time to make it. I took along a day-pack with a lunch and some odds and ends, together with a couple of fly boxes and a few extra leaders. It was a little after 11:30 when I set out from the Buckingham Campground (called Fourth of July Campground on the map). Hurrying, passing a father and son and, later, a young man hiking alone, I made the mile to the Diamond Lake trail in a little less than twenty-seven minutes. That is what altitude and slope do to the notion of hurry. Working that hard on a level Wichita street, I cover a mile in fifteen minutes.

The clouds, which made jagged formations, were white, though earlier, over the higher mountains, I had seen darker ones. The trail led to a pair of hewn logs over the North Fork of Middle Boulder Creek, a lovely, swift stream with a rocky bed. On the far side of the creek, hikers had trodden green-leaved marsh plants into the mud. I walked on them, too, unavoidably. The trail went through sun, then shade; I kept flipping my clip-on glasses down, then up. After a while the going leveled out, and I slopped through marshy meadows. I reached Diamond Lake at 12:35; that mile had taken me thirty-seven minutes. The lake was set amid nice firs and spruces. Above and to my right, I saw a cascade: the inlet, I told myself.

Suddenly it was raining. Hailstones hit my hat. I struck out to find a trail up the cascade, gave up, and traversed the open slope, avoiding vegetation as much as possible. It was steep enough that I edged my forward boot to establish each foothold, then let it flatten downslope. It thundered lightly; rain dripped; there was scarcely a breeze. Then a big clap of thunder came, so loud and rolling that I thought for a moment it was a rock slide and looked for a boulder to scramble under. I walked on. The flowers were gorgeous—a clump of columbines, surely two dozen flowers, growing out of a cranny in a ledge, and then more and more everywhere, the greatest profusion of columbines I had seen anywhere. I turned and climbed herringbone style along the cascade. The rain came harder; I put on my windbreaker. Then the sun came out. When I reached gentler ground, in the krummholz now, I picked out what must be the cirque of Upper Diamond Lake, discouragingly far away. But then I climbed a grassy ridge for a better view and saw a small lake directly below. *That* had to be Upper Diamond. How had I got north of it? Nothing looked the same as on my map. The altitude must have gone to my brain.

By the time I had climbed down to the little lake, it was raining copiously, a cold, cold rain. I took off my pack, sat on a rock, dug out my cheese-and-peanut-butter crackers, the kind you buy at a service station along the interstate when you're in a hurry—too salty and fat for high altitude, but I hadn't yet read that far in physiology books— and opened the plastic packages with my sheath knife. Nothing I was wearing shed rain—not my cloth hat, not the new windbreaker I had bought in Wichita. Within five minutes I was soaked except for my lap, where I had put the pack to keep at least one part of me dry. I hunched over to shelter my crackers, chewing, it struck me, forlornly. Lightning flashed and flashed among the rocks on the steep slopes above the lake. A couple of strokes came so close that the thunder followed, BAM, in two seconds. I was scared, and a Protestant voice shamed me for getting that irresponsibly wet and cold. I sat for twenty-four minutes before the rain dropped to a sprinkle.

Immediately, all over the lake, I saw the splashes of feeding fish. What insects could be flying in forty-five-degree weather with rain still prickling the water? I jointed up my fly rod, with stiff fingers tied on a number-twelve Royal Coachman, and began casting. A strike, felt but missed. Another, seen but not felt. I moved to the exposed end of the lake, farther from the head of the cirque, and cast into the riffle. Shortly I caught and released a nine-inch cutthroat. No point in keeping fish with no way to cook them, and anyway, I had an interview to conduct. After a few minutes, I walked back to the upper end of the lake, where my pack was, and put on a big buff-white fly, the first one being badly drowned by then. Standing on a quivering isthmus of grass and earth between foot-wide inlets, I missed a couple of splashy strikes, then got another. To hook it, I swept the rod up and at the same time stepped back. My left foot sank up to midcalf in lake water. Oh, well. As wet as I already was, it hardly mattered. The fish fought for just a

minute. Cutthroats, the native trout of the high Rockies, by all romantic rights ought to fight twice as hard and long as the government-
raised species in the warmer waters below. I have caught a few that
fought hard, but they usually come in about as readily as, say, yellow
perch, or as crappie that have not taken their vitamins.

This was a beautiful fish, a ten-incher with a vivid red V beneath
the gills and a hint of a rainbow down the sides. The hook was sunk
into the solid structure at the side of the mouth, under the eye. I
couldn't work it loose. The fish looked at me with what seemed a cool
awareness; damn it, I must remember to mash all my barbs flat. I laid
him on the wet grass and went to get some needle-nosed pliers out of
the pack. When I had unhooked him and eased him back into the
water, he swam away handily, to my relief.

I had fished a half hour, all I could spare and be sure of making
my appointment on time. I took down my rod, put away the reel and
fly boxes, and started down the way I had seen two hikers come up as
I fished, along the outlet from the little lake. As I walked, a stiff breeze
arose from the direction of what I had thought was Upper Diamond
Lake, scraping and whistling around the rocky cirques. I shook so
hard from the cold that my shoulders, of themselves, tried to join in
front and my chest ached with the tension. I made whimpering, gasp-
ing noises to myself. But at least this was a much shorter, easier trail
to Diamond Lake than the way I had climbed. I reached the main lake
in twenty minutes, already warmer and feeling better at the lower altitude. Later, on the familiar trail on the other side of the North Fork,
I was warm enough to enjoy the flowers again. It had quit raining,
though clouds loomed behind me, upstream toward Arapaho Pass.

A little farther along, I remembered something. In my pack, I had
a hard-finished reflecting blanket. It would have kept me dry. Later,
looking at the contour map at an altitude conducive to reason and in
the comparatively intellectual setting of my car, I perceived that I had
climbed along a lesser feeder stream of Diamond Lake, not the main
tributary. And the distant cirque did hold Upper Diamond Lake. I had
fished something too small to have a name. Just as well. If I had gone
to the right lake, I would never have made my appointment.

In Idaho Springs, I stopped for supper, then went to a Safeway
store for some gifts to take to Jim Palmer and Susan Austin: gouda
cheese, crackers, Valpolicella. He and she lived at Berthoud Falls, and

Jim did any kind of work he could find that enabled him to ski all day, all season. That was nearly all I knew about them. I had met Jim a few months earlier, in late May, on top of a mountain named Colorado Mines Peak. In Colorado for a long weekend, I had taken an hour or so to walk up the little mountain, which rises above Berthoud Pass. Jim was one of a ski-touring party of three on top. I had talked with him, made arrangements to come and see him again, and then watched him dip over the back of the mountain on his skis and make perfect jump turns down an impossibly steep chute in the breakable crust, as casual as a kid on a skateboard.

His cabin was a patched-together thing in a cluster of similar ones, along a dirt lane paralleling U.S. Highway 40 and maybe a couple of hundred feet upslope. In front were a small car and, as I recall, a small pickup, both with badly battered grilles; if you live at 9,800 feet in the Front Range and drive daily to 11,000 feet and back on snowy roads in the winter, you are bound to have collisions; if your work is whatever you can find after skiing hours, you can't afford either proper insurance or the services of a body shop. Jim stepped onto his log porch, grinning, and waved at me as I tried to jockey my car far enough off the lane to make room for other residents to pass. It was about seven o'clock, still light.

We sat at a round table in a corner of his front room while Susan, small and shy, sat on a couch in near darkness behind me. Their child, Abel, used his newly gained powers to feel his way along the wall, exclaiming piercingly every now and then at something he had found. The inside of the room was all unfinished planks. Wooden boxes contained assorted belongings, and a couple of wooden barrels held up a rough plank with books on it: *Diet for a Poisoned Planet; How to Choose Safe Foods for You and Your Family.* The gleaming blondness of Jim's hair, which fell to his shoulders in twists and mats, and of his impressive beard made a full-face solar halo like Apollo's. His skin was russet—as near to tan as it would ever get, I imagined. I gave Susan the sack of wine, cheese, and crackers. She set it down in the kitchen. Their big dog, Hobbes—named by his previous owner, though Jim had heard of the "Calvin and Hobbes" comic strip, all right—flopped on his side under the table.

I asked Jim how long he intended to live for skiing. "The rest of my life, for sure," he said.

I: You never get tired of it?

HE: Never. It grows on me. It seems it grows on me. I just try and do it more and more every year.

I: So you're doing exactly what you want to do out of life?

HE: Yeah.

I: And there're not many people that can say that.

HE (laughs): Yeah, there isn't, is there? Yeah, I'm totally satisfied with the way I'm living. I give thanks for that, you know. You've got to appreciate that, because, you know, a lot of people can't. But you know, a lot of people can change their lifestyles and do different things. But you know, they don't seem to want to, or they just want to meet in the middle; you know, like, say, a lot of folks that live in Denver and come up just a few weekends a year—they're totally happy with that. For me, I have to do it a lot more than that. But yeah, I want to keep skiing the rest of my life. Every day.

I: What is it about skiing that has that kind of pull?

HE: I don't know what it is. It just shows you—it's freedom, you know. It just shows you what life has to offer. For me, it's the ultimate.

Vacationing at a ski lodge in my youth, I found that after three days, skiing bored me; I had to stay in the cabin a day and read. On the other hand, I had never skied remotely as well as Jim Palmer. If I could have commanded all humanly negotiable slopes with his ease and daring, instead of merely surviving the repetitious challenge of the packed runs, I might have felt more nearly as he did. But not, I think, to the point of embracing a lifetime of dishwashing, and, worse, dishwashing during the hours meant for books and music.

I had already gathered that Jim was an environmentalist because of the medium of a cheery, misspelled note he had sent to me in Wichita. It was on the back of an old letter to him from the *Amicus Journal*. He told me he belonged to Greenpeace, and along with the *Journal* he subscribed to *High Country News,* a biweekly roundup of western environmental news. His and Susan's season passes to the Berthoud Pass ski area, at $290 each, caused them pangs even though, as he said, they did two or three months a year of climbing under their own power. "But the rest of the year we're riding the lifts, you know. Not every day, but we use them as a way to get further in, you know. And, yeah, it's a bit of a conflict there. You know they're all running off the electrical grid and that. I guess the ultimate, what we're going toward, is just strictly hiking and skiing." That would mean living where they could ski right out the door and not ride the lifts at all, he said.

Jim agreed that his abandonment to skiing was partly a dislike of organized life. They didn't have a television set. Once in a while he read a newspaper, but otherwise, mostly environmental nonfiction. Did his environmental interests affect what he ate? "Yeah," he said. "We're both strict vegetarians. And I don't drink alcohol. Suzy does, but I don't." Uh-oh: the Valpolicella. No problem, he said. "And I don't eat dairy at all." Uh-oh: the gouda. He laughed. I looked at Susan. "You can give him the crackers," I said.

About food, Jim said, "we're real spiritual." But he wasn't an activist on environmental issues: "I haven't gone out and done any protests or anything like that." I asked what his environmentalism sprang from. Was he worried about the future of the world? Yes, he said—about global warming, for instance. I said that might be rough on skiing, all right. "I've just got to keep going further north if it is," he said.

I went back to his remark about food and spirituality. Was he religious? "Yeah," he said, barely breathing the word. Did he go to church, or . . . ? "This *is* my church," he said, and waved a hand. "The outdoors is my church. I go to church every day." I asked Susan if she felt the same way. She tried to keep an open mind, she said. Religions were all basically for the same thing: "Mankind loving each other and peace all over the world."

I (to Jim): But you do believe in a . . . ?
HE: Higher power?
I: In a higher power.
HE: Absolutely.

I wanted to get back to his way of life. To confirm my memory of our mountaintop conversation, I asked him what kind of work he did at night during skiing season. His eyes flinched. "I dishwash," he said. I saw the same sensitive, retreating look when I asked him how big the rented cabin was (three and a half rooms) and what his father, back in Chicago, did for a living (he sold insurance; when Jim was old enough for college, he asked his father, "Why should I spend your money on something I have no interest in?" And he headed for the mountains to do the one thing he wanted to do with his life). He said he tried to ski until five o'clock every day and then work till ten.

Sometimes he operated the run at Fraser, where the tourists went down the hill on inner tubes. He worked four nights a week, Susan three, so they could trade off watching Abel. He and she had met at Telluride four years before. There and at Steamboat Springs, as here, he had been a ski bum; that was the term he used, and without the defensive look. He showed me photographs of him skiing beautiful S curves down a slope of new powder with Abel on his back. Tracks alongside, presumably the photographer's, had only half as many turns; Jim had skied conservatively to avoid endangering Abel.

In summer Jim worked days, but because he wanted to keep on skiing as late in the year as possible, he hadn't started work until well into June. It had been two weekends since he had skied: a long time. "My best year," he said, "I went every weekend all summer. I got two hundred and eighty-four days in for the calendar year. This year I'm right around two-twenty-five." He doubted that he could go every weekend for the rest of the summer. "This job I've got right now," he said, "it's just brutal on me. Roofing. I'm just so tired by Friday." The job was in Denver. He stayed with a friend two nights a week and drove home the other three so he could watch Abel in the evenings. He had to work hard like that in the summer to help finance his all-day winter skiing. "A lot of folks have day jobs," he said, "but it's just misery. They're working, and all snowy out, and they're just real unhappy with it." I asked him if he didn't worry about security. What if his health failed him at sixty-five or seventy? "The Creator will watch out for me, I know that," he said. "That's my security."

He took me out onto his porch to look across the valley toward Engelmann's Peak. The tundra on the far slope was aglow with the last of the day's sunlight, the air between as clear as a vacuum. Gazing, I felt something approaching the serenity of those few minutes on the Arapaho hike, and I could see that Jim was similarly moved. I had felt that way, now, twice in thirty years or so; he, every day since he had become a ski bum.

I reflected, as I drove back to Denver, that Jim wasn't just a pleasure seeker, a snow-going beach boy, though he had that element in him. Like Thoreau—no, more than Thoreau, who lasted at Walden Pond only twenty-six months—he lived according to his vision. He had steadfastness and enthusiasm. But I wasn't sure whom to pity, him or me. He struck me as a prisoner of his fears and taboos, barred from the varied, small, and mixed pleasures of most lives by his commitment to a way that offered a single large and unqualified pleasure. What did Jim know about the kind of life he had fled? What scope could he draw upon to justify his decision? He would have said, "The outdoors is, you know, a lot of scope." He made me think, no question. Still, I had long ago given up my collegiate notions of being a nature bum. It wasn't a mere surrender to duty; I had found out I couldn't be happy in separation from the works of man and the work of man.

Surprisingly fresh, considering the miserable experience at the lake and the lack of sleep the night before, I negotiated the down-curves of the foothills and took the straight line of West Colfax back to the motel and bed. I went to sleep quickly, not much disturbed by the noises coming from the adjoining room, which was now occupied by a couple with small children. I dreamed that I caught a fish and laid it out to admire. It took on the shape of a child or perhaps a fetus, with stubby, fat arms and legs and a face of indeterminate but piscine features. Then it became a living Greek statue of a baby. I had hooked it in the side. After removing the hook, I put the trout-child back into the water feet first. It sank straight down, statuelike, its eyes expressing gratitude. Must all my recreations be guilty?

CHAPTER FOUR

Alexander Drummond was not, I think, a recluse, and perhaps no more of an environmentalist than Jim Palmer and Susan Austin, but he lived in a big cabin without electricity, high in the foothills above Ward, Colorado, by himself. I say he was without electricity—he had a generator, he told me as we sat on his glassed-in porch, "a man-hating machine, which fails me whenever I have company." When he was alone, he didn't mind if it failed. The absence of power drew his evenings close about him. "Especially in the wintertime, when it's dark by five-thirty and usually storming outside, I'll finish supper by six o'clock and have a fire in the stove, and I'll settle down," he said. "I have five hours of completely open time to just sit and think and read and write and so forth, and with just kerosene lanterns lighting the place, you're not so tempted to putter and do distracting things . . . and if I put two kerosene lanterns side by side, I have enough light to sew and darn socks, fix my mountain equipment, things like that." He listened to National Public Radio for news, opera programs, and folk and country music. Not a bad mix of nature and art.

The cabin, as Drummond's guest, Forrest Ketchin, called to my attention, sat in an ecotone. A meadow sweeping up an easy grade merged with a grove of aspens and lodgepole pines a hundred feet or so from the porch. No other dwelling was within sight or hearing. An ecotone is a busy place in nature. I don't know whether I saw specifically meadow life and grove life as the three of us talked, but a chickadee hung upside down in an aspen close to the windows, and a small hawk flew down and perched on the very top of a pine a hundred yards away, then took off again, hovered three feet over the treetop, and lowered itself into the next branches down, getting comfortable.

46

A wasp kept bouncing its underside off a window at us. Aspens rustled in the breeze; I could hear them through the glass.

Forrest Ketchin is an applied anthropologist. Her doctoral work was on the interaction between people's settlements and wild places: a conceptual ecotone, one that concerns Jim Palmer, Texaco, everybody. Drummond had interacted with the wild by detaching himself from people, but not all the way. I had interacted with the wild by detaching myself, to about the same degree, from *it*, doing so out of a regretful sense of obligation.

On the subject of such interactions, Drummond and his friend told me about characters in Ward, the little town a few miles south and down from the cabin and thirty miles northwest of Boulder. One, he said, had recurrent two-week depressions and so couldn't hold a job, though he tried. Every so often he hitchhiked down the mountain to reapply for government benefits. The depressions occurred whether or not he was working, Drummond said, "but up here it doesn't matter." Another Ward character, he said, was "a fellow who had post-Vietnam syndrome"—"he was still so afraid of ambushes and so forth that he carried pistols and knives and everything, and he went around in the woods on his horse, and he wrote poetry, and—a very strange character, and he was also an alcoholic. He was definitely too scary a person for normal society. He looked fierce." Still, he said, the man never caused trouble in Ward. After his death at the age of forty-seven—he had said his body was "all used up" and had announced that he was about to die—"there was a very moving service for him at the Ward church," with congregational singing and a pistol volley.

Another, a fugitive from pressure to advance in academic administration, lived in a mine tunnel for a year or so and now "lives by himself out in the woods in a little tiny shelter." He sold the fish he caught and the rabbits he snared. He walked around wearing a big coat, summer and winter. "His teeth are gone now," Drummond said. "He doesn't eat properly. When he gets money, he buys Snickers bars. Again, a very peculiar fellow. And Ward is one of the very few places where he could survive." Then there were the two university professors who headed for Ward every year and turned hippie for a few months to get away from jobs, suits, and neckties. "They're part of the social fabric of the town in the summertime," Drummond said. His guest, a blonde woman in her midforties who grew up in Georgia and had a distinctively southern cast to her long face—maybe from the shaping of her pronunciations, though I didn't notice an accent— said some people laughed at Ward because of its fugitives from organized living, but there were also "a large percentage of people up here who simply opt for a life with nature. And that has nothing to do with whether they can function or not."

For some years, Drummond both abetted and fled institutional life, working as publications director for the National Center for Atmospheric Research in Boulder and commuting from the cabin. Now he was working on a book full time, keeping two years of firewood ahead, and laying in groceries when a big storm was coming. If he got surprised, he could ski to the store in Ward as easily as I walk my daily mile to the bus in Wichita. On the wall behind the couch where I was sitting were rows of photographs showing great, snowy mountains and semimicroscopic skiers. Drummond told me the pictures had been taken on a cross-country skiing expedition he led. It started near Durango, Colorado, and ended up in the mountains west of Fort Collins: six weeks and 490 miles, he said—"that was the adventure of a lifetime."

I asked him about skiing above timberline. It's tough, he said; on the ridges, it's often blown bare till spring, and there are cornices that can break off; also, the snow will vary unexpectedly from hard to soft: "You'll be skimming along the surface and suddenly your skis will dive into the soft snow, and you'll go over headfirst." Jim Palmer had told me similar things about timberline skiing, but I had hoped Drummond would say it was wonderful, a matter of tipping over a summit ridge onto a long sweep of perfect powder and making S turns like calligraphy for a couple of thousand feet of drop. Timberline slopes had always stirred me to such fantasies. It was appropriate that this trip was eroding them. At sixty-one, I could expect to be hit with clear sight, and worse.

If Enos Mills, the subject of Drummond's book, ever felt disillusioned about the high country, I gather he didn't admit it. Mills, who successfully pushed for a national park in the Rocky Mountains and also successfully ran the Longs Peak Inn, aspired to be the John Muir of the Rockies, Drummond told me.

He was a vigorous early publicist for the benefits of high altitude and encouraged people to come out to this wonderful high-altitude, elastic air in which you could move more easily, in which your thoughts were optimistic, where you would make acquaintances on the trail at a depth that you would not make otherwise, and so forth . . . He made it sound as if nobody ever gets sick at high altitude. In fact a lot of people at his inn got headaches and so forth, because they'd come immediately to 9,000 feet. But Edna Ferber, who stayed there a lot—the novelist—agreed with him that the high-altitude air was like a good martini.

The talk about mountain sickness reminded Forrest Ketchin of something, and in her deferential southern-lady way she reminded Drummond: "You were the first pulmonary edema case, and written up in what book?" It was *The New England Journal of Medicine,* no less. Before Drummond's case, hikers and mountaineers who developed bubbly coughs at high altitude and often died within two or three days were presumed to have pneumonia. At the end of 1958, when he was twenty-one, Drummond went on a cross-country skiing trip with a friend, camping in a tent at 11,500 feet near Snowmass Lake, a remote area in those days before the Snowmass ski development. They started from Aspen, at nearly 8,000 feet, and carried packs of forty pounds or more over a 12,000-foot pass in deep snow. On the second day, Drummond felt weak, developed a cough, and had trouble breathing. On the third day, he and his friend tried to ski down to the valley, but Drummond was too weak to make it. On the fourth day, the friend skied out for help while Drummond lay in the tent. On the afternoon of the fifth day, help came on skis, one of the helpers being Dr. Charles S. Houston, then an internist at the Aspen Clinic, who brought along his children's toboggan to pull Drummond out on. Houston wrote up the case in *The New England Journal.* (Drummond, who changed his name in the late 1980s to that of one of his grandfathers, is identified by his former initials, R.C.)

Three months after the experience, Drummond went back into the mountains above Aspen, climbed thirty-three hundred feet on skis, reaching 11,200 feet, spent two hours cross-country skiing, and then underwent another examination. Houston found him free of symptoms. But some people who once have high-altitude pulmonary edema (HAPE) seem more susceptible to it thereafter; when Drummond returns to Colorado from a visit at sea level, he tries to stay overnight in Denver before going to his cabin. Then he avoids higher altitudes for several days. He told me he could still go easily to 14,000 feet; the trick was not to hurry. "I have an old-man-of-the-mountain pace," he said.

HAPE is far more serious than acute mountain sickness. It usually develops just as Drummond's did, on the second to fourth day at high altitude after a fast climb. The symptoms are fatigue and shortness of breath to a degree uncommon even at high altitude; a cough that typically produces froth or blood, with a bubbly sound from the chest that can often be heard without a stethoscope; a high pulse rate; mental peculiarities; sometimes a slight fever. Coma and death can come within a few hours; Drummond was lucky. Physical fitness has no bearing on susceptibility. As Houston observed in his article, Drummond had trained hard for weeks before his skiing trip. And HAPE may be especially common in dwellers at high altitude who return, as Drummond did, after spending a week down low. Children through their teens are particularly susceptible to both HAPE and ordinary mountain sickness.

I turned to Forrest Ketchin, who so far had left the talking to Drummond. She told me that David Paddon, one of Paul Fretwell's friends who died in the June storm on South Arapaho Peak, had been an intern in a succor-and-teach organization that she had helped found—the Indian Peaks Wilderness Group. Every summer the organization puts forty volunteers to work hiking and camping in the wilderness area, making sure at the start that all are equipped with garbage bags. The bags are not for garbage. The participants in the program look for flatlanders who don't understand the tundra; they instruct them and, when necessary, help them get out of whatever fix they have let the elements get them into. "The garbage bag," Forrest Ketchin said, "is the instant raincoat: hole in the top and two arms, with a sweater underneath, and you've probably saved a life." (I should have taken a garbage bag on my hike above Diamond Lake.) She told me about the parents who left their eight-year-old daughter sitting at a trail junction in the krummholz on Mount Audubon at eleven one morning and went on to climb to the top, which looked just a short distance away in the insubstantial air. The sun was shining; they would be back in a half hour. One of the hosts found the girl shivering in a bitter storm in her T-shirt and shorts, took her down to the head host on the main trail, and went back for the parents. "Hosts come back every year with stories of encountering someone on a pass, and a lightning storm with hail falling everywhere, and the person not having even a poncho or a windbreaker," Forrest Ketchin said.

Drummond put in, "Because it was ninety degrees in Denver when they left."

"Women with babies," she went on. "And the little babies have on sunbonnets and little pinafores . . ."

Her remarks about ecotones had caught my ear earlier, and I asked for more. She seemed happy to talk about her ideas, though a shade doubtful that anyone would really be interested. She said the most popular destinations of visitors to the Indian Peaks Wilderness Area were Blue and Isabel Lakes, both of them in the forest-tundra ecotone, just at timberline. That ecotone, with the thousand-year-old krummholz trees, some of them "essentially a hundred feet tall except that they're along the ground instead of standing up," fascinates people, she said.

I have speculated that these ecotone lakes with the krummholz trees have to do with that human experience of coming out of the forest, having climbed and sweated, and suddenly being released into the expanse of the tundra, and here in front of you is a beautiful lake, usually in a depression surrounded by a moraine so you can stand up above it, and then there before you is a peak rising higher, with a snowfield.

It's more than merely an esthetic appeal, she said. "It has an emotional content that I think is evolutionary, because so many different animals seek these—seek edges—and humans particularly not only seek edges, they call them sacred."

Sometimes when people designate a sacred ecotonal site, she said, they feel the need of something more clearly above themselves. Mont St. Michel, for instance, "rises up, and when the tide's high, it's cut off from the land, but when the tide's low, there's access to it. So it rises up out of the ocean, and then they will build a spire on it to . . ."

"Emphasize," Drummond said.

"Emphasize . . ."

"How high . . ."

This is. Things like that; there are just numerous examples— Christian, Buddhist, Zen, Hindu, Native American, Australian aborigine—all over the world, of certain criteria being applied; and when those criteria cannot be met naturally—for instance, if a particular group of aborigines in Australia are wandering in a particular part of the Outback and they have to settle for the night, and they can't find a particular tree in a particular configuration, they have the leader carry the staff and . . . plant the staff in the center of the place where they're going to camp, and by that act establish this relationship between what's up there and what's down here, which—

and she returned to a theme that I thought had been lost amid the aboriginal wanderings—"mountains and lakes establish just by their very existence."

How many ways must there be of looking at a mountain? Hers was one I had never before encountered, and yet one as much at home on a mountain as vulcanology is inside it—a viewpoint that encompassed both ecotonal shrines and life-saving garbage bags. Drummond's, on the other hand, was familiar, and yet not a duplicate of anybody else's. I suspect that nobody's relationship with mountains is exactly the same as anybody else's and also that nobody's is the same twice, anymore than a mountain will ever again reveal itself in quite the same way it looks at this moment, or this.

But why must my own way of looking at mountains start so far from them? Why didn't I live in the country where those two people (she lived in Boulder) spent so much thoughtful time? Why didn't I live in a cabin in the subalpine woods and write books about mountain characters? On the other hand, I hadn't asked Alexander Drummond how he proposed to provide for his old age if he didn't hit upon a provident book or two. Maybe Social Security and a trickle of royalties would keep him in kerosene, ski wax, and beans. He was only fifty-three in any case. I, at that age, had scarcely begun to think about providing for my later years and my wife's. So I might as well have lived in a cabin above Ward all that time, mightn't I? I said goodbye to the biographer and the anthropologist, drove to Lakewood, and had swordfish and pesto and a glass of fat chardonnay for dinner.

* * * * *

Forrest Ketchin's ideas about the sacred overtones of timberline made me curious about people who had seen all the American timberlines long before her kind and mine. Indians may or may not have looked upon them as places more frequented by spirits than lower places. Some archaeologists say that the stone circles Indians built above timberline are oriented, like Stonehenge, to catch the rays of the sun at the solstice. I talked on the phone about that idea, and others, with two specialists in high-altitude archaeology. James B. Benedict, who is with the Center for Mountain Archeology at Ward, is not one of the believers. He has spent time among primitive mountain people elsewhere. "They're astonishingly oblivious to what I think is an esthetically wonderful environment," he told me. And E. Steve Cassells, whose doctoral research is on a hunting site in the Colorado tundra, said that although there is a wheel in Illinois that unquestionably lines up with the sun and the seasons, such an alignment would make less sense among the Indians he had studied. "These are just hunters," he said, "and so the sun and all that isn't going to be as important as it would be for planting."

Prehistoric Indians certainly did hunt at timberline. They liked the ecotone because it was more sheltered than the tundra and had fewer insects than the forests, Benedict says, and because animals liked it. Benedict has written about a site at timberline near the little lake where my own ecotonal urge got me soaked and chilled. The site contained tools for repairing hunting weapons, along with some projectile points. And Cassells's tundra site, also in the Indian Peaks area but seven or eight miles north of the part I visited, consists in part of a V-shaped chute made of rocks, something more than a half-mile wide at the opening. Indians probably used it for thousands of years. Some of the participants in a hunt would conceal themselves in stone blinds near the apex of the V. Others would get behind a flock of bighorn sheep (or possibly a band of elk) and drive it into the trap, probably so gently that the sheep would stop to graze along the way. When the animals were packed together in the narrows, the concealed hunters would jump up with their spears and kill them. There are almost fifty hunting blinds at the site, though Cassells says they wouldn't all have been used at the same time. A flock might have amounted to twenty to fifty sheep, if sheep were what they were; rodents destroyed any bones left on the sites, and sheep are small enough that the hunters would probably have carried the carcasses off the mountain and butchered them in camp. The tundra of the northern part of the Front Range is full of game drives—more than fifty have been found, according to Benedict, who writes about them in "Footprints in the Snow: High-Altitude Cultural Ecology of the Colorado Front Range, U.S.A."

One of Cassells's purposes is to test Benedict's theory that Indians stopped for late-summer hunting in the high country as they returned from the west side of the mountains to their winter grounds in the eastern foothills. The site Cassells is testing is remote enough to suggest that, as he says, Indians wouldn't have gone up there on a whim: "It's just a monstrous hike." And yet it's not tough enough to have discouraged treasure hunters who have the notion that every archaeological site must contain salable artifacts. When he went up for his second year of study, Cassells found that somebody had excavated all the holes he and his colleagues had dug. It was wasted work, he said: artifacts in that dig are few and unimpressive. He and I marveled that the tundra-hiking urge would be coupled with the despoiling urge.

In spite of Benedict's scoffing and Cassells's reservations, I still like to think that timberline exerted a special romantic or spiritual pull on Indians. It certainly must have exerted such a pull on the Incas of Peru, who named their mountains as real-estate developers would: the White Dart, Star of Snow, Sentinel of Stone—the last being Aconcagua (see Evelio Echevarría, "The Inca Mountaineers, 1400–1800"). And when Indians chose Old Man Mountain in Colorado as the location of vision quests, during which men fasted and invited their souls (see Benedict's "Footprints"), surely the view from the eminence, or of it, or both, was an influence. The mountain, rising behind a 7-Eleven store in Estes Park, is far below timberline, but, as Benedict observes, the view from the top is spectacular. If that view, along with the prominence and anthropomorphism of the peak, put spiritual thoughts into the Indian mind, why would the higher terrain and wider views of the tundra not likely have done the same? Benedict told me, in fact, that there are sites above timberline with the same "suites of artifacts" as the ones found on Old Man Mountain—"really exquisite" tools that might have been left as offerings—and he believes the sites were similarly used for fasting. What is lacking, to his mind, is evidence that Indians attached romantic or religious significance to the tundra or krummholz. More likely, he says, they went there because the game was there. Some archaeologists have interpreted certain game-drive structures as religious. "My own personal opinion is that that's a bunch of hogwash," Benedict said.

* * * * *

One day of my trip was an interlude in the foothills—a rest from timberline. My brother, Bob, was visiting his daughter at Fort Collins. He and I went in his pickup to Dadd Gulch, which Bob, like most others who live there (as he used to), puts in the filial possessive: Dadd's Gulch. We parked, opened a gate, closed it behind us, and walked up a Forest Service trail—a stock trail, though it showed no sign of having been used for that purpose recently. It was a swell, easy hike. We started at 6,900 feet in country with bare south slopes and sparsely forested north ones and followed a small creek bordered at first by willows and alders—I recognized the serrated alder leaves that grab your leader when you try to cast a fly. As we walked upstream and uphill, I saw a single aspen by the water and soon some nice stands of small ones. Aspens have white bark, slicker than birches'. They are slender and fresh, with tremulous leaves, among the most beautiful living things in the Rockies.

Later we found ourselves among big ponderosa pines, with also some Douglas firs. We were following a dry tributary by then. From the slope above it, as I looked down at the tops of a grove of good-sized aspens, a breeze created a Van Gogh shimmer among the leaves. We cut upslope, taking our time but soon pulling out on top of the first line of foothills—our goal, though only a thousand feet above the road where we had parked. We sat on a rock amid ponderosas and ate lunch. In the shade, the breeze cooled my back deliciously where my pack had been. The sun, between trees, brought out the aromatic smell of sagebrush. A grasshopper wavered past on a long flight without a steering wheel, buzzing a crackly buzz.

We talked about the hikes of our youth, when, as I remembered with guilt, Bob had always been not only the teacher but also the worker, showing me by doing it himself how to pitch a lean-to and thatch it with boughs (that was in the days when cutting foliage was not just permitted but recommended—a standard, rewarding technique of woodsmanship), how to scour a skillet with sand from the creek, how to squeeze all the air out of a down sleeping bag to make a tight roll of it. He had always been the enthusiast, the one of us whose eyes took on an explorer's look in conceiving the ruggedness of this or that remote range on the map, the one who, more than I, hung onto his boyhood delight in the free ways of aborigines and pioneers, and the one who gave his delight shape by making and using bows, boomerangs, atlatls, and muzzle loaders. I warmed to his fancies more readily than I originated my own, and although I admired his weapons, I knew better than to turn my awkward hand to copying them.

These days, having long since moved out of Colorado to the hill country of our native Texas, he teaches piano, gives recitals on the piano, plays also the harpsichord—one that he made, of course—and spends his spare time making assorted boats and trying them on the clear Guadalupe River near his house. Of the two of us, he is the more dedicated to the romance of the earth, the less willing to acknowledge the demands of organized life. But on the day of our Dadd Gulch hike, I suspect, we felt about equally free of such concerns. It was good to be kids again. After a while we bestirred ourselves and lazed back down the stock trail to the truck, feeling wonderful. Attaining timberline is not essential to the enjoyment of mountains.

A week earlier, when I had phoned Franklin and Mary Folsom, it had taken them a while to figure out a time for us to talk because both had deadlines to meet on books they were writing. Between them they had written more than a hundred books. He was eighty-four years old, she eighty-five. At their apartment in Boulder, we sat around a coffee table. He was squarely built, with powerful forearms and shoulders, and she was darkish, with an aquiline nose, a high forehead, and straight hair, still considerably brunette. They had both been born in Colorado, but although they loved the mountains, they had turned their backs on them: for fifty years, they lived in and near Manhattan: where the publishers were, where duty was. But in the summers they drove back to Colorado with their children and camped in the mountains. Once, after the kids were grown, they saw a For Sale sign on a big log cabin next to a lake. Knowing that the Forest Service was moving out all cabins there, Franklin Folsom inquired. The owner told him the only offer he had had was from hippies; he refused to do business with hippies; he would sell to Folsom for one dollar.

The Folsoms had the cabin moved to a piece of land they had just bought, a half mile upslope from Alexander Drummond's place. Shortly the Boulder County health department hit them with so many required installations that they decided they might as well go all the way, fix the cabin up for winter, and live in it. "So it was a somewhat accidental arrangement that we found ourselves with a permanent home almost up at timberline," Franklin Folsom said. They lived there thirteen years and then, finding it increasingly tedious to shovel their way down to the road in the winter, moved to Boulder. That was in the mid-1980s.

Maybe they had slowed down on the snow shoveling, it struck me, but surely they hadn't on the writing. As they worked on their newest books, they also were revising an old and well-known one: *America's Ancient Treasures*. The book is a guide to archaeological sites and museums in the United States and Canada. The Folsoms showed me, on a table behind them, a copy of it with sheaves of yellow correction slips sticking out of the pages. It is a work that E. Steve Cassells has since warmly recommended to me, specifically in connection with its account of Indian medicine wheels and the like; and I notice that it says without qualification that an astronomer has found that a stone medicine wheel high in the Bighorn Mountains of Wyoming is aligned with the rising sun at the summer solstice (pages 207–8, third edition). The Folsoms compose on old portable manual typewriters. He used to use pseudonyms, one of them Troy Nesbit. She, as Mary Elting, has written more than seventy children's books.

When he was attending the University of Colorado in Boulder (where the football field is named for his father, Fred G. Folsom, a professor of law and, for seventeen years, the football coach at the university), Franklin Folsom guided green summer students up the Arapaho Peaks. Once, he was leading a party of more than two dozen across the ridge between the peaks—the ridge where the storm hit Paul Fretwell and his companions—while another guide took a group of the same size down the mountain a different way. A woman sprained her ankle. Folsom helped the rest of the party down Henderson Glacier, having them stand and ski on their boots or sit and bump down the rough snow on their bottoms. (Henderson Glacier, Folsom tells me, is just north of Arapaho Glacier and is separated from it by a ridge.) He and the injured woman went last. They sat in tandem on the snow. He was in front, holding her legs with his arms. Halfway down, she somehow caught her good heel in the snow. The jolt swung them around so that they plunged head first down the slope. She was wearing a slicker. It zipped them along like a waxed toboggan. Looking at the sky, Folsom dug his heels into the snow, but it wasn't enough. Just before they would have hit bottom, the other guide, returning to see why they

were late, arrived from downslope. "He got to the snowbank in time
to run out in the snow and dive into us and stop us from going into
that moraine at the bottom," Folsom said.

I asked him when was the last time he had been in the Arapaho
Peaks country. "Last summer," he said; he had hiked to switchbacks
beyond the Fourth of July Mine, above timberline. Another hike he had
taken, five years earlier, was the peace march from Los Angeles to
Washington, D.C. At seventy-nine, he was the oldest to make the trip,
he said. "Not much of that was above timberline," he told me. I
thought that was humor, but no—they had hiked over Independence
Pass, 12,095 feet above sea level. Both the Folsoms love alpine country.
They have been to timberline together many times, in several countries.
Still, they went the world's way for fifty years, choosing the lowland city
for the sake of their careers. I imagine that when they lived in
Manhattan, their work in the absence of mountains made them happier
than mountains would have made them in the absence of work.

* * * * *

I opened my motel room door at 6:30 on Saturday morning—the
next-to-the-last day of my vacation—when Clare Gregg knocked.
After forty-five years, I would have recognized him instantly if I had
seen him on the street. Except for the one ascent of Cameron Cone
when we were teenagers, we had never hiked together. When we had
talked on the phone the day before, I had told him that I felt pretty
good, and if he wanted, we could climb a 14,000-footer. Of the fifty-
four mountains that high in Colorado, I had climbed only Mounts
Harvard and Columbia, and those on the same day—they are connected by a ridge. Clare said he had climbed, oh, twenty-two or
twenty-three. With some climbers, it's almost a matter of pride not to
keep count. Robert M. Ormes, who has climbed them all, expresses
annoyance in his *Guide to the Colorado Mountains* at the amount of
attention the fifty-four get. There are lesser peaks of just as great interest, he says. He says that when climbers have made all fifty-four, they
usually feel freed of a burden and glad they can start climbing for fun.
Still, I'll bet that Clare knows how many times he has climbed Pikes
Peak. He climbed it once, he told me, from Manitou Springs—seventy-seven hundred feet below—and in a single day. He had been a
superb athlete: state champion pole-vaulter when we were in high
school in Colorado Springs and later Big Eight champion. Even so,

that is a cruel amount of altitude to gain and lose in a day. Neither of us could come near it now.

Mount Evans is the closest thing Denver has to the dominance and majesty of Pikes Peak. It is in fact 154 feet higher than Pikes, and its breadth from north to south seems just as great. It falls short of the Pikes effect because it is farther from town and less cleanly enthroned among smaller mountains, less grandly naked. If the Laramide epoch had cast up Mount Evans in Pikes Peak's place and vice versa, tourists in Colorado Springs would look up Mount Evans Avenue and over the Antlers Hotel to a slightly more magnificent mountain than the one they see today up Pikes Peak Avenue, and only Denverites would ever have heard of Pikes Peak. Like Pikes Peak, Mount Evans has a well-used road to the top, or almost to the top.

Clare had climbed to 12,000 feet on the east side of the mountain— the Denver side—but never all the way. He had also hiked up the north-western approach before branching off to climb Mount Bierstadt. That was the approach we were taking. We could have chosen to climb Grays or Torreys Peaks, both of them higher than Evans, but Clare said they were easy and therefore likely to be crowded. Mount Evans suited me. Together with Longs on the north and Pikes on the south, it makes the third orienting point in the string of major peaks you can easily see from the right parts of Denver. When I was a student at the University of Denver in the late 1940s, I used to gaze at them from a semireclining position on a grassy slope outside the cafeteria after lunch, dreaming.

On the drive along Interstate 70 to Georgetown and then south on a lesser road to Guanella Pass, we talked, not about old acquaintances from high school but about glaciers. Clare, a geologist with an oil company, could tell me that a glacier shows little cracking and checking on top when it glides through a smooth valley but breaks apart like falling water when it crosses a ledge. I suppose that a glacier creeping along smooth granite will yield up a Bronze Age corpse some centuries earlier than a glacier negotiating crags and slabs. Clare and I, three decades past our prime and on the way to climb a mountain, talked glaciers but might have meant time. I'm sure that for him, as for me, the years seemed to have slipped along on waxed floors, the top ones even faster than the bottom ones. But we didn't articulate the connection. His reticence, as I was soon reminded, always pulled him up short of speculations that edged toward sentimentality.

It was brisk and clear when, a little before eight o'clock, we pulled into the parking lot on top of Guanella Pass, 11,669 feet above sea level. A glass-covered map of the mountainous skyline, fixed on a post, was glazed with new ice and illegible. In the valley below, scrub willows covered everything for a long way toward Mount Evans. We saw two hikers follow a trail into them and vanish. Willows are a wrestling match. We drove back to the second switchback from the pass, parked at 11,400 feet, walked down a couple of hundred feet to a creek bottom, found a place to teeter across the creek on two rocks, and shouldered and butted our way through a waterside fringe of head-high willows, getting soaked. It had rained the night before; when we emerged from the thicket, we saw a cover of snow, or perhaps graupel, on the north slopes above timberline. We climbed between small, widely separated evergreens on an easy slope. Every thirty or forty feet, the top of a buried rock stuck up. There were succulent plants underfoot; timberline was close.

We had talked a little about Jim Palmer and his environmentalism. Thinking of Jim, I told Clare in all seriousness that to avoid crushing so much vegetation, maybe I ought to be walking in his tracks instead of at his side. "Come on!" he said—close to an outburst, for him. He took a few steps and said, "Your ski bum friend would say we had to walk on the rocks."

I: I hadn't thought about that. I'm sure you have strong feelings for the environment, but you're in a business that some people think is harming the environment. Does that cause you any conflicts, or . . .?

HE: No, we have to leave a little bit of a print on the ground in this life. (he laughs) And we've got to be responsible for putting things back the way we found them. But the book that we write by the print of time and geology is, in some ways, much more harsh on its own self than we are as people. And to overdo it— overdo it in one direction—is just—ridiculous. (His reserve will not let him keep on with the metaphor.)

I: How do you mean, that nature . . . is tough on itself? I mean, fires and stuff?

HE: Fires and volcanoes, earthquakes and landslides.

I: This guy is utterly sincere, I'm sure . . .

HE: Oh, I'm sure he is.

I: Just completely wrapped up in it. But I kind of left with the feel-
    ing—as if I'd talked to a Hindu or something . . .
HE: Yeah!
I: Who doesn't step on ants . . . ("Yeah!") . . . and doesn't . . .
HE: Yeah, right!

I told Clare it was disgusting, though, to see places like the
Climax Molybdenum Mine, which had turned some magnificent tundra and krummholz into pools of poison and heaps of earth-offal. He
agreed; there were too many sites like that; they wouldn't be permitted these days.

But a lot of people think, you know, when we're going to drill a
well or something, that we're going to leave the wilderness, or
whatever, like that. They don't understand drilling an oil well
and . . . you can't even find the spot where we drilled five years
later. As far as geological time goes, it's a, you know, it's a second. We're not tearing down forests; we're not open-pitting anything; we're drilling a nine-inch hole in the ground.

"Well, really," I said, "those people aren't protesting petroleum
operations as much as they are a lot of other things, are they?"
"Oh, they won't let us drill," he said. "And they're trying to put
the whole world into a wilderness area."
We were above timberline by 8:45 or so, and I, talking, had barely
noticed the break. It was not sudden, anyway. A mile or so across a
sweep of tundra, in the shelter of a slope facing us, we saw trees at our
own level, or so I thought. Clare, who flies over mountains all the
time, said no, they only looked as high; it was a common illusion. A
passenger in a light plane Clare is flying will ask him, trying to sound
casual, if he's sure he can clear the ridge ahead. "We've already
cleared it," Clare will reply.
We had no trail but walked on thick hummocks of grass or sedge
that rolled beneath our boots. It was like stepping on inverted rag
mops. Maybe a trail down a rocky streambed was better after all.
Paintbrushes grew all around us, amid a scattering of other alpine
flowers—more than on Pikes Peak, as the summit-house proprietor
had said, but nothing like the profusion of my South Arapaho trip six
days before. Little springs spurted out of the grassy slope. I filled my

canteen from one. It wasn't quite deep enough to get the canteen all the way under, but I at least replaced city water with mountain water. Though giardia—a parasite that causes intestinal misery on the level of the *turista* of visitors to Mexico—thrives in the Rockies, neither of us could believe there was danger in water that had jetted from the earth only an inch before. In our youth, we had drunk any water we were sure no one lived above.

Suddenly, far above us in a patch of willow krummholz, we saw a deer—a buck with a fine rack. He stood in profile amid the willows for a moment and then stotted on springy legs almost straight up the slope, somehow keeping his antlers from snagging the brush. He ran to the saddle four or five hundred feet above us, taking only a minute for what at our pace would have been a quarter-hour climb. On top he stopped and looked back, then jounced along the ridge in silhouette for a quarter mile before finally disappearing over the other side. It was amazing how much ground he had covered. "I'd like to have his cardiovascular system," Clare said.

I had declined Clare's invitation to lead, partly because he was more or less acquainted with the route and partly because I knew my tendency to go fast early and repent later. After an hour or so, he said, "I know I have a seventy-five-year-old pace today, but it's been steady, you know." It had. We had scarcely stopped except to watch the deer and for Clare to change from shorts to corduroy pants in anticipation of tundra weather; the corduroy went *wheet wheet wheet wheet wheet* when he walked. It was a beautiful day, blue and brisk and not very windy. I felt fine. Striding out, though, expressing my energy, would have been a bad mistake. Once you get exhausted, as Clare said, "You're through, you're absolutely through. You try to keep up with some teenager, you'll kill yourself." Clare kept nibbling on Corn Nuts; I turned down his offer to share them. We talked the way all reunited old classmates do:

"Did you know so-and-so?"

"Yeah, I guess so. Wasn't he a sort of blond guy, always grinning?"

I asked him about his brother, Don, who had been a ski trooper in World War II. Though I never met Don, Clare had told me about him when we were in high school.

"I remember you said he used to be nuts about the mountains," I said, "but that when he got in the ski troops, he lost all interest." That was right, Clare said. Was he still that way? I asked. "Pretty much so," he said. He marveled that I had remembered so long, but that story had made an impression on me—the idea that mountains and snow, like sex, lost their charm when encountered under duress.

We walked along contours as if the brown lines on the U.S. Geological Survey maps were our trails. That meant that to get from a point at the mouth of a U-shaped cut to a point opposite, on the other leg, we hiked to the back of the horseshoe, around the curve, and out again, holding to the same level. The alternative would have been to cut straight across, dipping a few hundred feet into the willow bottom and climbing to the same contour on the opposite leg. Our way was much the longer, but I imagine Clare was right in avoiding the down and up, and the brush. If I had been leading, we would have done it the other way. Clare wouldn't have said a word, but we most likely would have ended the day more nearly exhausted, even, than we did.

As it was, we were getting a little tired by about noon; when we finally stepped onto the north end of the long, upward-sloping summit ridge, the crags and gendarmes ahead looked more forbidding than we had the energy to tackle. So we cut behind the ridge onto the west, lee side, overlooking Abyss Lake. That slope was all steep pink-stone slabs, with slivers of sandy terraces here and there between them. We traversed, edging upward, clambering more than I had done on South Arapaho Peak and more tiringly. Flocks of ravens soared beneath us in the updrafts and flew down to light on rocks around the lake.

For the first time I could remember, I felt woozy from the altitude. We were above 13,000 feet, which seems to be a decisive line for me. Every bend to find a new handhold made me fainter. (Clare said afterward that he had felt the same way.) I kept looking up at the ridge and thinking that, thank God, we were nearly there. When we at last did flump over the top of the ridge again, we saw that the summit was still a long, long way ahead. Most disappointing. "Let's eat," I said. Clare, who had never stopped nibbling, grinned. "I think I have a little left," he said. We sat on the lee side and ate. Right away I felt much better. I finished my apple and asked, "Think it's OK to throw away an apple core up here, do you?" "Damn right," Clare said. "The birds will eat it." I flung it, enjoying the little rebellion against environmental correctness. We put our packs on and walked up the summit ridge. The wind made me grab my hat a time or two but wasn't as strong as usual on a ridge that high. To our left, straight below, were snowfields at least as steep as Arapaho Glacier, but I jumped from boulder to boulder, one step from falling over the edge and not worried, though at home I refuse to stand on the top of a kitchen ladder. Altitude impairs judgment.

Finally, we hit the highway just where it ended. Several dozen cars were in the parking lot. Families walked up and down the trail between the lot and the summit, a couple of hundred feet above. We joined the walkers on that last brief climb. After a few minutes, a man coming down told us encouragingly, "You're more than halfway." We looked at each other and laughed the way high school boys do, feeling superior. From the top, I saw the burned-out summit house at the edge of the parking lot, its stone buttresses lodged not against a wall anymore but against vacant sky. Among the tourists on the summit with us were a group of a half-dozen from Germany and a young couple who attended Colorado School of Mines at Golden. He came from Medellín, Colombia, and she from La Paz, Bolivia. They made pleasantly belittling remarks about the altitude where we were standing.

No doubt their oversized lungs gave them a permanent adaptation to the thin air. I wonder, in fact, if Clare Gregg and others brought up in foothill towns 6,000 feet or so above sea level don't develop some of the same capacity, like the beagle puppies that the scientist took to Leadville to grow up. When I was a baby, I lived in El Paso, Texas, altitude 3,800; maybe it's more than an accident that I feel most vigorous at about that altitude. Maybe we all have lungs sized to the altitude at which we spent our puppyhoods, and that is the altitude that brings out the best in us. So what were Clare and I doing eight thousand feet above his optimal altitude and ten thousand feet above mine?

It was two o'clock. We started down. On top of Mount Bierstadt, a mile and a half away by air, we could just make out the silhouettes of three or four hikers. We met a climber on his way up from Summit Lake. He had on a T-shirt from the Olympic training center at Colorado Springs. Yes, he said, the center was still operating. I had supposed that the studies of Rusten Igor Gamow might have shut it down. Gamow, a professor (of chemical engineering) at the University of Colorado, had tested runners and concluded that it was a bad idea to train at high altitude. Train at sea level, he advised them, where the dense air permits you to give your muscles their utmost workout. But live up high, where you produce more red blood cells. When I had talked with Gamow by phone from my motel a few days before, I asked if his experiments had made him unpopular with the Chamber of Commerce in Boulder. "Very," he said. "Not to mention the Olympic training center." His findings hadn't been out long, and of course no scientific study is accepted without contest, especially when acceptance might mean you had to leave Colorado Springs.

"Look!" said the hiker, who was forty or fifty feet downslope from us. "Mountain sheep!" We picked our way down for a look. They weren't sheep but goats, a nanny in front and a billy a hundred feet back, walking a contour line below us, taking their time, ignoring us, and heading toward the parking lot. We supposed they went there regularly for peanuts and sandwich crusts. It was shedding season—a bad time to be seeing my first mountain goats. The nanny, especially, looked like a tramp. She had patches of white on her front shoulders, but the rest of her was mouse colored. The billy was all dark. A while after we parted from the hiker, I found a tuft of white hair between rocks and picked up a small tangle. When I separated the strands between my thumb and forefinger, they felt coarse and oily. Enough of them would make a warm mountain jacket.

It became a tough hike again. My faintness returned, and an ache developed at the base of my skull. We slanted down the grassy slopes, edging the right soles of our boots this time, instead of the left, and cutting across the mouths of the arroyos now that we were going down. Clare asked a couple of times over his shoulder how I was doing. "Pretty good," I said. He, too, he said. After another hour of slogging, when he asked again, I replied, *"Fair"*—how was he? *"Fair,"* he said. I was at the stage of looking down all the time, willing my feet to move ahead. Eventually, I kept telling myself, this will be over. It's amazing how long a descent of four miles and three thousand feet can seem to a nauseated person walking at the optimal altitude for mountain goats.

The rain broke loose. It was cold, heavy, and mixed with stinging sleet. My windbreaker was no more water repellent than it had been above Diamond Lake, as I might with sufficient mental effort have been able to foresee. I bent my neck and watched the ground just ahead of my toes. Slog, slog. Then we came to willows. They were taller than we, each leaf a trap for icy rainwater. Clare stopped and put on baggy nylon pants that unzipped all the way up each leg so that you stepped into them like shorts. I had on khaki part-cotton pants that soaked up water. Each willow bough I shouldered aside drowned me, froze me. I got my fur-lined leather gloves out of my daypack and put them on. In half a minute, they were as soaked as if made of chamois.

Finally we broke out of the willows. I peeled off the gloves, unsticking each leather finger and tugging at it. The rain stopped. In a few minutes, we were back into the sparse timber. We slashed sharply downslope, too tired for finesse, and bulled through the streamside willows, across the creek, and anaerobically up the last slope to the car. Man. Then down to Georgetown. At the Silver Queen restaurant, deafened by the competing blares of young people's voices and young people's music, we had a hamburger and a steak and beer and margaritas. On the drive to Denver, neither of us said a dozen words. No subject was worth the effort. Ah, timberline.

It wasn't until I washed my hands the next morning, Sunday, the day I had to drive five hundred miles home, that I made the discovery. My gold wedding band was gone. I looked in the bathroom, lay with my cheek on the rug and one eye shut to squint across the room for any object rising above floor level, and turned inside out the fingers of my left glove, still sopping wet. Nothing. I phoned the Silver Queen. Nothing. No point in going over my trail. I would never in a hundred years find a ring amid the willows or in the marmot dens beneath the boulders. Besides, I had to be at work before eight the next morning. I remembered that, once, on the way down, when my hands were shrunken with cold and slick with rain, the ring had slipped over my knuckle. "Got to be careful about that," I had told myself as I pushed it back up. And I remembered having to work off each finger of the wet, clinging gloves.

I packed the car and started home, feeling awful. All day the loss of the ring told me how irresponsible my mountain escapes were. I drove across dusty plains, a south wind plastering tumbleweeds against the fence lines to my right, nothing rising above the flatness to be the "what's up there" of my aboriginal cravings, as if I had not already put those cravings aside in disgust. When I finally pulled into the fringes of Wichita, the buildings ahead rose in a blur of pollution. Here, once more, was the abode of duty, of crabgrass, of touch-tone phones, of livelihoods—the optimal altitude of the dull and conscientious.

Part II

The Sierra Nevada

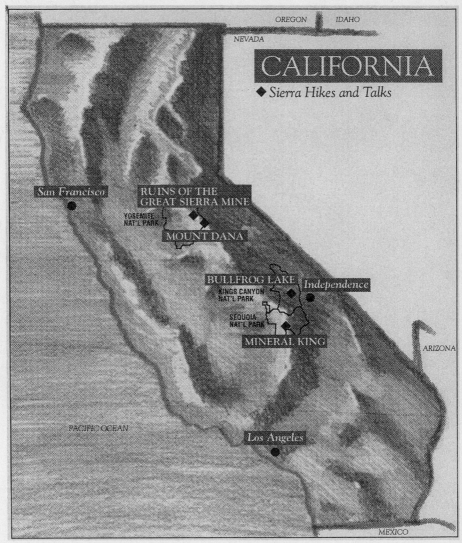

CALIFORNIA
◆ Sierra Hikes and Talks

OREGON   IDAHO
NEVADA

San Francisco

RUINS OF THE
GREAT SIERRA MINE

YOSEMITE
NAT'L PARK

MOUNT DANA

BULLFROG LAKE   Independence

KINGS CANYON
NAT'L PARK

SEQUOIA
NAT'L PARK

MINERAL KING

ARIZONA

PACIFIC OCEAN

Los Angeles

MEXICO

Brent Castillo

CHAPTER FIVE

Except that they reek of the lawless moments spent on them by fellow employees who are not supposed to smoke in the building, the darkest and least-used stairs at my place of employment make a fair conditioning ground for mountain hikes. They, like mountains, are cold in winter and hot in summer, and though the uniform height of the risers and the levelness of the treads are unmountainlike, the climb is plenty of work, and the descent provides realistic jolts. As I had done before my Colorado climbs, I spent twenty minutes on the stairs three times a week all year to get ready for the next round of summer hikes. That is enough to protect against excruciatingly sore thighs.

During a workout, I made ten round trips between the fourth floor and the street level, exactly a hundred steps each way, lifting myself 583 feet and lowering myself the same distance by the time I had finished. I took two stairs at a time, dragging up but hurrying down on the assumption that it was best to keep my heart and lungs working as steadily as possible. Also, the jolting is more pronounced that way and therefore presumably better conditioning, though before the summer was over, I wondered if I shouldn't have made it easier on my knees, not harder. When climbing, I put just the ball of my foot on the treads and let the heel sink into space, stretching the muscles in the back of my leg as happens in the wild. And remembering my out-of-breath clambering in Colorado, I pulled on the handrails during part of each climb so my arms and shoulders would get used to helping. For the last couple of months before heading for the mountains, I increased my workouts to twelve round trips. Those, along with brisk daily walks of a mile each way to and from the bus line, somewhat improved my condition, I'm sure, but it was as an anodyne that the work emphatically helped.

My first destination was the Sierra Nevada; the second, the Cascades; the third, after a two-week intermission, the northern Appalachians—three widely differing ranges in five weeks. I was excited and curious. John Muir's rhapsodies, the photographs in National Park Service brochures, and my memories of hikes forty years before had made me particularly keen to see the California and Washington mountains again. For part of the year I had drooped under the conviction that mountain expeditions were a breach of the commandment, Thou shalt not play. A punishable breach—otherwise, why would I have lost my wedding ring in the rocks on the back slope of Mount Evans? Time silenced such recrimination, and I took off with joy.

On the flight to Fresno, the clouds began to break over what I supposed was the Owens Valley. As I studied a large lake, trying to identify structures feeding in from the west and west northwest like tubes in a patient's mouth, the man next to me said, "Well, there's still quite a lot of snow up there." At that instant, we broke over the eastern escarpment of the Sierra Nevada. The world beneath us leaped seven thousand feet straight up. Almost as if I were among them, hiking the ridges, I saw jagged points, lakes, and spots of snow the same size and shimmer as the lakes; only that size, because it had been a dry year. There was lots of country above timberline and lots of bare rock that might or might not have been that high, since it wouldn't have grown trees in any case. The western slope had big trees just below timberline, probably lodgepole pine and red fir, and long, large lakes farther down. As promised in the books, the eastern slope reared up abruptly, but the western slope eased down toward the tawny hills and the Central Valley, giving me time to observe its zones.

The Sierra Nevada is a long north-south wedge with the straight side to the east, rising abruptly above Independence, Lone Pine, Bishop, and Big Pine, and the inclined face cutting west and down into the dense air of the Central Valley. We descended at about the same angle as the western slope and soon were low enough over the geometrical orchards of the San Joaquin Valley to make out individual almond, walnut, and citrus trees (my seatmate, an orchardist, told me which were which), each looking as if it had been molded of colored wax and set into place in a diorama. At Fresno the sun was still red in the western haze. I got out in fading light. The mountains to the east made a backdrop of one long purple ridge with a gray ridge behind it, and far beyond those, lighter and hazier, the real top. That would be alpine country, with the chill settling in, but it was hot outside the terminal building, where I stood and waited for a van to my motel.

The next morning I set out northward in my rented car, heading for Yosemite National Park. The trip would take me around a croquet wicket: north, then east, then south. My first stay would be in Independence, a small town only eighty-five miles east of Fresno, where I had started driving. But I couldn't drive directly there; for 150 miles the Sierra Nevada has no bisecting road. So I would go north along the western slope to Yosemite, east through the park and across the range, and south along the eastern escarpment to Independence— 234 highway miles altogether. I would hike west of Independence, up the escarpment by trail and over Kearsarge Pass to Bullfrog Lake, where, an archaeologist had told me, there were ruins of Indian dwellings. After that hike, I would drive back north to stay in Lee Vining, a town east of and down from Yosemite. At the east edge of the park, I intended to climb Mount Dana, a great red peak that had especially thrilled John Muir. I would talk with an archaeologist in the eastern part of Yosemite and then drive west across the park and again south, down nearly the full length of the Sierra to Mineral King, a valley once almost developed as a huge ski resort by Walt Disney. In the course of these drives and hikes I would get a good look at the Sierra Nevada and its timberlines, east and west.

Nearly always, the approach to a high mountain range is more distinctive than the top. That's not to say that timberline is timberline; if you set a reasonably observant hiker down on the highest ridge of any of the four major ranges in the contiguous United States in summer, in a cloud so he couldn't cheat by looking down at the foothills, he might yet guess which range it was by the density and form and tone of the alpine vegetation. A botanist could certainly do so. But nobody who pays minimal attention to countryside could mistake the dry sagebrush-and-ponderosa slopes of the Front Range foothills in the Rockies for the densely forested, steep western approaches to the Cascades or the boggy, dark woods beneath the peaks of the northern Appalachians in New England. The drive north from Fresno in my rented car took me through country at least as much itself as any of those. First came the hills, the grass brown and tall, with grain hanging from the stems like parched oats; this country gets only ten inches of rain a year. The folds

of one hill led my eye to a ranch-style house on top with small, graceful deodars around it. Then my eye traced a descending line of the slope
and at the bottom saw fat Herefords with their heads down, grazing.

The road kept rising. Suddenly oaks were growing on the slopes,
meaning that the altitude was enough to pull down an occasional bit
of moisture as the clouds cruised eastward at the level to which the
speed bump of the Coast Range had jolted them. The two-lane road,
State Highway 41, wound and climbed. Soon pines were mingling
with the oaks and head-high brush. Ahead a higher ridge had a fringe
of unmixed pines on top. A roadside sign said the altitude was 2,000
feet. Now and then I passed a seedy resort saying Affordable Rates,
and evidences of a touristophagous economy became more numerous
in the small towns as the road climbed: Nugget Cafe, Western
Clothing & Gifts, Century 21 Gold Rush office. That far south, in a
valley barred from most of the coastal mists and rains, the altitude
was just enough to furnish residents a living off the weakest wavelets
of city tourists—families looking for the kind of nature that comes
with swing sets and Sno Cones. But other signs offered homey services: well drilling, woodchoppers' supplies. Residents must collect
money from the tourists in town and then go back to their houses in
the hills and live the way the tourists dream of living.

At the 5,000-foot sign, the road had been in evergreen woods for
some time, the trees growing to the edge of the two-lane highway and
casting mottled shadows across it. At the same altitude on the eastern
slope of the Colorado Rockies, you're in plains country, with no vegetation taller than head-high junipers. The difference is partly that the
Rockies are far taller than the Coast Range, and so the remnants of
their storms stay higher after crossing the range, leaving the plains
dry, and partly that the Pacific storms that reach these Sierra foothills
have had only 150 miles or so in which to lose their moisture instead
of 850. At Big Creek, the first mountain stream on my route, I got out
and stood on the bridge to look for trout. I heard voices, and in a
moment a young woman burst out of the upstream brush, laughing
and making a face. Behind her, a bearded man in shorts emerged, carrying a squirming snake by the head. The woman shrieked. It was a
garter snake, I was sure. I hoped they would let it go.

In Yosemite I had planned to feel contemptuous of the tourists
who took pictures of the great rocks—the freak show—and ignored

the gorgeous forests and streams. But I stood and stared, too. I walked on a wood-chip trail from the road across an endangered meadow to get close to the base of El Capitan—the attraction of that abrupt, right-angled ecotone, I suppose. A small meadow mouse scuttled across the trail in front of me. At the end of the trail, the slickly flowing Merced River interposed itself between me and the rock. I wished to have been there with a fly rod before the touristing of the park. Muir would have tolerated my trifling in view of the greater good it was doing me. "Trout fishing regarded as bait for catching men, for the saving of both body and soul, is important, and deserves all the expense and care bestowed upon it," he said.

Before resuming my drive, I stood alongside the one-way road down the valley floor, counting, and in one minute, fourteen vehicles, one of them a motorcycle, passed. It was not the Long Island Expressway but not the Old Waco Highway, either. So onward and upward through the forests, which with increasing altitude changed from magnificent to exquisite. I crossed Yosemite Creek, a typical mountain brook here with no hint of the sculpturing ability it was to show downstream. At Olmsted Point, many tourists had stopped in the wings to view the hunched backs of the performing rocks going onstage, and I stopped, too. It was a world of bare rock. I wanted to go over to the city people and say, "Listen, this isn't what it's like to be up in the mountains. Mountains are green and have flowers." But this was spectacular in its granitic way. I got back into the car and drove over Tioga Pass and down, the trees on the slopes growing sparser with every mile of progress onto the east side of the divide. The west side at 6,800 feet had looked like a Disney fantasy of a forest. This, by the time I reached Lee Vining at the same altitude, was sagebrush country with big, but few, red-barked pines. It might have been possible, after all, to mistake it for the Colorado foothills.

The Sierra Nevada, rising to the west now and paralleling my drive south from Lee Vining, looked toothy and forbidding but still, in the beginning, like a mountain range rather than a great thrust-up mesa. One mountain, out to itself and looking only a mile away, was above timberline but had no timber—just sagebrush and then rock and snow. At Bishop the range got steeper , and at Independence, the end of the drive, the peaks looked still less hospitable than before: gendarmes, precipices, overhangs, and chimneys, with scarcely a level ridge—"everywhere," as Clarence King said in *Mountaineering in the Sierra Nevada* (1871), "the greatest profusion of bristling points." Yosemite had been a display of masonry; this was one of dentistry. I was glad I would be on a trail.

After gassing up at tourist prices in Independence and finding in lieu of a water fountain only soft drinks, which, out of grouchiness and on principle, I refused to buy, I headed west toward a collision with the Sierra wall. At the last minute, like an automatic door at a shopping mall, the mountains slid apart, and the road wound steeply into them, gaining five thousand feet in the thirteen miles to Onion Valley—a prosaic name for the setting of a pack station amid pointed evergreens with a creek foaming past. I looked unsuccessfully for drinking water, then started up the trail in my town pants and soft shoes to get a preview of the next day's route. It was an easy trail, much easier than office stairs. The air was cool and exhilarating. I met hikers on their way down: a woman and a man, he with a fishing rod on his pack; a teenage boy, burned red, pulling at a right-angled plastic straw that was stuck into a water bottle like a self-administered therapeutic drip; a young man and woman, carrying daypacks, who said they had gone almost to Kearsarge Pass. Feeling springy legged and energetic, I turned back after twenty minutes and swung down to the parking lot.

As I walked across the lot to my car, a woman hailed me. She said her friend had lost the key to his truck. I had met them near the top of my walk as they were coming down. I gave them a ride to Independence. Her name was Julie (not really; out of compassion, I am misidentifying both of them), and she taught at a university; his was Jack, and I think he taught somewhere, too. They were in their thirties; they lived in Los Angeles—together, I think. They told me the key had probably fallen out of his shorts pocket when he sat on a rock along the trail. They had to be back in Los Angeles the next day; they would look for a locksmith in Independence. There was plainly tension between them. Poor guy, I'm sure he was cursing himself.

When we pulled into the Shell station/grocery store in Independence they told their story to the blondish, middle-aged woman in charge. She got on the phone and tried to find her husband, a wrecker operator who might bring the truck down the mountain to get the lock picked. Jack and Julie stood outside the store and talked. He had thought of going back up, breaking into the camper, crawling into the cab of his truck from there, and hot-wiring it. But with the complicated computer wiring under the dashboard, that would be tough. Julie admonished him for being too ready to accept the wrecker-driver's services; couldn't he at least have looked for alternatives in the *Yellow Pages?* He bridled.

I left them, used the pay phone on the lawn outside the sheriff's office to call my wife in Kansas—there are no rooms with phones in Independence, the woman who ran my motel told me—and took a walk through the little town at sundown, all the Sierra Nevada a silhouette except for Mount Williamson, which stuck out eastward and so was detailed in the alpenglow. It had two X-shaped incisions filled with snow, up high. It was a tremendous mountain, as bulky as Mount Massive in Colorado. The town had modest houses with cottonwoods, deodars, fences, grass, and dogs.

Jack and Julie had the truck towed down during the night, and when I got back from breakfast the next morning, they were waiting for nine o'clock, when they could call the car dealer and get the key code for a locksmith. I noticed that the back of his camper was hanging loose and supposed he had had to pry it open and now couldn't shut it. That would cost him, and I suspected that he had little money. I drove back to Onion Valley, the clear light from the east revealing all the details of the mountains. It was a rocky, forbidding scene, without the charm or intimacy of, say, the mountains around Colorado Springs. "You'd be a fool to come up here," the voice of the country said through tyrannosaurus teeth. When I started up the trail at six minutes after eight, my legs felt dead, possibly because the hotcakes I had eaten at The Pines café sat heavy, possibly because I was wearing a daypack, light as it was, but most likely because hikers, like golfers and batters and singers, just have bad days and good ones. The creek roared alongside the trail, and I passed a fine, fat red fir and, a little later, some foxtail pines, their needle-encircled twigs forming brushes for cleaning a shotgun. It took me twenty-four minutes to climb to the place on the trail where I had met Jack and Julie; the evening before, I had made it in twenty. There was a cool downslope breeze. I saw a jawbone of rock ahead with snow lodged like tartar between the teeth.

Jack had told me that he had hiked up here quite a lot. Once he hiked clear to King's Canyon, fishing, taking seven days, though he could have done it in five if he had tried. It was wonderful fishing:

golden trout; rainbows; he thought brookies. I told him I hoped to climb Mount Dana. Had he been there? Oh, yeah, he said. He went there ski touring in the spring once with a girlfriend (not Julie, I gathered) and a guide (so he must have money after all). The guide took them along a slope that terrified him, with cornices everywhere. In one place, a cornice had fallen into a slide path, and the guide wanted to go down that way. Jack didn't. Oh, come on, Jack, the girl said; you can make it. He did, but at the bottom the girl laid out the guide thoroughly for taking them that way. For the sake of Jack's confidence, she hadn't shown her feelings earlier.

A solitary hike in the mountains makes you forget people and their problems. The flowers, for one thing, absorbed me, though they were nothing like as lush as the ones in the Indian Peaks; the Sierra Nevada, especially the east side, just doesn't get enough summer moisture for such a display. Still, there were enough that I wished for a handbook or a learned companion. I knew a few names and figured out a few later, using Stephen Whitney's *A Sierra Club Naturalist's Guide to the Sierra Nevada* and Tracy I. Storer and Robert L. Usinger's *Sierra Nevada Natural History: An Illustrated Handbook*. There were Sierra shooting stars, growing in a seep that crossed the trail; purple thistles; Indian paintbrush; a pair of small columbines whose spurs were red, not blue like those of Colorado columbines. I recognized the cluster of pink phlox growing in the shade of a cranny between a rock and the trail, and up high I saw a twiggy plant with dark-pink blossoms forming a round saucer: alpine laurel, the books say. Alongside a trickly stream on the west side, to get ahead of my pace, were the most graceful flowers of the hike—lustrous purple ones with gold centers, growing singly at the tops of their stems and shaped like vases when I bent to get a side view: Sierra gentians. It was a pleasure, later, to find them clearly described in the books. Though I stopped and gazed at flowers, talking what seemed like every observable characteristic into my pocket recorder, I often found afterward that I had picked out exactly the features that made no difference to a flower book.

The trail got steeper. I stopped to rest and look. In some places, I noticed, people had cut across switchbacks; the Green Berets of environmental correctness still had some mopping up to do. Looking down through the notch, where the road I had taken twisted and curled, and then across the valley beyond Independence, I saw the

southern extension of the White Mountains, a dry range that fascinated me in part because Indian dwellings had been found in it above
timberline. Indian families or groups of families, starting sometime
after A.D. 600, laid circular rock footings, erected timber houses on
them, thatched them, and lived in them for possibly more than two
months a year, the men hunting bighorn sheep and marmots, the
women digging roots out of the hard soil. (Robert L. Bettinger of the
University of California-Davis tells about the settlements in an article
in *American Anthropologist.*) Unfortunately, I would not be able to
manage a hike in those mountains on this trip. I drank from my World
War II surplus canteen and looked around. The krummholz was
beginning, though I could still see fair-sized trees three or four hundred feet above. When I held out the canteen to gasp after swallow-
ing—I was that short of breath at something over 10,000 feet—the
wind whooshed across the top like a pigeon's call.

At Bullfrog Lake, my destination for the day, Indians laid rocks to
form five rings that seem to have been footings for dwellings. The
anthropologist who discovered them, C. Kristina Roper Wickstrom,
told me about them on the phone from her office in Santa Cruz and
later sent me a draft of a paper she had written about them. She said
Indians went there because, after a population explosion in the Great
Basin, the increased competition made marginal grounds like the timberline country more attractive than before. (This was Bettinger's
explanation also.) It was an easy hike, she said—a couple of hours over
the pass and then a half hour down to the lake. The trail, she said, went
right through the site of the rock dwellings. The Sierra Club had held
camps at the lake at the turn of the century, according to her paper, but
the basin had been closed to camping since the late 1970s to give vegetation a chance to recover. I promised her that I would not give away
the exact location of the dwellings; she, like Cassells, was worried
about vandals. Imagine, though, that with campers for close to eighty
years pitching tents against the very rock foundations of the ancient
houses, none of them before her had ever reported to any scientific
institution the patterned courses of rocks they had seen. Possibly they
supposed the shelters were made by early-day Sierra Club campers.

I had been gone a little over an hour and was already starting to
put both hands on my hips as I walked. Tired hikers walk that way
because, I think, the arm position spreads the rib cage and makes

more room for air. Stunted trees were about me. Though the morning breeze in summer is supposed to go upslope, here it was meeting me as I climbed. I came to a lake and stood to look. A six-inch trout jumped. In an evergreen near me, small birds, olive green on top and dusty yellow green beneath, flitted about. A marmot ran a tight semicircle around a tree trunk ahead, vanishing, and another stuck its head up from a rock at the side of the trail. I lingered. Possibly it is my fishing instinct that brings home the beauty of such lakes. The breeze riffled this one but left a slick spot in the center. A fallen tree angled down the steep slope of the bottom until its bleached form disappeared. A trout swam along like a turtle, the ripples distorting it—maybe it was a turtle. At the far edge of the lake, gray boulders rising from the water were reflected, sitting on a foundation of themselves.

Up the trail, when I had started walking again, a sign said Matlock Lake. Two men were folding a tent close to the lake, breaking camp. A napkin-size sheet of clear plastic from some kind of food lay on the trail: disgusting. I walked on, feeling superior. Several hundred feet lower, I had thought I was in the krummholz, but here was a grove of thick-boled, red-barked foxtail pines, fifty feet tall. One near the trail must have been four feet in diameter, maybe five. Such stout trees did not belong so high. I stopped at ten o'clock and backed against a rock, letting my pack slip off on top. My wet shirt felt like ice against my exposed back. To eat an apple, out of breath and with my nose stuffed up by dryness, I chewed a moment, breathed with my mouth open, chewed a little more, and so on, an ungraceful spectacle. I wrapped up the core in plastic and stuck it into my pack—no doubt a decisive moment in my environmental-esthetic maturation. There were plenty of boulders, cracks, and mats of dwarf trees to hide it in, but I thought, what if somebody should find it, be disgusted, and feel superior to me? This was California, after all. Everything was orderly; everything took into account the fact that there were great masses of people, a fair percentage of whom hiked in the mountains.

I went on, stopping again soon to gaze at a deep lake—either Heart or Flower Lake—about three hundred feet below. The far side was a rock slide that sloped steeply into the lake and vanished far down in the dark-green water. When I started again, I felt a miniburst of energy from the apple. The sky was a deep blue. I had not seen a cloud all morning.

Here came a hiker down the trail to meet me, still far enough above that I could barely be sure of his sex. All around, at last, was real krummholz, waist high and sparse, spaced out by patches of lichens, bare rock, and flowers so small they barely deserved the name. Two more hikers popped into view, closer than the man I had first seen; they had been concealed by rises. They said they and the man trailing them had been in the mountains eight days and were ready to get home. They and I went our ways, and soon I met the hiker behind them, a smiling fellow. His name, I learned, was Bob McGavren.

HE: You're going the hard direction.
I: Maybe not too much more of it.
HE: There really isn't. You can see it from here.

Good. I had hoped the crest ahead was really the top, but you can never be sure.

McGavren said he lived in Cathedral City near Palm Springs, was a pilot, and tried to get together once a year with the couple I had just met, who lived in Bridgeport, just east of Yosemite. A jet flew over us, heading south down the line of the High Sierra. An F-15, he said, an Air Force twin-engined strategic-attack bomber called the Strike Eagle. Probably the pilot was on a cross-country flight and decided to take a sightseeing excursion, he said. McGavren was thirty-eight. When he was seventeen, he said, he hiked the whole John Muir Trail, down the High Sierra from Yosemite to Mount Whitney. It took him six weeks. Curious about that trip but not wanting to make him stand on the trail any longer—though he had shown no sign of impatience to be going— I got his phone number and arranged to talk with him later.

The pleasant talk at trailside, together with the bit of rest, gave me another burst of energy. I sped up, got winded for my cockiness, and slowed down. My feet were tired and too warm, beginning to swell inside my boots. Here, now, was the uppermost of the stairstep lakes, Big Pothole Lake, deep and green blue. The slope that rose from it went under my feet and on up to what I felt sure was Kearsarge Pass. I straightened up and trudged on. Note the touch of self-pity; "trudged" connotes gameness in the face of undeserved adversity, possibly oppression. I was not really very tired and certainly not oppressed, unless by my own willfulness in hiking uphill at my age and in my shape. In *The*

Mountains of California, Muir wrote about oppressed people—the women of the Paiute tribe:

> It is truly astonishing to see what immense loads the haggard old squaws make out to carry barefooted through these rough passes, oftentimes for a distance of sixty or seventy miles. They are always accompanied by the men, who stride on, unburdened and erect, a little in advance, kindly stopping at difficult places to pile stepping-stones for their patient, pack-animal wives, just as they would prepare the way for their ponies. (64–65)

I had seen women carrying huge packs in the mountains, but it was presumably by their choice. Also, they had shoes. On the other hand, the Paiute women didn't wrestle computers all day and then go home to cooking, dishes, and Little League.

Three hours after setting out, I was nearly over the pass. Kristina Roper Wickstrom had said two hours, and I imagine she meant with a pack full of archaeological tools at that. Across the uppermost lake from me, two rock pinnacles had minipinnacles on top, poised against the blue sky as if preparing to crash down the sheer, crumbling drop below them. "The most stupendous rock scenery," Muir said, comparing Kearsarge to the other four or five passes across the High Sierra. It was certainly forbidding. But the pass itself had seemed like a highway to Muir, who ordinarily scorned passes anyway, crossing the range instead at "nearly every notch between the peaks," using an ax to cut steps in ice and hard snow if he had one, otherwise hammering rocks with other rocks to knock off the ice glaze. Sometimes he carried a blanket; sometimes he burrowed into the krummholz amid surprised little birds and slept uncovered on the needly ground. Ahead of me a hiker rose, his pack so big he looked like a bear. He must have been lying behind a rock. He moved west, out of sight. Then I was at the pass. "Anybody here?" I called into the boulders. No answer. The sign said the altitude was 11,823 feet—a bonus of 500 feet, since I had misread the small type on my map. I had climbed about 2,600 feet from the car. I felt pretty good.

To the east, where I had just been, all looked bleak and sparse, the few trees nothing like the gorgeous Engelmann spruces below the Arapaho Peaks. Still, it was wild, magnificent country. I could see why it had enchanted Muir, not that enchantment was a rare condition with him as he told about his explorations of the range that he, above all other men, promoted into the consciousness of the public and, eventually, the proprietorship of the federal government. When I looked over the other side of the pass—and it was a clear division, a fairly sharp ridge—I saw a basin with one, two, three, four lakes down in the ecotone. The two nearest me were almost joined. Quite a way down the valley was the one that must be Bullfrog. It was shaped like my memory of it on a map I had forgotten to bring.

I started down, stopped to hook up the chin strap of my hat in the increasing breeze, and went on. I was shambling, almost running. The difference between running down a natural slope and running down stairs is that in nature you land on the ball of the foot instead of flat footed, and your knees roll on over the front of your foot. Also, your big toes drive themselves into the toes of your boots. I could see that I would have sore toes that evening, a kind of mountain gout. But I was moving along—looking across the uppermost lake already, or so it seemed. A tremendous system of crags and teeth came into view to the south and southeast—to my left and back. I had not yet found a level, vegetated, inviting ridge above timberline, the kind of terrain that more than any other calls me to those heights. But beyond the toothed ridge, which seemed as high as aberrations of the earth could get, was a higher one yet. It must be Mount Williamson. It occupied more sky than Pikes Peak, I judged, but it lacked the charm, the grand, rough symmetry of The Peak.

I was getting into the upper edge of the krummholz again. As close as it lay to the divide, this already looked less arid than the east side. More and greener grass grew between the rocks. Ahead of me, a marmot was lying flat on a rock, sunning himself and lackadaisically hiding at the same time. A sign just above the easternmost lake said, "Bullfrog Lake Closed to Camping and Grazing." Then I won't graze, I told it. The altitude had not only made me silly but was beginning to charge me with the mix of contentment and energy that I used to feel above timberline: the altitude, and the beauty of the lakes, and the carbohydrates, and the fact that I had hiked there without much trouble, and the perfect day—dry, about seventy, with a breeze. My stomach no longer felt overloaded; my legs were barely tired. My only problems were a slight case of the hiccups and an overinflated feeling around my fingertips, probably from the several hours of dangling and the tightness of the pack straps. I raised my hands and felt relief.

At seven minutes before noon, I was at the first lake, sitting on a rock and eating fig newtons. I looked around for ruins but found only some rocks the size of a loaf of bread piled between two larger rocks, probably to prop a grill on. Down among the rocks was a sardine can of the Paleo-Discount era. I could find no signs of grinding on rocks. But I didn't know what I was looking for, didn't even know whether this was the right lake. Deep in the lake, I thought I saw, and then thought I hadn't seen, dark, mysterious forms. Indians might have given them a name and a ritual. But the mountains, when I looked up at them in the hard light, seemed devoid of mystery. One, at the western or northwestern end of a ridge to my north, was as red as a West Texas courthouse. It looked like mine tailings, as if the mountain had been turned inside-out—ugly and forbidding. I liked it better where I was, and the footing certainly had the advantage; straying from the trail, I walked to the other lakes on soft meadows, receptive to the boot. Nowhere did I have to fight through entanglements of willows such as the Colorado Rockies fling up in moist places.

Here was the biggest lake, beautiful like the rest. The shallows near me were yellow green, giving way to darker and darker green toward the middle; then a patch of bright green with blue-black all around it. North along the shore, a sign said, "Revegetation project . . . Please stay off"; a century of hikers' boots had worked like slowed-down Agent Orange. It was a little after two o'clock. I had left the parking lot six hours before. I knew I would be tired by evening, but just then I felt fine, and it delighted me that one of John Muir's ouzels flew past in dips and rises, singing a chirpy song. All the time, in the background, I heard the high-pitched *grack, graaack* of jays—a sound familiar to me from the Rockies. The weather had held, as it seldom does during stretches of many hours in the Colorado high country. The dry summers of California climb the slopes to bless hikers.

On the trail back, not far from the lake, I stopped to watch a mule deer buck, which seemed barely concerned about my presence. As I sneaked from tree to tree for a better view, he looked up, then lowered his rack again and went on grazing. A couple came toward me on the trail, he brandishing a camera and beginning to stretch into a cautious lope toward the deer. She was a blonde woman with a huge pack. Her name was Ragni Pasturel, she told me as we watched him walk up and practically stick his camera into the rib cage of the deer, and she and Marc had been married thirty years. They came up every year for two weeks "to be halfway between earth and heaven." They lived in Palo Alto; they were starting an educational-software company. (The buck, a fine one, with a yellow-brown summer coat and a wide, thick-boled rack, held his head up and posed in profile for her husband's camera.) I saw a cloud—the first I had seen all day, I told her.

She said they often encountered thunderstorms but were hoping this would be the right two-week window to avoid them. In the seventeen years they had been coming up here, she said, they had run into sleet only once. They were going past Bullfrog Lake—the one I had just left, she confirmed—then toward the part of Kings Canyon that was accessible by road from the west, turning off before they got there, going to East Lake and on to Lake Reflection, "one of the most beautiful lakes in the Sierra." Then cross country over Longley Pass, then down through Cloud Canyon, then along contours on the north slope to Deadman Canyon. Her husband, a dark man and either not friendly or in a hurry or just distracted—he had barely grunted at me when we met on the trail—yelled for her. "OK," she yelled back and started off to join him, wishing me a good trip. She was born in Norway and he had grown up in Morocco, she had told me. I got her phone number, as I had Bob McGavren's, wanting to talk more with her. Hikers one meets on trails are generally interesting, decent folks. I don't know how the banes of the archaeologists and environmentalists and estheticians sneak past.

So that had been Bullfrog Lake. I had found nothing there, no granite ledges of the kind described, no rocks laid in circles or parts of circles. I went on east, toward the pass. Now the cloud had become an accumulation of clouds, a white cauliflower head growing up into a notch to the northwest. It was the hottest part of the afternoon, and though the wind was at my back as I hiked upslope, my pack blocked everything but my arms and the back of my neck from its benefits. Being hot at timberline is not a common experience. I met three boys in their late teens, going in, they said, for four days; a man with a ten-year-old boy, just down from Rae Lakes, where they had caught fish until their reel broke and where the man had sunburned hotly—an unpleasant augmentation of the effects of high-altitude dryness; and another man who was going in for four days and seemed impressed that I had walked all the way from Onion Valley to Bullfrog Lake and was going back. "Pretty good day hike," he said. He was heading for Harrison Pass, he said, and he pointed toward the forbidding crags— the Kearsarge Pinnacles. He would go around those; he liked to get above timberline because then you could cut cross country. He did find pleasant walking up there, he said, even amid the great rock piles. He and I went our ways. The closer I came to the pass, the harder the wind blew. I plodded, stopped to double over and breathe, plodded, and made it to the top a little after four, eight hours after my start. I looked both ways, east into aridity, west into forests. Then I started down.

A young man overtook me. His dark hair was in a thick braid down his neck; a bandanna was tied around his head—he had no hat. Wearing sneakers or running shoes, he walked smoothly and a little bent, his arms hanging in front of him. His pack was small, with a rolled-up khaki sleeping bag at the bottom, not at the top as with fancy hikers. A real mountain man, he seemed, outfitted not much more extravagantly than a Muir. He said he had started that morning from Cedar Grove, twenty-two miles to the west, at 5,000 feet above sea level. Twenty-two miles of hiking and close to seven thousand feet of climbing, then. He would have walked, by the end of the day, from the end of the road on the west to the end of the road on the east, clear across Kings Canyon National Park. I kept up with him awhile, talking. His car was at Onion Valley; he had started his outing five days before. He lived around Lone Pine and had been coming up often lately because he had the summer off. For the previous six years he had worked summers as a firefighter for the U.S. Forest Service or the National Park Service. I saw that I was holding him back, and after a while I let him stride ahead at his natural pace and vanish.

Like a tenderfoot, I had allowed myself to get a blistered heel. I stopped to bandage it and went on in reasonable comfort. Finally I stumped down to the parking lot. On the outdoor bulletin board at its side, a hand-lettered sign said, "Hot [red letters] Shower [black letters] $3.00 [green letters]. Onion Valley Pack Station." I imagined they sold a lot of those. Another sign gave the life expectancies of various kinds of litter: aluminum cans and tabs, eighty to a hundred years; glass bottles, a million years; plastic bags, ten to twenty years; orange and banana peels, two to five weeks. A handwritten notice from Mike

Baas, Onion Valley ranger, said backpackers must get wilderness permits; the trail quota was twenty-five drop-ins and thirty-five with reservations. "This quota keeps the trail from becoming another L.A. Freeway," the sign said. Another sign warned about bears, which had been active lately; hang up all food, using a counterbalance, it said. A personal message in terrible German said, "Roger und Andreus, wir haben auf Unit 11 gebleiben. Honda Accord Weiss."

In Independence, back at my motel from The Pines café, where I had enjoyed a hamburger supper—I was entitled to the protein, since I wouldn't hike the next morning—I asked the woman who ran the place how Jack and Julie had made out with the key problem. Well, she said, a locksmith had come down from Bishop and made two new keys for the truck. Jack had hiked back up the trail to look for the old key (maybe other keys were attached to it). But a friend had come from Los Angeles and picked up Julie, because she had to get to work. The motel woman had told Julie consolingly, "Well, he's not your husband." Julie replied, "Well, he *was* my fiancé." There were two beds in the unit where Jack and Julie had stayed, the woman said, "and I noticed this morning that both of them had been slept in." (I had always wondered if motel keepers noticed such things.) Julie, she said, was really angry. Too bad. I feel for people who lose things, since I lose things. I am convinced that their self-hatred is punishment enough that no one should scold them. Think how my wife would have withered me over the wedding ring I lost on Mount Evans, if my wife had been Julie.

CHAPTER SIX

Though the highest ridges and peaks around Kearsarge Pass seemed uninviting to me, in an earlier day it was exactly their hostility, together with the fact that they were comparatively little known, that invited climber/explorers whose boldness later made them luminaries. Bob McGavren, the cordial pilot I met on my way up the pass, told me that some of them left their signatures on those heights. He found the signatures—he and a friend who climbs long-neglected peaks to read the registers, the literal registers, of far-off days. A few weeks after I met McGavren on my little day hike from Onion Valley, he and the friend went into the mountains on a name hunt. "We found registers in place on peaks of the Sierra that have been there since the 1890s," McGavren said. "Some of them haven't been touched since the twenties and thirties."

That hiatus showed how unstable a vogue mountaineering has been. The Sierra Club, from the turn of the century until the late thirties, took huge groups into the mountains to spend the summer climbing. But interest declined during the second World War. These days, McGavren said, climbers tend to concentrate on named peaks (I suppose this is one more case in which the willingness to start from the bottom and work up, to serve an apprenticeship, has given way to the insistence on instant riches). He wouldn't tell me where he and his friend went register hunting; I think he dreads vandals as the archaeologists do. But in a telephone conversation after I had gone back to the Plains of Duty and when he was in one of his interludes between airline flights and hikes in the Sierra Nevada, he told me what they found some of the old registers in: bouillon cans. Some cans were tubular, some shaped like old Prince Albert tobacco cans. "Oftentimes they've been struck by lightning, there are burn holes in them, and they're rusted closed," he said. But the contents were likely to be well preserved.

Among the signatures and messages McGavren and his friend found were those of a Sierra legend, Norman Clyde. Clyde often led the Sierra Club's early-day High Trips, which to judge by old photographs must have had as much the tone of church picnics as of hikes— in a characteristic one, a mixed group, including young women wearing broad-brimmed hats and beribboned blouses, sits in the shade of evergreens while a hiker, "Signor De Grassi," stands in his boots and plays the violin. But Clyde liked best to climb alone. He carried a hundred-pound pack at a terrific, nonstop pace up and down mountains. The pack was heavy because it contained heavy reading: Homer, Virgil, Dante, Goethe, all in the original. Clyde had done graduate work in the classics at the University of California. His speech is said to have revealed that background in its aptness and fluency. An article by Harold Gilliam in *Voices for the Earth: A Treasury of the Sierra Club Bulletin, 1893-1977* says that in 1961, when he was close to eighty, Clyde was still rambling the mountains alone, carrying a fifty-five-pound pack. Gilliam characterizes Clyde as the unquestioned leader in first climbs of American peaks.

I think Bob McGavren is an adventurer from the same cloth as Clyde, only adapted to a society nine-tenths of a century further removed from the habit of walking to the post office, the market, and the bank. (Another of the old photos of High Trips shows several dozen insouciant-looking picnickers sitting on the rocks at the summit of Mount Brewer, altitude 13,570 feet. They might have been the office staff of an accounting firm, taking a lunch break in the park around the corner.) Mountains were his first adventuring outlet when he was fresh out of high school in Los Altos. He took long backpacking trips, including the one he told me about when we talked on the slopes below Kearsarge Pass—the hike all the way down the John Muir Trail. But the next year he got engrossed in rafting. He worked five years for a river-touring company in the Grand Canyon. Then, in the late 1970s, he began hiking again, mostly short trips. For seven years in the 1980s, he and his wife, Laura, lived at the Bear Valley ski resort in northern California, skiing all the time. With a couple of friends, he once skied from Piute Pass, west of Bishop, to the Yosemite Valley, a three-week tour.

But the big trip was the John Muir Trail hike when he was seventeen. He and two other boys had placed caches of food along the way. One cache was at Onion Valley, which had a store and campground at the time—since obliterated by an avalanche, McGavren said. They set out from Yosemite. One boy left the party, as planned, at Red Meadow near Mammoth Lakes. McGavren and the other boy continued what had become an unhappy hike. They got along badly. "We were looking for different things, I suppose," McGavren said. "He would be irritated by things that just seemed meaningless to me—whether it was how fast you walked and whether you stopped and waited or didn't. I just saw no merit in that. I couldn't see why a person would get irritated at things like that. And yet I was probably just as much aggrieved at his attitudes." At the Mono Hot Springs pack station on the west side of the mountains, above Fresno, they stopped to pick up food from a cache. Sorting through it that night in a cabin, they got into yet another argument. That was enough for McGavren. "I just flat out told him, 'I'm going to go tomorrow morning, and you're not going with me,'" he said. McGavren went the rest of the way alone.

When I saw McGavren and his friends, Mort and Sandy Testerman, both of whom teach school in Bridgeport, California, they were coming out after a ten-day trip to East Lake. The lake is in the transition to timberline, about sixteen miles from Onion Valley, a long day's hike. They had hired a horse packer to carry their gear in while they hiked with light daypacks. It rained on them all the way that first day. They stopped at one point on the trail and built a small fire to dry themselves. It was against regulations to build a fire above 10,000 feet in the Kings River drainage in the national park. Here came a park ranger. "And we were at ten thousand, one hundred," McGavren said, "and he found it worthwhile to write a citation. They're more involved in writing citations than they are in preserving the parks." The fire cost them fifty dollars. "Of course, it gave us something to talk about the whole trip," McGavren said. His party climbed Mount Brewer on the second day, or almost climbed it; the fog was so heavy that they turned back when they were probably a hundred yards from the summit. The next day they hiked over Lucy's Foot Pass, named for a woman who walked it in 1896.

Another of the party's climbs was up the third crag of Mount Ericsson, where they roped together for protection on one or two pitches. They ran the rope through chocks, which are flimsier-looking life supports than pitons and are not driven in like pitons but wedged into the narrow part of a crack. Among their other climbs were Mount Stanford, 13,973 feet, and Deerhorn Mountain, 13,265. McGavren said that on every climb except Deerhorn, they were the first climbers to register that year, and this was toward the end of July. If Colorado had as many people living at the foot of the mountains as California, every summit would be carpeted with apple cores by midsummer every year. Of course, California has the equal and opposite attraction of the Pacific to cut into the ranks of climbers, along with its own breed of urban pleasures; in Colorado, mountains are overwhelmingly the main attraction. At any rate, McGavren and his friends spent the last night at Charlotte Lake, a couple of miles west of Bullfrog Lake, where they encountered bears the only time on the whole trip. "The bears took whatever we hadn't eaten," McGavren said. I didn't think to ask if he and the others hadn't felt pretty hungry by the time they made it over the pass. They looked hale enough.

Flying must be a third outlet for McGavren's adventurousness. He is a pilot for SkyWest, a commuter airline that feeds Delta flights. He was a building contractor in 1982 when he learned to fly. His wife sometimes goes into the mountains with him, he said. Not often, I gather. "I tend to drive her crazy," McGavren said, "so she takes separate vacations." They have no children. McGavren went to junior college a year, then lost interest when river running grabbed him. "I'm finishing now," he told me: he was nearly through getting a bachelor's degree in business by mail. He struck me as a vigorous character and a real appreciator of mountains. A bit of a hard fellow to get along with on the trail, though—to judge not at all by his demeanor when I talked with him but by the stories he told about himself.

Ragni Pasturel: another mountain character and also a lowland one. She was the woman who talked with me while her husband was photographing a deer, and she told me later about her life in Palo Alto, where she and Marc have a 3,200-square-foot house on a half acre, with pool, in a cul de sac. She said they lived in south Palo Alto, which they chose because of its diversity; they didn't want their children to grow up exclusively with children of white doctors, white lawyers, and white engineers. Among their neighbors were black people and Japanese; Mormons, Methodists, Jews, Catholics, and Buddhists. The Pasturels lived examined lives in environmental terms as well, trying not to have too many automatic devices: a dishwasher and a washing machine, yes, but no electric knives or can openers. Their garbage can was no more than a quarter full each week; they recycled yard trimmings, glass, metal cans, cardboard, newspapers, even polystyrene; even junk mail and junk magazines. Usually they didn't buy meat, though as dinner guests they ate it if it was put before them. They did buy fish and poultry. "I think our bodies are telling us something, because we're getting more and more vegetarian," she said.

They attended a church presided over by a former priest, seventy-five years old, whom they had met at Stanford and who hiked the Sierra Nevada carrying a sixty-pound pack. It was he who introduced them to the mountains. The priest had got married and excommunicated, in that order, she said, "but to us he's a wonderful spiritual leader." She believed absolutely in a supreme power but did not place that power into the framework of any particular religion: there was room for everybody. She and Marc, examining everything else about their lives, examined their marriage, too. They set considerable store by a book named *The Working Relationship,* coauthored by a Palo Alto woman, Lisa Stelck, which told how to organize one's relationship. They made one-, three-, five-, and ten-year plans, setting priorities and each summer looking back to see which goals had been achieved.

They had met in France, where she had gone in 1959, at the age of nineteen, to study electrical engineering at Lyons. He became interested in the mountains when they took trips into the Alps; she was already interested, having spent her childhood on an island in the Oslo Fjord. The nearness to mountains was an influence in their choice of Palo Alto, but also they had already lived there once, when he was attending Stanford in the early days of their marriage. When I talked with her on the phone some months after we met on the trail, they were devising educational software for children, trying for a holistic approach that included natural science, reading, and mathematics—all, I think, with sound and animation intended to make learning like exploring. Marc was a product manager with a high-technology company. He was involved with an instrument that made measurements in hundred-millionths of centimeters and was used in semiconductor and hard-disc manufacturing. Could a couple be more Californian?

The love of mountains had grown on both of them. "It's a place where you have the space," she told me, "and not only the physical space but the mental space, to be who you really are and to find out who you really are; and also find out more about our relationship and who we are and who we want to be." They went on a two-week hike every year. They used to take their three children, all of whom, by the time we talked, were also electrical engineers and married. The mountain trips had contributed to the closeness of the family—the "moments where you put everything aside, there is no façade, there is no superficiality, you really are yourself." I remembered how my brother and I would be growling at each other after five or six days of a backpacking trip. Did the Pasturels have none of that experience? She laughed at the idea. "We really enjoy each other," she said. They had a very good life, she said, "but up there it's almost like perfection, almost like it's between earth and heaven." They didn't have to ask each other to do anything in the mountains; everything just fell into place. There was a harmony between each of them and between them and nature. In the mountains, she felt close to God, "whatever that is, whoever that is."

For a couple of summers, they took cards because they were used to playing bridge. They quit: "It wasn't necessary." But they took books, at least two of them, choosing ones they both wanted to read so they could swap. The year I saw them, they had taken Steven Covey's *The Seven Habits of Highly Effective People* and Jeffrey Iverson's *In Search of the Dead: Scientific Investigation of Evidence for Life after Death*. The Covey book, she said, presented a way of getting back to a principle-based and value-based life. (I didn't say that it sounded to me like a way also of keeping a finger on the earth they were supposedly getting away from.) Since they hiked hard, two books were usually all they could manage. Also, she loved to write and never had time to do so except on hikes. She used to fish in the mountains, but she had put her tackle away after the previous summer. "It just hurt too much to kill these beautiful fish," she said. I sympathize, but I fish.

After I had talked with her and exchanged grunts with her husband on the trail, they had stopped for the night at Vidette Meadow along Bubbs Creek, a three-mile hike from where I saw them and a thousand feet lower. The next day they went west to Junction Meadow, about three and a half miles down the trail and a thousand or fifteen hundred feet lower. Then they cut south four and a half more miles, climbing past East Lake to Reflection Lake and camping on the north side, where there was a beautiful waterfall. During the night, for the first time she could remember in the mountains, dense fog came in, so dense that when she woke up at two o'clock she couldn't hear the waterfall. They got up at 6:30, the fog turning pink and dissipating in the sun. They took their time, strolling along the lakeside trail for two hours and admiring the scene. Then they went over Longley Pass, about 12,400 feet, slipping on the scree, some of the rocks only an inch in diameter. A snow cornice blocked their way in the middle of the pass—an obstacle that gave the passage a Class 3 mountaineer's rating, meaning ropes and pitons were needed. The Pasturels never take such equipment. They crossed on all-fours, having some tense moments. "We always get into those situations—it seems to me every year," she said.

They started west toward Cloud Canyon, feeling by this point that nobody had been there in a long time, but stopped, worn out, and camped at about 11,500 feet on the far side of the pass. They didn't get mountain sickness; they never do. On the fourth day they hiked on to Cloud Canyon, then south through a tangle of dwarf willows that discourages travel (so those do exist in the Sierra), getting views, she said, that few people get. (The feeling of exclusivity, of earned privilege, is one of the rewards of backpacking. On a tough hike, you imagine that no one else could have had the fortitude to precede you.) They stayed at Big Wet Meadow on the Roaring River.

Looking at a "Recreation Map of Sequoia and Kings Canyon National Parks" now, tracing the Pasturels' route, I imagine with excitement what that remote country must be like—the basins behind ridges behind basins behind ridges—and how wonderful it would be to have it to yourself for a while. The names, the steep faces shown by the dense brown contour lines, and the gentler green-tinted slopes beneath, all convey mystery and splendor to me. The Pasturels experience them, or places like them, yearly. Their next stop on this trip was Colby Lake; then on to the Kern-Kaweah River; then northeast across fabled wild country to Forester Pass; then on to Onion Valley, the starting point. During one four- or five-day stretch, they did not see another person.

Ragni Pasturel had planned the trip with solitude in mind. She told me she customarily picked routes over trails that showed on old maps but not new ones. That way they could be fairly sure the routes were passable and fairly sure of not seeing many people. But at one point on this hike, along a stretch of the John Muir Trail, which is comparatively well traveled, they came upon a party with eleven horses. "The first thing we woke up to in the morning," she said, "was the leader galloping up and down the trail, which just killed me." Another encounter was pleasanter. As they started over Forester Pass on the homestretch, they met above timberline a British couple whose camp a bear had raided the night before, cleaning out everything edible. The couple asked to buy some food. The Pasturels, who had precisely measured cheese, crackers, and everything else for a thirteen-day trip, nonetheless had some food left over, and they gave the couple gorp and cocoa, among other things. The Britons said they had been so tired the night before that when they hung their food in a tree, they weren't careful enough to keep it away from the trunk. Restored and secured by the Pasturels' generosity, the couple decided to go ahead, as planned, and try to climb Whitney. They made it, as they told the Pasturels later in a letter from London.

The year before, Ragni and Marc had hiked in country to the north of the Kearsarge, heading west and south from Bishop and spending several days crossing passes from one wild basin to the next, hitting into territory where, again, they expected to see no one else. They started over Cartridge Pass on what Ragni describes in her journal as the old John Muir Trail, which she says has not been maintained since the 1930s. They stopped for lunch, enjoying the view of Arrow Peak and the Bench Lake plateau.

We are soon surprised by a lone ranger, who is even more surprised to see us. A young woman of 29, she is on a solo 9 day tour. We invite her to rest with us and we discover a delightful, funny and energetic person. We laugh at her bear stories, her own panics sometimes, and we feel she is happy to talk to someone. She carries a radio for daily communications with her headquarters at Mineral King. Tonight we are camped a few feet from each other and she'll share our dinner.

They camped short of the pass because of a thunderstorm. "So after a rush to set up tent and camp, we now enjoy the late afternoon sun together. The ranger has done her inspection of the lake surroundings, surprised to find horse droppings. No stock is allowed up here! A few camp fires also, that she cleans out and conceals. We are above 10,000 feet and no fires are allowed."

In camp, Ragni and Marc had time to read Thomas Merton and some meditations by Meister Eckhart, the thirteenth-century mystic. They found their minds more active than at home. "The amount of creative thinking that goes on in both of us is amazing. We are able to discern priorities, set them, come up with new ideas, prioritize our lives, practical and spiritual. It is amazing. If only we could do the same back down on earth[,] Palo Alto."

They hiked and camped with the ranger, Hannah Merrill, for two and a half days, sometimes taking shelter from hail and thunderstorms together in the Pasturels' tent. In the Lake Basin, they were surprised to encounter more people: Al Nicolaus, a man of seventy-eight, and his wife, Evelyne Mae. "They are, especially Al, just as surprised to see us. Al considers the Cartridge Pass and its surroundings a place where very few people come. Al has travelled through the Sierra for over 60 years (since the 1920's), and this is the second time he meets someone in this area." There was one more surprise:

> Soon we are joined by yet another couple, an American history professor at San Jose State and his Dutch woman friend, on her first backpack trip. She seemed exhausted already, and ahead of her, she had the steep Cartridge Pass and then quite a few miles before their next planned campsite. We all felt it was unusually cruel to take someone on such a difficult route for the first time.

Hannah Merrill left them at eight o'clock on the third morning to hike alone back to headquarters. She had less than two days to climb two or three passes and make the steep descent into the Cedar Grove area (west across the mountains from Kearsarge Pass). On trail maps, it looks like at least twenty miles. "As I transcribe my journal, we have heard from Hannah that she walked out from Marion Lake in ONE day . . . her feet sore and full of blisters. She simply did not want to face the storms alone."

The Pasturels also had a tough hike to make as they headed northward to return to their car.

> It is after 9am when Marc and I finally start on our steady 4,000 feet descent from Marion Lake along Cartridge Creek. In

some places we find the old John Muir Trail, but most of the time we hike cross-country, sometimes over piles of boulders, other times through jungle-like thick brush and young willows. Add to that the rain, and we end up with the worst day ever in the mountains.

They saw a mother bear with her cub and passed by Triple Falls. "But all the misery of the day's hike," she says, "was not worth these two exceptional sights."

It impresses me that this middle-aged couple, carrying packs of close to fifty pounds at the starts of their hikes, take such pleasure in penetrating deeply into forbidding terrain. But consider the case of their predecessors by nearly a century, Bolton and Lucy Brown. After several days of preliminary hikes, during which they climbed a number of peaks more than 13,000 feet above sea level—one that Bolton climbed alone, Mount Gardiner, had apparently never before been climbed—they decided to hike over the Kings-Kern Divide and climb Mount Williamson, the hulk that had impressed me as I looked up from Independence at sunset. "Though Lucy had never before been in the mountains," Brown says, "yet already she had become so hardy and skillful a climber that I hesitated at nothing on her account." (His account is in the *Sierra Club Bulletin*, 1897–1899, of which I have seen a reprint.) Back in camp that night—earlier in the day they had climbed Mount Brewer—they "baked up all the flour into eatables." The next morning they put the eatables into whatever primitive approaches to packs they had and headed south from their camp at East Lake. They were in the same country that the Pasturels covered after I met them on the trail.

Brown tells the story of the climb to the Kings-Kern Divide in a few casual lines. It had rained all morning, he says, and from the divide it was so misty that they could not see any of the many peaks surrounding them. They traveled "pretty much by guess," going southeast "through an immense labyrinth of lakes, ponds, pools, and puddles," including a lake "shaped just like South America." That is the name the lake bears on maps today, and their way across the divide is labeled Lucy's Foot Pass; this was a historic hike.

Still hiking blind, they followed a long red spur south to a plateau overlooking the beginning of Kern Canyon. "Descending from the plateau," Brown says, "we tramped eastward along the timber-line, past several small lakes; and at last, as night was approaching, and we had only the vaguest notion of where we were, we prepared to bivouac."

> The elevation must have been more than 11,000 feet; and a cold, steady rainstorm was blowing, with no signs of improvement. We had neither blankets nor even coats, and no tools with which to make a hut, and as there were no caves, nor even a protecting ledge, we said nothing at all about the matter. Lucy, bending over to shelter them with her back, handed me dry matches, wherewith, however, I failed to get a fire, because everything was too wet to light . . . But now, rather than lie all night there on the rocks in the storm, we determined to go back a mile to where we had seen a burning log, probably left by some herder. On the way, however, we came across a big log which looked rather promising, and, to our great joy, we actually fired it up. Then we piled on so much wood that it became a roaring furnace which drove us back and back, and scorched the bag of provisions, and made us so hot and steamy that we were veritable pillars of cloud. (22–23)

They ate as darkness fell and then "were so tired that we just lay down among the dripping stones, and, even while the storm beat upon our sun-burned faces, fell asleep." All night they kept turning, looking for more comfortable places to lie and warming the side that had the more recently been exposed to the cold and wet. The rain stopped a little before dawn, and as they ate breakfast, "the sunrise came so glorious that we were repaid over and over for all the dreary night." They were still not sure where Mount Williamson was but decided to climb a peak to the north that appeared to be about 14,000 feet high. (I assume that this was Junction Peak, altitude 13,888 feet.) What amazing people these were: "Lucy was not at all used up by our twenty-four hours of hardship and exposure," Brown says, "and would not hear of returning to camp without climbing something." But when they had climbed a few hundred feet up that mountain, they saw the unmistakable form of Mount Williamson to the southeast, "a stupendous pile," and rushed toward it, crossing a basin, climbing into a saddle on the easternmost, main crest of the Sierra, then down again into another bowl to start the climb. They climbed a slide on the northwest slope, then cut upward to a notch near what Brown saw as the western eaves of the mountain—he endows Mount Williamson with the shape of a house with gables on each end.

> Looking through the notch, we saw the southern face of the peak—a wilderness of vertical crags and gullies, seemingly impassable. Yet the hope of finding there a line of ascent carried us out among them, where, after some really ticklish cliff work, we got upon the lowest seat of a bottomless amphitheatre with very high and steep sides. Wallowing up to the top of a big snow-bank, we managed to squirm from it onto the next ledge; thence we edged up a crack to the one above, whose smooth slope was ascended by sitting down and shoving ourselves up backwards with the palms of our hands. The next step we reached by cross-bracing ourselves against the sides of a vertical crack; everything the gymnasium ever taught us, and several things it neglected, now came in play. Eventually, up the bottom of a narrow, steep chûte, over patches of snow and ice, with plenty of all-over climbing we got up the highest and steepest part of the southern wall of the peak—through the eaves, as it were,–and upon the more moderate slope of the roof. From here to the ridge-pole, and thence westward to the summit at its end, was easy. (25–26)

All this was done without any notion of equipment such as pitons, which would not come to the Sierra Nevada for three decades, and without decent packs or a semblance of a map. Scarcely anyone had been there before them, though the Browns did find a register of names on the summit from three previous climbs, all of them apparently made from the east side. On the way back from the climb, they were tempted by the neighboring peak, Mount Tyndall, which is also above 14,000 feet. It was only midafternoon, after all. "Probably we could have done it, ascending in two hours and descending in one," Brown says. But they decided against it. Their shoes were "worn to tattered wrecks," Brown says, and besides, "our labors were beginning to tell on us." They decided instead to try to hike back to camp that day. They ran part of the way and were in darkness for the last few miles. It was about ten o'clock when they reached East Lake. "That day," Brown says, "we tramped and climbed, at speed, for fifteen hours, during the last six or seven of which we had not paused for two consecutive minutes."

If the Browns and Norman Clyde were alive today, I wonder what sort of relationships they would have with the mountains. Would they be like Bob McGavren and the Pasturels, bound by duty most of the time to the altitudes of software and metal detectors but living for their annual flings with timberline? And what hikes, in a day of contour maps and featherweight tents, would seem challenging enough for people who a century ago thought nothing of striking off blanketless into unknown country? The most an adventurous hiker in the Sierra Nevada can hope for today is a chance to rediscover some remote lesser peak and find a historic bouillon can on top.

Still, the fleeting solitudes and self-imposed primitivenesses of hikes such as the Pasturels' may be as much a contrast to the congestion and automation of Bay Area life today as hikes into the unmapped Sierra Nevada were to the coastal ways of 1896, when even California had unpopulated spaces and when people accomplished work by using muscles. Adventure is relative. My little strings of day hikes gain me points in my scoring system because they originated in an office in Wichita. Lucy Brown, on the other hand, wins too many points to count because she hiked when female hikers were practically anomalies. And yet, mere hikers and explorers, even of the Lucy Brown stripe, are game players alongside Muir's burdened squaws, to whom a Sierra pass must have seemed like necessity raised to heights of misery. Necessity, to me and to the people I meet on trails, is what you leave behind when you go into the mountains.

CHAPTER SEVEN

I cruised the roads north of Independence, trying to find the trail Bob and I had taken in the summer of 1948 on our only backpacking trip together into the Sierra Nevada. We had ridden a bus from Los Angeles to Bishop, one of the few towns at the eastern foot of the mountains, and hiked up a steep trail that started near a power plant on a creek—that much I remembered. We had camped on the far side of a pass alongside a west-flowing creek. We had cooked wonderful biscuits made from a mix our mother had prepared and had spread them with dried apricots we had stewed at the campsite. And one day, while I fished a lake near timberline above our camp, Bob had climbed farther yet, into jagged peaks far above timberline. When he hadn't returned at midafternoon, hours after he was due back, I ran to camp, looking for him, ran back to the lake—a thousand-foot climb—and had just pressed two other fishermen into search duty when he broke through the patch of scrub timber above the lake, repentant and almost as worn out as I. He had accidentally started a slide as he crossed a rocky chute and had taken a roundabout way back to avoid crossing there again. We went back to camp. The next morning I woke up with chills and fever. My high-altitude runs had weakened my resistance to some stowaway virus from the low country. We broke camp, hiked back to town, and caught the bus home.

A vivid memory, all of it. But where had it started? Searching now, helped only to a degree by a small-scale topographical map, I ended up at South Lake, southwest of Bishop. Nothing looked right anywhere in the vicinity: no power plant along Bishop Creek, no white house, with flowers, by the road, no footbridge over the creek and onto the trail, no trail going steeply west up a canyon. I saw that during that forty-four years, new civilizations had buried old and that finding our traces would require not memory and map reading but archaeology. South Lake was wrong, too. I sat in the parking lot for a moment, making up my mind to drop the search. As I backed out of the parking space to head down to Bishop and on to Yosemite, a hiker came up and asked if I would take him to his car a few miles down the road.

This passenger, a bearded man in his early forties, turned out to be a geology professor at Stanford University, a pleasant, interesting guy. He and his wife had been on a five-day hiking trip, and I think he was going to drive back to the lake to meet her after he retrieved his car. They took such hikes a couple of times a year, always getting above timberline for the scenery and solitude even though it gave him headaches to go above 10,000 feet or so. He liked the contrasts of the high country—the cold nights and hot days—but, he said, "It's nice to come back down where it's green and there are trees." He used to live in Seattle, and he remembered spending several days high in the Cascades and then descending into the relief of forests where a sweet, soft rain was falling.

Since he was a geologist, I asked him about the outcroppings of black rock between Lee Vining and Independence, which had looked volcanic to me. Yes, he said, they were from the Long Valley caldera, a volcanic crater that erupted six hundred thousand years ago and flung up several thousand cubic kilometers of magma, laying a foot of volcanic ash over the ground as far east as Nebraska. It left little obsidian domes all around Mono Lake, at the eastern foot of the Sierra Nevada. Yes, he said, it could happen again: "There was a big to-do a couple of years ago—there's a community of Mammoth, a resort community, which is on the edge of this big crater, and there started to be a lot of earthquakes, and the U.S. Geological Survey issued a volcanic-eruption warning and really had the property owners really mad because it lowered property values. They built an extra road into this town as an escape route." But he said if a big eruption was coming, there would be a lot of warning. He told me about the red and white slopes that were all around us—told me more than I caught, geology being a mystery to me—and also about "this old brown stuff out here," which he said was "the old rock that all this granite intruded into."

Geologists lose me when they talk about old and new rock; it's partly because in the perspective of many millions of years I have no power to conceive a difference and partly because rock looks neither old nor new to me but timeless. Mount Dana, I was told, was made of "what used to be sedimentary rocks that got cooked and squeezed and then uplifted." Again the imagery was too large for me to focus on. Geology, like the national debt, needs pie charts for me, or those illustrations that show a primitive man rising into existence a second ago on a scale that takes in the whole hundred years of the earth's life so far. I let the geologist out and drove back to Bishop, still frustrated over the obliteration of my old traces in a period too small to show on the evolutionary charts. Maybe an earthquake or an avalanche had changed everything.

I stopped in Lee Vining long enough to find the motel room I had reserved. A sign said the town was 6,780 feet above sea level, which was just right for sleeping because it would help prepare me for higher altitudes. Sleep between 6,000 and 7,000 feet the first night, the formula says, and then increase the sleeping altitude a thousand feet a night, no more. The hiking altitude isn't so important. I bought a one-day fishing license for the next day's climb of Mount Dana and drove up to Tioga Pass, the eastern entry to Yosemite.

Not far west of the gateway, I parked and walked into the evergreen woods on the north side of State Highway 120, where I had been told a crew of archaeologists were working. They were—only fifty or a hundred feet from the road but behind a ridge just tall enough to conceal them from the eyes and cameras of the many tourists who drove past. Two young men and two young women were working around a square hole with a rim of piled-up dirt. One of the women, Sonny (rhymes with Bonnie) Montague (two syllables), told me they had found a few tools and a lot of obsidian debitage from tool making. The obsidian had to have been brought from the valley floor, she said. She was a small, smiling woman with a chipper voice that became downright pert when she told me, "We also, on this side, might have remains of—it might be a house." It was only a hundred feet farther into the trees, and she showed me: several embedded rocks in a line six or eight feet long and some larger boulders at right angles at one end. "Definitely a rock alignment," she said.

I knew then why I hadn't been able to find the dwellings at Bullfrog Lake; I would never have noticed a pattern in the rocks she was showing me. She said she had no idea how long ago the work at our feet had been laid. Why were the rocks partly buried? Well, she said, stuff blows and needles fall. (And, I suppose, all turns to soil in time.) The dwelling could have been of brush over the rock foundation, she said. Indians from the dry valley to the east and from the wetter country of the Tuolumne drainage in the forests to the west would have come up here to trade and hunt in the warm months. They might have looked for plants to eat, too, she said when I asked her, "Or there could have been just all-male hunting groups coming up here."

"And *they* wouldn't have messed with the vegetables, would they?" I asked.

"Probably not," she said. She had a bubbling laugh that came into her voice as she was making perfectly straightforward remarks— a nervous habit, I think—as well as in response to a notion that amused her, but in either case it conveyed a nice merriment. I asked whether she and her crew had found evidence of tools around these rocks. Well, she said, they hadn't really started to investigate the site. But she bent over and picked up a flake of stone from which, as she showed me, a couple of smaller flakes had been removed. Why hadn't it been buried like the big stones? Because of various disturbances, she said: freezing and thawing of the ground pushes things to the top; growing roots do the same; rodents could have done it. I looked without success for a tool or a flake. "You kind of develop an eye for it," she said. When she and the others were ready to investigate the site, she said, they would mark off a square meter and then study the contents of the soil in successive ten-centimeter thicknesses. "First we'll probably move the duff off," she said.

"With what?" I asked, envisioning a delicate brush.

"With a shovel," she said.

While she walked off through the woods to finish laying out another site, I watched the two men working by the square hole in the ground. Next to it they had set up a tripod with wooden legs seven or eight feet long. A screen was slung across the bottom and anchored to the legs. One man was on his hands and knees scooping dirt out of the hole and dumping it onto the screen. Afterward they shook the screen. They usually found at least a flake or two in every screenful, they said.

I told John Vittands, the blond young man with the shovel, that I was curious about prehistoric Indians' response to timberline— whether they found it inspiring as we were likely to do. He responded with enthusiasm. Nearly all the sites of Indian activity he had seen at timberline or above, he said, were in beautiful, exciting places, and he couldn't believe it was by accident. He told me about one such place, an unrecorded, unexcavated site a few miles from us and well above timberline. "There's this one lake that's back a little bit in a cirque," he said, "that's gorgeous, probably the most beautiful lake in the park. And there's this big site right on the edge of it." He shook the screen, peering. "I would certainly say that the native people had just as much appreciation of the wilderness as we do. In many cases, more appreciation." I mentioned a *National Geographic* article, "Sacred Peaks of the Andes," about the evidence of human sacrifices up high; the article said the mountains seemed to have been considered (and still to be considered) gods. He would certainly suppose that, he said: he had seen Machu Picchu.

I walked down a short slope and up another to rejoin Sonny Montague, whom I found squinting through a transit and giving instructions to a younger woman thirty or forty feet away. I stood looking over the highway and across the broad Dana Meadows to the mountains. "They camped where they could see the game, didn't they?" I asked. Yes, she said, that was probably what they had in mind. She squinted into the eyepiece again. "Now you have to come back this way," she called to her helper. "Another five. Now one back. No, the other way. A little bit more. Little more. There we are. OK, that was perfect." The younger woman drove a spike where the centimeters had come out right. Sonny told me the federal government wanted to improve the highway through the park—the highway fifty feet from where we stood. Because widening might "further impact the sites," the archaeologists were trying to determine how significant the sites were. I asked if it would worry her if the highway work cut into any of the fourteen sites they were studying. She gave the big, joyful laugh as she answered. "Well, yeah," she said. "Personally I don't think the road needs a lot of improvement." The laugh again. "That's my personal opinion. We don't have any analysis done on any of the sites yet, so I'm withholding my opinion until then."

She said she lived in El Portal, at the west entrance to the park, but the crew was staying in cabins in Tuolumne Meadows, only a few miles west of the sites. She broke off to show me part of what had been a large obsidian projectile point—found just a few minutes before, I think. A little of the point was broken off, and so was the base, where the notches to aid in lashing it to the wooden shaft had been. It glistened even in the shade. She told me it was probably intended for an atlatl shaft, bows and arrows not having come in until about A.D. 500 or 600.

"You're thinking that this might go back before that?" I asked.

"The size of it suggests that it does," she said. We talked a little more. Cars kept passing noisily along the highway, and one of them stopped. After a moment, a young man in shorts bobbed over the ridge, and, carrying a camera, approached us.

"What you doing out here?" he asked in a German accent. "Surveying for something?"

"Not I," Sonny said, "I'm just sort of . . ." She gave the big laugh again and looked at me. I finished what I had been saying, thanked her, and left. She turned to the newcomer, smiling—a patient young woman, willing to take time from her science to be gracious to his kind of tourist and my kind.

It was only 4:15. I went back to the Tioga Pass entry station, parked, and started up the Gaylor Lakes trail, beginning right away to meet hikers—better, walkers—coming down. A woman in her forties with a seven- or eight-year-old boy assured me that the climb was well worth it. It was an easy climb, as it turned out, and soon I was above the lowest lake, walking a trail worn into the meadow. In the bottom of the rut, some grass persisted in spite of the continual trampling; not all timberline vegetation is delicate. Still, when I met people, I looked for a rock to step out on so they could pass without gratuitous trampling. They didn't comprehend; they stepped out, too, and walked on the plants. This was green country, far greener than around Kearsarge Pass. It was a perfect afternoon. The temperature was probably sixty-eight, and the sun was shining. I saw a few clouds in the west and southeast.

Above the third lake, after a fairly steep, short pitch, I stopped to examine a fallen-in rock cabin with roof beams and a rock fireplace. It was above timberline and nearly to the krummholz line in a saddle overlooking the lakes and giving fine views to the south, where I saw in the distance the biggest snowfield of the trip so far at the base of a tall, pointed peak. Another hundred yards up the trail were two more rock structures, in worse shape than the first—just rocks piled up. More climbing revealed a whole encampment of them: the ruins of the Great Sierra Mine, I later learned. It had gone out of business because of inadequate financing and rough weather. The cabins were on beautiful sites; did miners 110 years ago appreciate the mountains as we do?

This day was beginning to be one of my small peaks of appreciation. An exhilarating wind was blowing; I fastened the chin strap of my hat. I climbed a small rocky ridge for a view and looked over the side into a different drainage with an exceptionally beautiful lake. Enchanting; a discovery. Oh: cars and a road; I was looking at Highway 120 close to where I had parked. It was 5:40. I started back, pushing through pine krummholz, and then stopped for a long look. It struck me again that this country had the great advantage over the Rockies that lightning and sleet, though they occurred, were not daily probabilities. It was huge country, and the weather made it more readily accessible than the same terrain in Colorado. It was also rocky country, even apart from the weird formations of Yosemite; rockier than the Rockies. Its firmness, near and far, undergirded my human shakiness as I stood amid failed habitations.

The wind had stopped as sunset approached. A glow suffused the plateau around me and softened the distant views as well. I found myself practically holding my breath in raptness. For all its ability to stimulate, the quality of timberline that most stirs me is the rarest one: its serenity. I think the mood—outer and inner—might have lasted until dark if I had had the boldness to make an achronological leap. Time guilt had me back on the trail after a few minutes, heading for the car and supper.

An electrocardiogram reflecting the history of the Great Sierra Mine would look like segments of the Sierra escarpment separated by long stretches of Death Valley. Two men in the early part of 1860 found silver a few hundred feet to the north of what later became the site of the rock cabins and left a tin can bearing a notice of their intention to develop a mine. A silver strike in Nevada lured them away, and they never returned. Fourteen years later, a young shepherd, William Brusky, Jr., found the can and took home some ore samples, which his father told him were worthless but which an assay three years later found to be rich in silver. In 1878, backed with sixty thousand dollars from fellow residents of Sonora, the young Brusky located four claims. The money gave out before he could start mining. In 1881 he committed suicide, presumably in despair over his friends' lost money. By then the lode to the south, at the site of the cabins I saw, had overshadowed his find, and mining companies had bought both claims.

A weekly paper, the *Homer Mining Index,* tells about a goofy bit of heedlessness that must have occurred in one of the rock structures that I saw above the Gaylor Lakes. In mid-November 1881, three miners were injured in the explosion of six sticks of nitroglycerine powder they were thawing on a stove. "Dr. Walker reached the scene of the accident on the evening following the occurence," the *Index* reported, "after a most fatiguing climb of more than a mile up the steep mountain, up to his neck in soft deep snow and in the dark and proceeded immediately to dress all wounds, including that of a mule, for the doctor is as good on mules as he is on men." This is quoted in what appears to be a term paper—it is marked History 124—by Bill Gibson. It is entitled "History of the Great Sierra Consolidated Silver Company."

The Great Sierra Consolidated bought out Great Sierra and set out to drill a horizontal tunnel into the slope below and to the east of the ruined site I saw. The operators repaired an old pack-train trail to use as a road for heavy equipment. When winter advanced enough to freeze the lakes and coat the rocky slopes with snow and ice, they built sleds, bought forty-five hundred feet of cable, and wound the loads up and down steep slopes with capstans for something like twenty miles southwestward from the town of Lundy. The job took two months and cost one life. Bears, blizzards, and avalanches threatened the miners, but the greatest hazard was impecuniousness. Work finally stopped in the summer of 1884, when, according to a court document, "the heading of the tunnel was . . . without doubt within 200 feet of the great Sheepherder ledge, doubtless one of the largest and richest ore bodies at present in existence in this country." A report from the state mineralogist in 1888 said "the comparative inaccessibility of the mines and consequent high rates of freight and the rigorous climate of the high Sierras are all unfavorable for a profitable mining experience." In 1933 the daughter-in-law of one of the early owners tried again, extending the tunnel several hundred feet but never striking the lode.

That was all. "No ore ever came out," Gibson says in his paper. The Indians who built their own rock-based dwellings close by, on the other hand, must have gone back to their winter camps with exactly the ore they had come up for—the hides and jerked meat they had extracted by atlatl and perhaps game drives; the baskets or obsidian implements they had mined by barter. And presumably, since none of them solicited money to support their analogue of mining, none committed suicide.

* * * * *

After hotcakes at Nicely's Café the morning after the Gaylor Lakes walk, I started up Tioga Pass at 7:20. I wanted to ask at the Forest Service station, partway to the pass, about routes up Mount Dana. The log ranger station was closed, but an old man in overalls, with a Forest Service patch on his shoulder, was working in the garden out front. He waved, smiled, and came over to my car, a pleasant fellow in his middle eighties. We spread my topographical map out on the hood. I asked him if it was feasible to climb Mount Dana from Tioga Lake, next to the highway a mile this side of Yosemite, and to do a little fishing on the way in Dana Lake, at the foot of the mountain. "I wouldn't advise it at all," he said. "What you want to do is to—yeah, I'll tell you how to get up there, and it's a lot better than—well, it's somewhat the same idea you've got." He turned and pointed over a ridge. "Dana Lake's right through here, right?" I told him that it seemed to me from the map that it was over *that* ridge, some distance from his. No, no, he said—no lake there, just a hanging valley.

Anyway, he told me, I'd better figure out where to leave my car first. Go back down the road toward Lee Vining, he said, and park across a bridge beyond a drinking fountain. There was a big, pronounced road up there, he said. "Not a big one. There's a lot of travel on it." I was getting confused, but he went on. "And, now, I haven't been on this doggone road," he said,

> but it used to go right up to the top of the hill right in here. There was a relay for a telephone up there. Take that. Go up to the top of the ridge, and then . . . Darn it, there's all kinds of ways you can get up there. Let me see now, what's the best way? Well, you've got to come back to your car. So I guess I would do like I said. Go up to the top of the ridge. And what happens to that road after it gets to the top, I don't know. But anyhow, it'll be good walking, if that's what you're after.

I told him fine, I had a compass and a map. But he was still pondering.

ANCIENT FORESTER: You want to end up back here?
I: Well, yeah, back where my car is, of course.

He said something about the road's going right into Horse Meadow Road.

I: Is it pretty good fishing up there?—Dana Lake and thereabouts?
HE: I'd advise against it. No.
I: Would you really?
HE: I've been up there, and I caught some of the most beautiful golden trout I've ever had. They were all about like that [he shows me]. But it was just one time. I've been up there about three or four times after that, and I just catch little fingerlings. So I don't know as I'd even bother to take my pole.

He thought that over and said, well, it might not hurt. If I caught one of those big ones, I would never forget it. I thanked him and got into the car, folding the map.

HE: It'll be a beautiful hike.
I: Well, pretty near everything up here is.

He had known that country about sixty years, he said. He was proud of being able to give me detailed directions. "If you'd ha' went inside there, they couldn't have told you that 'cause nobody in there knows it," he said. I waved, drove onto the highway, turned back toward Lee Vining as he had directed, got out of sight, stopped, turned around, and headed on toward Tioga Lake. Good: he didn't look up as I drove past the station again. He was a sweet old man, the kind of affably addled character that strangers in southern books call "uncle," and I didn't want either to hurt his feelings or to make him think I was an idiot. But if I had followed his advice, my hike would have taken me at least two days.

When I got out of the car at the parking area at the upper end of Tioga Lake, put on my daypack and swung out, I saw frost glittering silver-and-rose where the early sun touched the grass. A worn sign, legible only because the letters were cut into it, said, "Glacier Canyon" and "Dana Lakes." But I saw no trail. I cut upslope, picking my way among small trees and clumps of brush—not yet krummholz. There was lots of soft, springy grass underfoot; also a good many flowers. I saw a ground squirrel, a robin, and, down by the lake, a gull. Across the lake and across the road behind the lake, two red peaks rose above timberline. I would try to remember them and, coming down, steer between them, I told myself, since I probably wouldn't be able to see the lake around various bulges of terrain from above. As I climbed, I saw the two red peaks change shape, one of them acquiring a long gray ridge that descended into rock country. A gray peak, smaller than the red one that had extruded the ridge, appeared along the ridgeline. Every time I climb, I am reminded that the shapes of landmarks shift. It is easy to misplace a whole canyon.

Soon I was walking through red and pink heather flowers and then a field of lupines growing so densely it was hard to avoid stepping on them. I was still not quite in krummholz. Now and then a trail presented itself and I followed it up the level valley along Glacier Creek until it faded. Ahead was a grove of tapered alpine spruce or fir. The sides of the valley were fairly steep, but I could climb out if need be. First I wanted to get to the lowest lake and try the fishing. I had my disjointed fly rod in one hand. A cascade came whitely down, more air than water, for fifty or sixty steep feet close to me; if there were trout in the lakes, they hadn't got there by swimming. I remembered what the Ancient Forester had told me: "I wouldn't advise it."

These lakes were deceptive, like most alpine stairstep lakes. As I walked upstream, I kept coming over a rise onto level meadow and not finding the lake that had to be there. But here, in the scooped-out place at the upper end of that kind of meadow, there most certainly would be a lake. I hiked confidently, puffing, until I was on the same level. Disappointment: rocks and stream. I would have to clamber another hundred feet up the rocks to the next certain lake. I had nothing like the energy of the previous afternoon, when I had walked to the Gaylor Lakes and the old mine, and the wind was raging down the stream, as much an impediment as the grade. I stopped and looked across to the landmarks I had chosen. The gray peak along the ridge now looked higher than the red one. The solid mountains were flowing like magma.

Trudging again, I saw someone ahead, a woman wearing shorts and a blue-green parka. She was looking upstream and didn't see me. By the time I struggled over the moraine, she had disappeared into the slabs like a marmot. Here, at last, was a lake, small but beautiful, the clear water looking tan above a shallow rock shelf that extended thirty feet out and then turning to a sunny light green like honeydew flesh at the edge of the shelf. Honeydew green was too shallow; trout would be encased in ice in the winter. I would have to hike on to what must be Dana Lake, the top one. I walked straight up the fall line on slabs, keeping my feet flat for adherence and feeling the muscles in the back of my leg stretch with each stride. I was glad to have done the stair work. To my right, the northeast face of Mount Dana looked nearly sheer above what must be Dana Lake. But I veered off before I was high enough to see the lake. The shoulder of the ridge on my left tempted me because I knew from my maps that the Dana plateau was just beyond it. A large expanse of nearly level ground at or near timberline would have to be interesting, with twisted little trees and many flowers.

It wasn't. The ridge, attained by flatfooting up more and more of the slabs, was a hundred feet above the plateau, and I stood there disappointed amid thigh-high krummholz, looking downslope at mere dirt and dry grass. I decided to stay high and make my way through the small amount of remaining krummholz as I aimed for the head of the cirque above Dana Lake. The ridge there would give access to the easy-looking south slopes of the mountain. But before going on, I dropped into the shelter of the rocks and ate an apple. It felt good to be out of that terrific wind. Mount Dana loomed like a rising planet, so close I surely could hit it with the apple core. But no; I remembered my responsibility and packed it up.

Back on the exposed ground and walking, I could finally see Dana Lake ahead and to the right. It was long, narrow, and dark as a well. Above it a large glacier rose steeply, nearly to the summit of Mount Dana. The mountain showed its dark side from this angle, though it had looked red from the highway. The glacier was dirty white with a bay window of polished, stratified ice. Below Dana Lake, four smaller lakes were strung down the canyon. At my feet, tiny white flowers grew out of a gray-green cushion of their own leaves and stems—the configuration of tundra flowers, with variations, that appears in Colorado and everywhere else in the alpine areas of the West. The wind was trying to blow me back to my car.

Across the way on the glacier, about 40 percent of the way up— what was this?—two slender figures stood. Were they people or strange, upright rocks? Did they have on skis? The distance was far greater than it seemed. I couldn't be sure I had seen them move, couldn't be sure I hadn't. I wished for binoculars. But after a few minutes, I could see that they had been moving. As gingerly as spiders crawling out of a porcelain sink, they climbed, one beneath the other, up the steepening wall toward the mouth of a couloir that came down from the summit ridge. They entered the couloir, where they moved in and out of the shadows of the tall rocks that jutted up from each side. The airline distance between me and the porcelain-scalers, to judge by the minuteness of details, was a mile or more. They were so small, a strong gust would surely dislodge one of them from his tenuous grip and send him flailing down the wall to Dana Lake, snow spurting with every bounce. I felt an empathic acrophobia. In spite of the distance, the figures looked not arachnid, protected against injurious falls by their lightness, but human and altogether too heavy for what they were doing.

At the upper end of the plateau, where it narrowed, I cut across to my left to look through a notch at the far edge, where the land dropped off almost sheerly. I could see Mono Lake far down on the alkali-salted and obsidian-peppered floor of the valley. When I turned to look back, the climbers had disappeared. They must have made it onto the summit ridge. From where I stood, Mount Dana loomed nearly featureless. But at my feet, the barren plateau showed details I had not seen from the ridge: yellow flowers less than a half-inch across in little clumps, the outer ones shielding the rest from the wind; lupines with blue blossoms, the heads the size of pencil erasers— lupinettes, really. I turned and walked up the easy slope toward the merger of plateau and ridge. Here, ahead, was an outbreak of little white flowers. There were two kinds, one with separate petals in a blossom close to a half-inch across, the other smaller and with united petals, each one rounded like a coney's ear so that a line traced around the outside of the blossom would form a scalloped circle. Together the two kinds made the ground almost solid white.

I approached the top of the plateau, where the ridge began. With little slope left to modify it, the wind staggered me several times. I was carrying my two-piece bamboo fly rod in its cloth wrapper, holding the pieces in the middle, and the wind bent the two ends away from my grasp into an arc like a bow. If my son had been walking ahead of

me, as had happened on a good many hikes, I would have said the
paternal thing: "Don't let the wind blow you over the side when you
get to the top." But when I reached the top, it sloped down for a couple of dozen feet on the far side of the roof tree. I walked to the edge:
a real dropoff. Below me was a snowbank, and far below it was a
deep, blue, kidney-shaped lake. Some Olympian had a gorgeous
swimming pool. Beyond that lake, I could see far across the valley to
a ridge of buttes so white they looked like eccentric icebergs. Beyond
them was forested terrain, probably piñon country. Beyond that were
a ridge and a much taller ridge, probably the White Mountains.
Failing a knowledgeable companion, I needed to look at a map, but it
would have been impossible to read one in that wind.

I found a place where the outcroppings provided shelter and sank
down to have fig newtons and a drink of water. It was nearly noon. I
had hiked four hours. I felt pretty good in spite of the sluggish start.
For the first time I could remember at that altitude, I had no
headache. The loading up with carbohydrates, the sleeping at the right
altitude, and the fairly frequent tipping of the canteen must have had
their effect. As I rested, flies buzzed all around me, but these were tundra flies, not interested in cookies. A bee with a black abdomen
vibrated among the small flowers. I saw lots of crawling ants. The
tundra is full of life.

I climbed a nipple at the near end of the ridge that went across to
the slopes of Mount Dana. It was pretty steep, and I did notice the altitude—tired legs, scant breath. I had to rest often. On one stop, I looked
back to the landmark mountains I had memorized that morning. They
were hardly distinguishable. A whole tundra landscape had opened
above them: a gray pinnacle and, to its northwest, a set of five spires
with a sharp, tall one in the middle. None of that had been visible from
the starting point or from halfway up. But so far, at least, my route finding with the USGS map had worked fine. Though a park ranger at the
Tioga Pass entry booth had shown me where the trail to Mount Dana
started—just beyond a certain garbage can across the highway from the
booth—I had found my way to what seemed a more interesting route.

It was too interesting. The nipple turned out to be the prelude to
a narrower, steeper ridge than I had expected. It fell away almost
sheerly on both sides. It was not a real knife-edge ridge—I couldn't
have hung one foot over one side, the other over the other, and

scooted along as if riding a rock rail. It was more like a saw edge. I couldn't go over the teeth, I quickly saw. I would have to go around them. That meant hanging over one edge or the other. Beneath me on the left was Kidney Lake; on the right were rocks and chimneys down to the cirque containing Dana Lake. My occasional queasiness about heights—the imagination that makes the bottoms of my feet break out in sweat—began to stir.

Nonetheless, I picked my way for a few feet, setting down my fly rod in its bag a time or two to free both hands and making sure my daypack and the two canteens on my belt didn't give me an unexpected nudge outward as I completed a stride across space. Having crossed one gap by virtue of some self-persuasion and a little plotting of footholds and handholds, I stopped to plan the next advance. Ahead I saw a larger gap, a place where I would have to clamber along the exposed left side above a steep drop and then do a longer self-portage across nothing. Could I make it? I thought so, but I wasn't sure vertigo might not hit me in the middle of the crucial stride. I wasn't sure a rock at the start or the finish might not pull loose. I wasn't sure what lay beyond the tough place, and if it should be impassable, I wasn't sure I would be able to return the way I had gone. Should I take the chance of getting ignominiously and dangerously stuck far above timberline on an exposed, vertiginous ridge? I thought of my wife and of how irresponsible it would be to go on just to show myself that I wasn't afraid. Besides, I was afraid.

I turned around with difficulty and stepped back across the long step, resolving to stay calm; panic might be fatal. At the far side, I wrapped my arms around a small rock pinnacle and pulled myself up, having laid the rod down in a notch. That was it. Nothing would persuade me to turn around full of shame and adrenalin and bull my way across. The Eternal Footman had held my coat, and snickered; I had imagined dead climbers before me and declined the honor.

What was this? At my elbow was a pint bottle stuck into a cranny. It had a register inside, left by a Sierra Club chapter and dated three years earlier. "High Point of Dana Plateau," it said, "12,400 feet plus." Somehow I had missed it before. I read the dozen-or-so entries. One said, "From Lake Arrowhead, Cailf. Jesus is Lord & is mercy endures for ever." Another was signed Edan Dean and "Ossi, the mountain climing dog." Another said, "Almost got run over by fighter jets." That experience might really have jarred me loose, I thought. One entry said, "Rock & ice fall all around, good stuff!" Another: "Clouds rubbing against the top of my head, better run!" And, in a small, neat hand: "Registers such as this are incongruous with these environments. That is all should be removed. Besides, who in their right mind would have this place as their final point of destination? I guess they just couldn't go any further." What should I put down—"Lost my nerve and turned back?" One thing: I could beat my predecessors across Syntax Ridge and up Orthography Peak. I wrote approximately, "I had intended to climb Dana till I got a look at this ridge. At least it was a nice climb to here." And I entered my name and my city for the jeers of posterity.

The backtracking should give me time to fish. Though the park ranger had told me there was no trail to Dana Lake, and the Ancient Forester had advised against it, I would take a look. I jounced back down the edge of the plateau, and before long I came to a group of hikers. They had stopped and made a circle several people deep around a speaker. They looked down at Dana Lake and across at Mount Dana while he talked to them. This hike was part of a week-long seminar sponsored by the Yosemite Association, a man on the fringe of the circle told me. He didn't know whether there were fish in Dana Lake. I wanted to ask the guide but could never catch his eye. After a while I headed over the side and down the slabby pitch toward the lake. The top of one foot hurt where I had wedged it between two rocks. Even my leather boots, heavier and solider than the half-fabric ones that are popular these days, hadn't been enough to protect me.

At the bottom of the pitch, I got out of the slabs and into a terrain of loose rocks the size of my feet. Later I went through hundreds of yards of rock trash bulldozed aside by the glacier. The process had left slabs arrayed in heaps, stacks, domino trains, Rolodexes, and poker hands—numberless shoved-together cromlechs and dolmens that presented my feet with as many edges and points as they did flat surfaces. This trailless going at the outrun of the cirque was tough. Rocks rolled beneath my feet; edges dug into the sides of my boots; capstones slanting forward instead of backward forcibly compressed the tendons in the back of my leg—one of the day's many varieties of leg torture that stair walking had not prepared me for. To get past a tarn the size of my living room, I took a short cut along a dike that rose from beds of jagged rock. I picked my way without hesitation, grabbing a handhold here and a foothold there, stepping across empty space, and not worrying in the least about the prospect of merely falling fifteen feet and breaking a couple of bones, though it was probably as hard a route as the ridge whose challenge I had declined. Such are phobias.

After more and more of the rock jumble, at last I came to Dana Lake. As much angered as wearied by the tedious going, I decided to sit and have some water, then try a few casts. The wind made fishing an unpleasant prospect. I watched the surface of the lake form strange patterns that skimmed this way and that, quick as interference across a television screen. The water near me was blue green. Farther out, it was the deep blue of the Gulf Stream. That was where the ripples played. They flitted like spirits of sailboats, whole flotillas starting at one spot, darting a hundred feet in formation, and suddenly vanishing. Some were green, some blue; all had shimmering tops. Some fled me; others charged me, and just as they smashed into the rocks at my feet, the gust that had driven them also hit me. Waves formed instantaneously and slapped the shore to my right. Now and then for an instant the wind stopped dead and the water became almost glassy. Then the frenetic dance resumed.

I ate an apple and watched for fish. Not a sign of life. But then, without prelude, here before me was an incredible sight: a huge school of magnificent trout. It appeared just below the surface and finned in parallel files, thousands of foot-and-a-half-long fish, each one slender and perfect, heads quartering away from me to the right. I could hardly believe what I was seeing. "Some of the most beautiful golden trout I've ever had," the old ranger had said. But this many? I took off my polarized clip-on glasses and peered, put them back on, took them off again. All right; getting the two perspectives solved the mystery: it was more wind sculpture, a school of ripples chopped into fish-sized segments. When the wind changed, the fish vanished as suddenly as the other water fancies. I gave up all idea of fishing. Against that wind, I would have had to eat my fly.

Dana Lake had no above-ground outlet. I climbed down to the tarn below, which narrowed into a creek three or four feet wide. The creek headed down canyon, and I followed it until, in the middle of a level rock field, it simply vanished. There was no sinkhole, no visible descending stream, no whirlpool. Rock had said to water, "Stop." But when I had followed the fall line a few hundred feet, I heard the creek making treble gurgles under the rocks. Circling the end of the moraine for relief from rock walking, I clambered down to the next tarn on a sunny and grassy slope out of the wind, refreshed by the mint smells the sun drew from the herbiage. At the head of the next little lake, here came the creek back, babble-babble-jug, not leaping out with a show but emerging from the rocks full flow as if it had never been interrupted. From far up in the moraine, though, under the rocks, I could hear a waterfall. What a sight that would be if you were a gnome. Alongside the tarn and below, I at last came to tender grass. I wanted to take off my boots and walk through it barefooted.

Soon I got onto the trail I hadn't been able to find on the way up from Tioga Lake. It was an easy walk through woods and then through a grove of head-high willows interlaced with deer trails, each of them good for a hundred feet or so before I had to find another. Then through a flowery meadow and into more woods before I came to the lake. I had hiked eight and a half hours. If I had gone on across Nemesis Ridge and not fallen into Kidney Lake, I would have made the summit of Mount Dana by then and started down the civilized trail toward the highway. At least the route down the canyon had been plain; I hadn't had to rely on the morning's fickle landmarks. When I got to my car, I shed my pack and loafed a minute. I could see the seminarians hiking toward me around the head of the lake, and I waited. When they had come up to their vehicles, close to mine, I walked over and asked the leader, Mike Ross, if there were trout in Dana Lake. "Nope," he said. A woman looked at me and said with an arch emphasis, "It's sure pretty, though, isn't it?" I got it: one should be satisfied with the beauty; one should not murder the little fish. But I pretended innocence. "Sure is," I said.

The next morning, when I was on my way from Lee Vining back to Yosemite for the drive west across the range and then south, far down to the Mineral King Valley, I stopped at the Inyo National Forest ranger station again, this time after it was open, and asked a middle-aged employee about the lake. Yes, he said, there are fish in there. So I don't know. When I asked him about the ridge I had decided not to pursue, he said he had crossed it. It got a little tougher, he said, then easier. No, he said, he knew of nobody who had been killed there. On Dana Glacier, yes. That didn't surprise me. I saw no sign of the nice old man of the fancied road. I don't know what I would have told him, anyway.

CHAPTER EIGHT

I remembered the road east into Mineral King Valley because I had driven it once, forty years before. It is not a road that you forget in such a short time. Also, I had read accounts of the Walt Disney organization's fight to build one of the world's biggest ski resorts in the narrow valley, and I had read about the obstacle that helped defeat the plan: the same road, a twenty-five-mile writhe, one and a half cars wide. Being therefore prepared for what lay ahead, I set out to count the curves. After I turned off State Highway 99 near Three Rivers, northeast of Visalia, the road led me into the canyon of the East Fork of the Kaweah River amid oaks and shortly alongside great prows of rock that thrust into the roadway, blocking the view around the turns. It was close to eight in the evening but still light. At curve 61, which came after a very few minutes of driving, a small animal scooted off the road on the canyon side, holding high its long, kinky tail. A ringtail? It was ringtail country, rocky and pungent with the hot smells that the sun cooks out of the shrubbery of semiarid canyon walls. The slalom continued. Driving through the seven curves starting with number 99, at twenty-five miles an hour, took only thirty seconds. By curve 112, the first visible line of foothills across the canyon had evergreen forests starting halfway up; so I was climbing fairly fast, as the heat gauge of the small Ford verified. But I was still in oaks. At curve 150, a tarantula as hairy as a gibbon crossed the road. At 209 a man in shorts sat on the doorstep of a log house, looking across the canyon with the habituated gaze of a television watcher. What had it been—four dwellings in these eight or nine miles?—wilderness living, practically, and no more than 250 miles from Los Angeles. Nine curves later I met a station wagon coming down, the first vehicle I had seen; fortunately there were turnouts. A

117

little farther and I entered Sequoia National Park. Right, left, right, left, right, left, right, with never a break. The sun was close to setting, a silver pocket watch suspended in light-gray smog. The canyon had turned to a gorge thousands of feet deep. Two tall cedars appeared, the first evergreens I had passed, and soon thereafter a pair of magnificent sequoias next to the road. The trees, I had forgotten; the road, no. At curve 442, the surface turned to dirt. Thereafter it alternated between washboard dirt and patched pavement. It grew dark, but I could still make out the huge trees by the road. At curve 519, I reached the Silver City resort and stepped into chilly air, 6,800 feet above sea level. Driving that road eight hours a day would be a sure, though magnificent, route to repetitive stress syndrome.

What had attracted me was partly the lingering memory of extraordinary alpine terrain and partly a desire to see close at hand the valley that Disney, if permitted, would have bulldozed and bedizened into a resort probably more festive and efficient than anything in Colorado, Utah, or Switzerland. I did not look back at the failure of the project with unmixed joy. I well remembered the days when skiing had been so important a part of my life that I plotted my career moves on the basis of snow conditions almost as much as working conditions. If the Disney project had been in the making when I lived in the Los Angeles suburbs as a young man, I would have given it a great cheer, because it was more than three hundred miles to the nearest Sierra ski runs (at Mammoth Lakes), and skiing in the little Southern California mountains was sporadic and mediocre, with no high-altitude bowls and with rarely any off-track snow more hospitable to the ski than crusted Slurpees. I would have risen early on many a smoggy weekend to drive to Mineral King for parts of two days of skiing, and so would no-telling-how-many thousands of others from Los Angeles, San Diego, and the cities of the Central Valley.

At twenty, though I did realize that the wilderness was shrinking, I also realized that only the healthy and well equipped could enjoy it. Fat people, people with pacemakers, people who did not own boots or a pack deserved a shot at wonderful country, too, even if they stood to achieve only a modified exaltation the way they would see it, through the bars of its cage. So I reasoned in my youth; and I still have reservations about the attitude, "Let's save it for the people who can get to it." On this trip, I wanted to check out the slopes from above and imagine myself skiing them, to picture a chairlift up this slope and a warming hut in that saddle, and also to imagine hamburger wrappers blowing across parking lots where great trees had stood. I had not decided what I thought about the Disney project, though the government had some years since made the question moot by folding the valley into the national park system.

Before, the valley had been part of Sequoia National Forest. The United States Forest Service invited bids in 1965 on the construction of a winter and summer resort, and Walt Disney Enterprises won, proposing a thirty-five-million-dollar development designed to handle fourteen thousand visitors a day. An architect's drawing showed chalet-style buildings around a courtyard. In the foreground were outdoor café tables with umbrellas. Tall flagpoles displayed the flags of many nations. Handsome pedestrians carried skis along a snow-bordered walkway between perfectly tapered evergreens. Though *Harper's Magazine* in 1972 entitled an article about the project "Mickey Mouse in the Mountains," cartoon characters were not visible in the drawing.

Before leaving Wichita, I had asked a National Park Service man, William Tweed, what kind of resort he thought Disney would have built but for the road, the courts, and the various discouragements that cooled the project. Tweed, a management assistant who joined the permanent staff at Sequoia National Park in 1978, when the project had been dropped, said, "I would have to assume that it would look very much like the sketches. The Disney folks were not casual developers. I think it would be a well-run, intensively used, carefully managed, manicured mountain landscape, very different from the wild place, or the semiwild place, it is today." With the contemplated number of visitors a day, he said, it would have been "a very urban place in the wilderness setting." Would Mickey and Donald have had a part in the decor? "Ah, it's hard to tell," he said. "But personally, my guess is no. I don't think the Disney folks are generally that careless with their image." When I put the same question to Disney's project manager for the planned resort, Robert Hicks, he at first said much the same thing. Newspapers loved to play up that angle, he said, but no—the decor of the resort "would have been appropriate for a ski country-, not a Mickey Mouse- or Disneyland-, type amusement park." All right, I thought, that settles the question. Then Hicks went on, "But they obviously would have used the characters, I'm sure—in some way." Hmm.

The resort would not in another sense have been a Mickey Mouse operation. A cog railway would have taken visitors a mile and a quarter from a nine-level parking structure to the ski village, according to a 1969 article by Arnold Hano in *The New York Times Magazine*. The development would have had five ski bowls, each of them with more skiing room than an entire large-scale ski area, Hano said. Hicks, planning the layout, went into all the Mineral King bowls by helicopter and Sno-Cat and skied them, along with Willy Schaeffler, who was later to be coach of the United States' men's alpine skiing team and who had charge of charting the Disney ski runs. The planning trips meant skiing deep powder or breakable crust or ice or corn—whatever the season and the day offered. Hicks, though he grew up in Visalia, not far away, wasn't a skier as a youth. Later he became, he told me, "a survival-type skier" rather than a stylish one. He could go where Schaeffler went, though not always easily. By the time the Disney proposal was finished, he had skied all the resorts in the western United States and most of the big ones in Europe, studying and comparing. Mineral King ended up on top. "I can't think of anything that would have been better, even in Europe," Hicks told me.

Disney's resort evaluators put it more strongly at the time, according to Hano's article : "They came back [from Europe] contemptuous of what they had seen: overcrowded facilities, a hopeless mix of auto and pedestrian traffic, cumbersome ticketing procedures at the ski lifts, primitive luggage handling, what Disney's John Hench calls 'a general disregard of a guest's comfort.' All of this, of course, will be vastly different at Disney's Mineral King." The article also says Hicks "is adamant that the natural beauty of the area will remain unblemished, and that the numbers of visitors will not unduly tax the small valley's dimensions." Hano says that Hicks often spoke to service clubs about the project, devoting part of his time to correcting accounts in the press. "One such 'misstatement,'" Hano says,

> is the inclination to prejudge the Mineral King project as a transplanted Disneyland—cute, colorful, supercalifragilisticexpialidocious and out of keeping with the rugged setting of the High Sierra. Nothing so infuriates the Disney people. Says

Hicks: "It is unfair to think that Disney did a good job at Disneyland, but will do a bad job elsewhere. Why not assume this project will be just as appropriate for Mineral King as Disneyland was for the recreational needs of Anaheim?" (56)

That was then. When I talked with Hicks by phone, he was older and no longer a Disney employee—he had taken early retirement in 1977. Also, he was part owner of a cabin in Mineral King Valley, where the road ends and the trails start, a few feet from the proposed site of Disney's chalet. He had just spent the Fourth of July weekend at the cabin when we talked, and he said he and the co-owner had discussed whether the Disney development would have been a good thing. What had Hicks concluded? "I'm happy," he said. "I do think it serves the public better as it is." True, he went on, it struck him as a bit of a tragedy that the best ski terrain in the nation was not being used to the best advantage. "But on the other hand," he said, "I can see how intense development, which would have occurred there, would be a—well, I kind of like the peace and quiet up there. You can't have it both ways. So sometimes people say, 'You must be terribly frustrated.' Well, I've never even felt that."

It was in January 1969 that the Forest Service approved the Disney plan for ten restaurants and a complex of motels, swimming pools, and parking lots on eighty acres of the narrow valley floor, with twenty ski lifts on the slopes above the valley. To provide better access than the wondrous and terrible road, the state proposed to build a new, comparatively straight highway. Six months after the approval of Disney's plan, the Sierra Club asked a federal court to issue an injunction against the project, saying, among other things, that the road project would destroy timber and other resources. The court complied, but an appeals court reversed the decision, saying that the Sierra Club representatives who filed the suit had not claimed that the project would harm the club or any member of the club, "other than the fact that the actions are personally displeasing or distasteful to them."

The Supreme Court agreed, four to three. One of the dissenters, Justice William O. Douglas, argued that nature ought to have the right to sue for its own preservation. Ships and corporations could do that, he observed.

So it should be as respects valleys, alpine meadows, rivers, lakes, estuaries, beaches, ridges, groves of trees, swampland, or even air that feels the destructive pressures of modern technology and modern life. The river, for example, is the living symbol of all the life it sustains or nourishes—fish, aquatic insects, water ouzels, otter, fisher, deer, elk, bear, and all other animals, including man, who are dependent on it or who enjoy it for its sight, its sound, or its life. The river as plaintiff speaks for the ecological unit of life that is part of it. Those people who have a meaningful relation to that body of water—whether it be a fisherman, a canoeist, a zoologist, or a logger—must be able to speak for the values which the river represents and which are threatened with destruction. (Sierra Club v. Morton, 92 S. Ct. 1361 (1972), 1370)

Though that was a defeated eloquence, the majority on the court gave the club a way to win: just refile its suit to show how the ski resort would damage its or members' interests. The club did so—it had refrained in the first place in the hope of establishing the principle that Douglas asserted—and the injunction was reimposed. As the legal fight continued, protectionists held hike-ins to Mineral King (no doubt damaging the environment) and took their campaign to the prints and screens. Tweed, the Park Service representative at Sequoia, told me that the Forest Service, trying to overcome public opposition, made various proposals for scaled-down developments and different transportation systems as the Disney organization waited "with increasing frustration and with a fair amount of financial loss." The Disney people did not like the idea of less; they were convinced that only a huge operation would have a chance of succeeding. By 1975 they had given up, according to Tom Turner in *Sierra Club: 100 Years of Protecting Nature* (page 190). In 1978 the valley became part of the national park system. The crucial road stayed as it was.

Another of the Supreme Court dissenters, Justice Harry A. Blackmun, said that if the Disney resort materialized, the successor to that road would bear a load of at least one vehicle every six seconds. I took a count at the Silver City resort where I was staying: in three minutes, at a busy hour, two cars passed. A brochure at the resort said the road was built in 1879. There was a Mineral King stage into the valley in the 1890s, when mining had pretty well blossomed and faded. People had resort cabins there by the turn of the century. I think mine at Silver City may have been one of them. It was all bare pine planks, the floors and walls and roof full of holes—no need to open a window for ventilation. It had a propane light, two kerosene lamps, and a woodstove. It had a sink with running cold water (the restroom and shower were up the hill). A sign on the wall said, "Please conserve water. Our well is low." The bed was narrow and humped, not unlike the road. It had four blankets on it, and this was late July. When I was a child, my family used to escape the parched plains of the Texas Panhandle for vacations in the cool mountains of northern New Mexico, full of the smell of pines. This cabin reminded me of the ones we had stayed in on those occasions; it was just as inconvenient, just as cramped. I absolutely loved it. Not in more than a half century had I felt so much on vacation.

I sat on the bed, ate half a box of Sun Chips and an apple—carbohydrate loading for the next day's hike—and drank the wonderful water. Then I went outside and looked past the converging tips of tall trees at the stars, as huge and bright as childhood stars, undimmed by the lamplight from the few other cabins, though surely the smog must be leeching a little of the clarity, even at that altitude. Think how close the night sky must have looked to miners and surveyors a century ago. There was the Big Dipper; there was Orion. I stood a long time, looking up, looking around, breathing the sharp thin air, hearing nothing. Finally I went to bed to get warm.

It was morning. The four blankets had not been quite enough; I had dreamed I was ice skating. I dressed, putting a Band-Aid over the half-healed blister from the Kearsarge Pass hike. After hotcakes at the restaurant/store/office of the resort, I drove four miles east to the parking area at the end of the road: sixty-seven more curves. Two young horsemen along the way were leading a string of twenty pack mules. At the Silver City resort, a sign had said to beware of marmots, which ate radiator hoses. Here at the parking lot, a sign said, "Warning. Marmot area. Damage to your cars engine is possible. Check under hood before starting engine." There were a dozen and a half other cars and pickups in the lot. A portly scoutmaster was helping small scouts adjust their packs.

When my dad and I had come up here one June in the early 1950s, we had parked the car by a stream and slept—I on the ground, he in the car, nobody else around. All the next day, we had hiked and not seen another soul. Forty years later I was headed for the same place we had gone: Eagle Lake. I started hiking at 8:35 and stopped to tighten my bootlaces at the first boulder in the sun. It was too chilly to stop in the shade. I was on a sagebrush slope with the creek sounding below. Across the way, a pack station sat at the foot of steep slopes bearing the scour marks of long rock or snowslides. Ahead, southward up the trail, I could see symmetrical peaks above timberline. The air, the peaks, the familiar sage with Douglas firs above and the narrow, forested valley below all made me feel very much in the mountains, just as I had felt in the cabin.

There was scarcely a breeze. Only the tallest, slimmest grasses stirred. On the far side of the canyon, when I had hiked twenty minutes or so, I saw cascades coming down whitely; heard them, too. That would be Crystal Creek, according to my trail map. At a trail junction, I looked northeast to what would have been the ski runs nearest the Disney resort. The slopes were bare—whether from altitude or slides, I couldn't be sure. Snowslides had always been a peril on the steep slopes above the valley. A tremendous one had nearly killed one of the Disney snow surveyors, and it had buried and suffocated a young man in a neighboring cabin. I hiked on, feeling good. Soon I passed a man fixing his teenage daughter's ingrown toenail with moleskin. A mile farther, beyond a stand of Douglas firs that looked exactly like those of the Rockies, a young mule deer, a two-pointer, saw me approaching and sprang upslope beautifully, then stopped and turned his muzzle and fine big ears toward me.

I caught up with two other hikers and walked with them: a man and his eleven-year-old daughter, each of them carrying an alpenstock made of a ski pole with the basket removed. He was tall, with a three-day beard, and he had a vertical profile: a ruler would have touched forehead, nose, and chin; even the segment from lower lip to chin was straight. He looked like a man of firm opinions. His name was Greg Lathrop. I mentioned the proposed Disney resort; he said that when he was fifteen he had circulated petitions against it. Stronger opposition in the beginning—including that of the Sierra Club, which did not initially object to a development—would have blocked the whole attempt, he said. He was glad the proposal had finally been defeated. "Having hiked all the southern Sierra," he said, "there is no valley like this anywhere. You can put a ski resort anywhere, OK?" No, I thought; but I was beginning to agree about the valley. Access, he said—that was the crux: "Anybody in L.A. who's not a country person is scared by that road, because it's not a two-lane road. And they drive up very tentatively, and the best sign in the world that exists is 'No RV's and Trailers' at the start. So that only makes a whole class of couch potatoes, OK? So you have a much better class of party that's up here." Just look at the people "camping" in Yosemite, he said: "Color TV sets, generators cranking away at night." Yes, I said, but in the high country above the Yosemite Valley, it's different, because you meet people who are willing to work to get there. He agreed.

I asked about his business. He was a bank vice president, he said, a San Diegan and a Republican. He quoted me a college saying that "if you weren't a Republican by the time you were thirty, you were destined to be poor." He disliked the Sierra Club because, he said, it had become totally political. "And they tend to every year endorse Democratic candidates irregardless of who they are and where they are, and that pisses me off." Surprised at the phrase, I glanced at his daughter, Betsy, only a yard behind him on the trail. She didn't react visibly. "Therefore," he went on, "they have lost their vision of what they were." I asked him if there was irony in his being so stoutly a businessman and having worked against the Disney development. No, he said: "I vote for a Democrat once in a while. I'm more of an issues person. I want to look at the whole thing, I want to analyze."

He was quite a hiker, I gathered, and he was trying to recruit his daughter. She had started hiking at the age of eight. When she was ten, he said, she hiked from the south rim of the Grand Canyon down to Phantom Ranch and out with a full backpack. Soon the two of them were going to hike from the north to the south rim of the canyon. "And she's going to go to the top of Whitney," he said. That would be in less than a month. Mount Whitney, northeast over the ridges and canyons from where we were walking, is 14,495 feet above sea level, the highest peak in the lower forty-eight states, but he had more ambitious plans yet for his daughter. He had climbed the Matterhorn seven or eight years earlier when he was in his midthirties. "Now what I want to do is go back and do it again at fifty," he said, "and I want to convince her to go with me."

"Is that going to take some persuading?" I asked Betsy.

"I don't know," she said.

"Right now," her father said, "she doesn't mind going up rocks. But coming down, she doesn't like."

"Well, I can understand that," I said.

"The beauty of most of your rock climbs here, in Yosemite and places, you go up rocks, you hike down," he said. "The Matterhorn, the real thing I had to face for the first time in my life is, you go up, and you hike down facing out. And it is a very weird sensation."

He showed me a rock with inlays of darker rock. "It looks like chocolate marble," I said. Betsy, to my pleasure, laughed. I had walked between them so that I could hear her father clearly and was worried that her silence meant resentment. He said the two of them had gone to Olympic National Park the year before and found it exquisite. But, he said,

> I like this best. I like it above treeline . . . We always plan a full moon; in fact, last year I hiked Whitney under moonlight, up and down; left at ten at night. You get up there, and the color of these rocks, and the shapes, and the power of nature just seems to overwhelm you . . . And what I tell people is, I says, "You cannot understand what I'm talking about until you go there. You cannot drive a motor home there, you have to get off and walk to appreciate it."

We had been hiking at a steady, slow pace. I told him I tried to stay halfway in shape by climbing stairs. He said a Seattle lawyer who had climbed Everest did the same, carrying a pack, and considered it the perfect exercise. That was good, I thought, but if I carried a pack up and down the office stairs on my workouts, I would worry about falling; also about being seen. We talked diet; he said he ate carbohydrates and drank Gatorade. He said a woman who had climbed Mount Whitney with him suffered from altitude sickness on top.

"We couldn't get her to drink fluids," he said. "She was stubborn."

"Maybe she's worried about her privacy beside the trail later," I said.

"Yeah," he said, "although they have a little thing for women now." (It's essentially a plastic cup and tubing, from what I have read.)

I asked if he had scruples about treading on vegetation. "Oh, yeah," he said.

I won't walk through fields of wildflowers. And I definitely hate people cutting trails. It drives me crazy. In fact, what I have on one of my packs is, I have a U.S. Department of Forestry patch that makes it look like I'm a quasi-ranger . . . and I'll smoke people. I'll nail them. What it is, there's so few dollars left to maintain these trails, the damage that is done from erosion after you've trail-cut a few, people just don't realize.

Going overland, really bushwhacking, was different, he said, "because you're no different than a deer or a bear."

We had reached Eagle Lake, which was set at the foot of crags, just as I had remembered it from the hike forty years before. This time I had been on the trail barely more than two hours. It was an easy hike. The banker and his daughter began putting fishing rods together. She had said little. I imagined that she wished I would go away. But when her father told me that after they finished fishing they were going to go over the pass and down White Chief Canyon, she looked at me and asked, "You want to go with us?" Especially since he said nothing, I declined; but I was pleased again; it's nice to gain the favor of a child. I had another question for her father: did he throw apple cores away in the high country? "Darn right I do," he said. (Something about the question seems to elicit emphasis.) Followed by his daughter, he worked his way around the lake and started spin-casting—flinging a hard lure into the water with an uncompromising splash.

I studied the surroundings. The lake lay at 10,000 feet, a little below timberline. The walls of its cirque were fairly steep. How to get up? I decided to try traversing the rock slabs on the west side—to my right—cutting south toward the saddle below Eagle Crest, the peak that would have been the top of a Disney gondola lift. I could see Eagle Crest from the lake, I thought: a small peak but dominant because it practically hung over the cirque. Having had a rest and an apple at the lake, I felt confident. It was twenty-two minutes before noon when I started. Shortly I passed through what had to be the last stand of fox-tail pines, red barked and thick boled. Then I was striding up large, sloping tabletops of pink-gray granite—or I took it for such—my boots gripping the nubbly surface like a cat clawing a rug. The efficiency makes that kind of walking a gratification—the soles holding firm, the leg muscles pulling. Now and then I used my hands for steadiness or to hitch myself around a corner. If I fell, it would hurt me, maybe kill me, but I didn't worry; granite assures. I walked an inclined slab to its juncture with a steeper slab, on which I found a foothold, a ledge, a corner to grab, and then a couple of handholds for which I had to half lunge, taking it for granted that my groping foot would pick out a foothold at the same time; and it always did. It was the kind of surface that can be relied on to have something for you.

Still, I found myself backing up now and then, having picked my way around curves and then found that that route led around too steep a barrel of rock. The second route always worked. It was a delightful climb. I traversed upward, turning my ankles to keep my boot soles flat, and soon came out in the saddle. Strange: I was five hundred feet above Eagle Lake and nearly that far above what I had thought was the last grove of foxtail pines, and yet here were more of them, burly and stunted. I sat in the shade of one to eat chips and drink water. The ground was sandy and strewn with pine needles, pebbles, and twigs. The top few inches of embedded rocks stuck out here and there.

Rested, I headed up the lake side of the peak I had picked out as Eagle Crest, then decided that that route was too steep and rocky and peeled off toward the gentler south slope. The weather was perfect. I kept waiting for a timberline blast that did not come. There was just enough breeze to have stirred the used-car dealers' banners if this had been a city; not enough to have dispersed smog. I saw a flower composed of horizontally oriented, tube-shaped purple blossoms arranged like angels' trumpets around a half-inch of head. It is a flower that, with variations, I fancy I find in all western mountains, though I suspect that actually I see only the superficial similarities and that the less-apparent details would show a botanist that each flower is profoundly unrelated to the others. I also saw a slate-colored junco, a black-headed bird with a broad white bar down each side of its tail, flitting among the boulders.

I stood still and looked all around. The terrain where I was would make marvelous skiing: timberline ridges, easy slopes, steep slopes, a bowl sweeping down into sparse trees, briefly leveling off and then plunging. Even to the south, toward Los Angeles, I saw sharp summits and alpine ridges, and in country that had to be outside the national park. Maybe some successor to Disney would take on the battle of trying to put ski lifts there. Ski lifts, and a road. I moved on up the open, easy slope. Little lupines with deep-purple petals, white-toothed at the bases and with miniature rosettes of leaves, made a mat extending three or four feet out from a boulder. I skirted it.

Then I was amid the great pines again. They filed singly up the slope, astounding trees with red boles thick enough to have borne a hundred feet of wood above them but able in that climate to nourish only a fourth that much; trees as burly as Odysseus when he stripped to the waist to fight Iros, the hulking beggar. It was impossible not to anthropomorphize them. They marched erect, fifty or a hundred feet apart, like soldiers making an advance of centuries on the peak and exposed almost daily, year after year, to the blasts of the defending elements. I had never seen such timberline trees before, never suspected they existed, and their power and fortitude, sculptured in that Suribachi eloquence, moved me as if the heroes of my childhood had turned out worthy after all. One tree almost at the top of the file had been felled long before, cleanly cut with a saw by some incomprehensibly crass person, some murderer. It was hollow. The rings in the thick rind of wood that remained were compressed so tightly by the straitjacket of the brief summers that it would have been impossible to count them without a magnifying glass. Still, the tree, like the others, had survived and grown. In my susceptible condition, I was moved again when it came to me what way it had fallen: directly upslope.

Onward and upward. Above the last of the pines now, I jumped from boulder to boulder as I climbed. That was easier than climbing off one and onto the next, and it spared the vegetation between. Soon I pulled myself up a final rock to the top, and right away I perceived that the top was the wrong one. The little peak I had meant to climb was to the east, just above the lake; I had drifted into another watershed. I looked down at a string of three lakes, a long one first and then two round ones: the Mosquito Lakes, by my map. So I was on Hengst Peak, only 11,120 feet high—barely a mountain by Colorado standards. I studied the map and decided that Eagle Crest wasn't the little one I had seen from the lake but the rounded one to the east, the same height as the ridge I was on.

From where I sat on the edge of a rock that would fill a small room, the northeast face of Hengst dropped eight hundred feet. I squirmed gingerly to look in this direction and that. Toward the ocean, I saw mountains, then forested foothills, then a ghost of the tawny hills, then nothing, and above it all, a brown horizontal line for as far north and south as I could see—scum on a lake of air. Traces of the smog were probably above me, too, far from the cities though I was; there seemed to be a hint of a white haze in even that fine blue sky. I started down toward the saddle that connected Hengst with Eagle Crest, sometimes descending half my body's length by sitting on a boulder and dropping my feet over the side to the next, where I couldn't see. This high country, I reflected, had an advantage over my native Texas: you didn't have to worry about getting snakebit ankles when you did that. The saddle, when I got there, was painted with fields of practically solid lupine. I couldn't avoid walking on them. The slope up to Eagle Crest was gradual and not as rocky as the one I had just come down. The warm, agreeable breeze made the going pleasant.

What was this? On the slope a quarter mile or more from any of its kind lay another dead foxtail pine. The wood was red and had been deeply, selectively eaten away by weather, the harder wood forming a high relief of twisted veins. I saw not a trace of bark. It was a tremendous corpse, as sad and mysterious as a dead whale on a beach, and it must have lain on the slope a century. What had brought it there? What had made it fall?

And how was this, a moment later, for a contrast to that massive rigidity: a hummingbird came out of nowhere and hovered frenetically in front of me on its sugar-driven wings, checking out the nectar potential of my bright-red pack before thrumming out of sight like a rock shot from a Wrist-Rocket. Soon I was on top of Eagle Crest, where the Disney gondola would have ended. There was plenty of room for a summit house, all right, and there were skiing slopes of all descriptions, an endless supply. If I were a better skier, I would have liked to drive up the wondrous road in winter until drifts stopped me, ski the remaining miles up to the valley, and then, painfully, climb the trails to this summit, from which I would recompense myself for all those uphill miles with an orgy of downhill swooping in the untracked powder. With a lift here, the snow would have been not only tracked but packed, the swooping unearned and social—nothing like the thrill of puritanical deserving that makes ski touring what it is, but still a joy, still a superb way to achieve the pleasure of effortless, silent speed.

I considered the moot arguments about development again but did not conclude, and I chose a route back to my car, deciding to go south around White Chief Peak and down to the little lake at the head of the White Chief Canyon trail, then north to the parking lot. That must have been the way Robert Hicks and Willy Schaeffler skied. I walked through a field of upright slabs as if across the top of a shelf of books of various sizes, disliking the experience as always and weary legged as I usually am by the stage of a hike at which I have such encounters.

But it was a gorgeous day, a perfect day. I saw a paintbrush under a rock, and an anonymous yellow flower, and, again, dense fields of lupine. Across the way, on the far side of White Chief Canyon at the upper end, was a red mountain that met a gray mountain, the marriage occurring on the steep face of a ridge. To the far northeast was the great jumble of spires, fangs, ax blades, and bicuspids that I had seen from the other side on my Kearsarge Pass hike. It struck me that since I had left Eagle Lake, a little before noon, I had seen no one. It was a Friday in late July, and, 250 miles from the second-largest city in the United States, I had the easy high country, the hummingbirds, and the noble foxtails all to myself. Wonderful.

I ate an apple, sat in the curve of a boulder at the top of the slope down to White Chief Canyon, and watched cloud shadows in the form of amoebae and a swastika move north along the top of the far ridge, some of them sprawling a thousand feet down the slope. Until then I had scarcely realized that a few harmless-looking clouds had formed up high. I leaned on an elbow and put aside everything not visible. This—I felt it creeping over me—was becoming one of the great mountain experiences, the kind that I undergo only when in sheltered places above timberline, alone. At leisure, removed from human shapes or sounds, out of even the breeze, I dropped my ties to time, duty, and other artifacts of low-altitude culture and felt as light as air, as free as John Muir or a mountain lion, happy to lie there, irresponsible and in fact separate from the possibility of being responsible, merely an organism of contentment. I felt the way I had felt in the breathless moment out of the wind and out of view of the other hikers on South Arapaho Peak a year before. Altitude is part of this feeling, I think; in the thin air, you are less dependent on the oxygen that fuels the ordered life below. Thin air in an airplane or a space shuttle is not the same, because the air reflects human technology. Besides, technology in those situations is all around, keeping you from falling, talking jargon to you from its flat, low place on earth.

In any case, real timelessness, the chief element of freedom, must live higher in the mountains than my vacations take me. Looking west across the top of my sheltering rock and toward the coast, I saw that something substantial and ugly was drifting in. It had pushed past the timbered ridges, beginning to obscure them. Beyond the ridges, there was nothing now, just filthy gray air. It was frightening. I lay back and shed my connections for another moment, listening to a bee I couldn't find and watching a red bug smaller than a pinhead scurry along in the lichens. I felt a sublime carefreeness begin to settle in again, but it wouldn't stay, not after what I had seen. I surrendered my freedom and sat up. That gray effusion of downslope cities was moving eastward and upward like time embodied, and I remembered the propriety of getting back to the car before dark. At nine minutes and fifteen seconds past four, I stood and began picking my way down damp rock slabs and grassy interstices to the narrow bottom of the canyon, eleven hundred feet below.

When I arrived and looked at my trail guide, I decided the way to proceed was straight down the creek bottom. Before I had tried that route for long, the trail was gone and I found myself being squeezed more and more tightly between the sides of the arroyo. The red shale pressed in on me from its mountain to the east, the white marble similarly from the slopes to the west that contained the old White Chief Mine. I let myself down stair steps in the arroyo as if lowering myself into a deep armchair, and I found that my right hand was resting on red rock, the left one on white: a two-tone arroyo, the seam between two masses. Growing things contributed other colors. I saw large purple, trumpet-shaped flowers that I of course couldn't identify, and once I saw a damp slope covered with a hundred yellow columbines. Water appeared in the creekbed; I moved up and traversed the steep sides. The volume of water increased. Soon I saw a pair of ouzels that flew scolding down the course of the stream just as in Muir's depiction, not cutting across the curves but sticking to the stream like streetcars to a track. They stopped and chattered: *tis-uh tis-uh tis tis TISK tisk tisk*. I wanted them to walk into the water and under, but the best they would do was to stand on a rock and do knee bends.

Then the stream went underground again. I was still clambering and armchairing myself down rocky steps between the steep banks, sometimes on a bottom so narrow that I couldn't put one foot next to

the other. It was a tedious route for all its colorfulness, and I shook
my head at myself for having taken it. Finally I saw the trail ahead,
and greenery, hooray. I also saw a bread wrapper on a rock in the
middle of the stream, out of reach. Disgusting. Beyond the mouth of
the arroyo, two people were hiking downstream in the meadow where
the trail went, too far away for details to show—the first people I had
seen since leaving Eagle Lake. When I finally emerged from the narrows, at 5:32 P.M., I looked at the map again. The real trail, I now
realized, traversed the white, western slope a couple of hundred feet
above the arroyo. I am always missing trails.

Now it was easy, at any rate, and it was a pleasure to put my foot
down whole on the dusty path instead of stepping on edged or
pointed rocks. The trail led through pretty meadows with many flowers, including lupines fourteen inches high, and through a grove of
magnificent red firs. The Crystal Creek jumped whitely down the red
slope to the east. A grouse waddled down the trail ahead of me for a
couple of hundred yards before it flushed, showing a broad band
across the end of its tail. I saw a marmot.

At 6:50 I was back in the parking lot, where my car was one of
twenty-six, every one with a California license plate. Across the narrow floor of the valley, a pack string was getting home, the horses
neighing at those still in the pens. My hike had taken ten and a quarter hours. I could not tell that the sky was dimmed, though the smog
by now must lie all above me. No doubt it had dissipated considerably by the time it had moved that far east and up. I drove back to the
cabin; had Brunswick stew—I was free of the carbohydrate regimen
because I wasn't planning to hike the next day—and fresh-baked
bread at the lodge; walked up the road a few hundred yards and heard
an owl in the dark woods going *wuh, wuh, WOO-uh;* returned; took
a last look at the amazing stars, which were still not discernibly
affected by the smog; and went thankfully to bed.

Back up the road on the way to the Eagle/Mosquito parking lot
the next morning, I stopped at the park-ranger station and talked with
a dark-haired young ranger who said the red rock was, yes, shale, or
any of "a whole series of metamorphic rocks." In places where the
creek disappeared, the water had dissolved the marble and created
caves, he said. I told him I hadn't seen anyone up high; was that usual?
Yes, he said; people got up there maybe two or three times a week. He

was a visceral fellow with a broad smile and perfect teeth, healthy as
a bear, and yet dead-serious and army-conscientious when he talked
about safety and sanitation, as he did, at length, to each backpacking
party that stopped in for a wilderness camping permit. Bears will get
into anything, he told them—they will tear the door off a car if food
is inside. Don't feed bears, he said; fed bears become aggressive and
have to be shot. Don't leave aluminum foil in the mountains, because
it crumbles and rangers have to pick up all the little pieces and pack
them out. When you dig a toilet, make it at least six inches deep and
burn the paper; cover it all with dirt, not rocks: animals will dig it up.
Marmots, especially, have a taste for human excrement (and radiator
hoses, I thought). Don't soap yourselves or your dishes in a stream or
lake, because soap leaves a scum on the bottom; you can see it, and if
you go up later and drink, you can taste it.

He gave his lecture to one party of three—a man, a woman, and
an adolescent of indeterminate sex—who told him they were going in
for twenty-five days to the Upper Kern and other places and would
end up at Cedar Grove. The ranger was impressed and pleased. They
listened patiently to his admonitions, though people ready for a
twenty-five-day hike would presumably know all those things.

I drove on to the Eagle/Mosquito parking lot, where my hike of
the previous day had started, because I wanted to talk to people who
had cabins next to it. The pack station, one of them told me, lay
where a mighty avalanche had buried two cabins in 1969. I looked
again at the avalanche tracks all down the steep slope and close to the
runout above the station and stables. In the tracks, sparsely, small
trees grew; they looked the right size to have grown there since the
avalanche. The information about the avalanche came from a nice
gray-haired woman who answered when I knocked at the cabin
someone told me was Robert Hicks's.

She and another man showed me where the Disney chalet would
have been built. It looked like a perfect place, if there had had to be a
chalet. It was at the bottom of sagebrush-covered, sparsely forested
slopes and just across Eagle Creek from the pack station. From the
parking lot—from the chalet, it would have been—I saw sharp, rocky
peaks to the northeast with fine steep ski terrain but also with courses
of snowslides that had swept away trees. The slides had left gray rocks
exposed. Some slopes had so many slides that the trees were just strips

between. The danger of slides had of course concerned the Disney people. Tweed, the National Park man, told me that he thought avalanches would have been the major challenge to the development. But Hicks, Disney's project manager, said he was convinced that the problem could have been solved.

Disney sent a couple of snow experts to the valley for the winter of 1968–69. One of them, Wally Ballenger, nearly died in a cabin buried by that season's huge slide. Ballenger grew up a well-off Chicago boy who was supposed to become a doctor but was interested only in working outside and writing, though when he was young he played drums in jazz bands. His widow, Faith Ballenger, tells me that after graduating summa cum laude from the University of Chicago, a philosophy major, he ran a rare-book store in Chicago, married, moved to Monterey, California, wrote and sold short stories, then went to Squaw Valley and worked for the ski lodge because one of the perks was lift tickets for his children. His enthusiasms resembled those of Jim Palmer, the ski bum in Colorado (another Chicago product), though the two struck different balances between the ethereal and the worldly. Ballenger soon became an expert on snow—a nut on snow, in fact, living for it and for his writing.

A powerful man with wide shoulders and with stomach muscles like an eighteen-year-old's, he was almost wordless at home, though he talked a little with his wife at the table. On Sundays he read and listened to his collection of classical, jazz, and blues records. "You didn't bother him," his son Jeff told me. Otherwise, he was either working on the mountain or writing in his studio. He was not a pal to his children. "My dad never threw a ball with me outside," Jeff said. But if Jeff wanted to go upslope with him, he never said no: "In the worst storms, he'd take me up the mountains when I was ten or eleven years old. That was the only time I ever saw him." On those occasions, Ballenger finally relaxed. "If I accidentally swore and looked at him like I would if I did that at home," Jeff said, "he wouldn't even look . . . All the barriers that kept us in line at home changed. He would smile. He loved working with young men, training them, finding out about snow."

Tom Anderson, now director of base operations for the Squaw Valley resort, was in his early twenties when he worked two summers with Ballenger, who at the time was head of the ski patrol in winter and was in charge of avalanche control. Ballenger would sit and talk snow phenomena by the hour. "Wally was always pointing out to me in the summer where the anchors were and where the slide paths were, how the lay of the land and how the topography generated energy and inertia for the slides," Anderson said. But Ballenger never talked with him about his past, which at that time included the frightful avalanche at Mineral King.

When he went to Mineral King in October 1968 to spend the winter gauging snow conditions for Disney, Ballenger left the two oldest of his four children with Faith Nitz, who had three of her own. His first marriage had dissolved—because his wife, Joan, could not match his passion for mountains, Faith told me—and Faith's marriage had also broken up. At Mineral King, he stayed in a cabin on the valley floor where the pack station is now. As he wrote in an article in *Quest 79* (1979), his companions for the winter were Dave Beck, the other Disney snow expert; Beck's wife, Susan; and two young men who, wanting to learn about the mountains, shared a cabin and helped with the work. One of them, Randy Kletka, who was about twenty, became close to Ballenger. The Disney operation had weather instruments and also instruments to set off avalanches: dynamite, a compressed-air gun to fling explosive projectiles, and a .75-caliber recoilless rifle. The last, on loan from the Forest Service, could be fired only when a Forest Service chaperone was present.

The first substantial snow, eighteen inches, fell on November 15. Then it was clear and cold for almost a month—conditions, as Ballenger observed, under which the snow could turn into crystals down deep and lumps of ice could form at the bottom of the pack. With enough weight, such snow collapses and grinds downhill on crystal skids. By Christmas, avalanches had started rumbling. By the end of January, seven more storms had come, one of them leaving more than fifty inches of new snow. By mid-February, it had snowed four more times and the snow lay ten feet, eight and a half inches deep. The danger of a major avalanche hung on the tops of the slopes, including Miner's Nose, a summit I had seen in looking north from my uneasy perch on Hengst Peak. "Even though no avalanche had touched the village in Mineral King's 70-year history," Ballenger said in the magazine article, "I was worried and I wanted out." On the phone, in fact, Hicks, the project director, ordered him and the others to leave. The snow was too deep for further measurements to mean anything, and danger was imminent. A new storm was predicted for February 22, a Saturday.

Beck and his wife left by Sno-Cat, taking one of the young men with them. The other, Randy, stayed behind, saying he wanted to look after Susan Beck's dog and puppies. It's not clear why Ballenger stayed; I think it was not clear to him, either, though he said he hoped to keep records through February. On February 22, eight inches of snow fell; the next day, at least twenty-five inches; the next, ten inches by eight in the morning, and the snow continued, sometimes at the rate of three inches an hour. Randy moved into the Becks' cabin during the afternoon, he and Ballenger having managed to clear the snow from the entrance. That night they radioed the Forest Service to arrange for a helicopter to pick them up. The snow lay seventeen feet deep around the cabins. The edge of a passing avalanche had already broken a window in Randy's cabin. At 9:45 P.M., when the two men were talking on the phone—the line had somehow stayed in operation—Randy said, "What the—" and the phone went dead.

Ballenger heard the avalanche coming off Miner's Nose, and when it hit his cabin he heard glass shattering. Rafters broke; the slide creaked and groaned internally for ten minutes, then stopped. Ballenger started digging out. Five hours later and twelve feet above the roof of the cabin, nearly exhausted by exertion and lack of oxygen, he broke through, opening an air hole. At six o'clock, he went looking for Randy on skis. He saw nothing but snow and, disoriented, went the wrong way—Hicks told me of flying over afterward and seeing Ballenger's misdirected tracks. The helicopter came for Ballenger on the morning of February 26. It went back later and returned with Randy's body. His cabin had caught fire when the avalanche overturned his stove, and he had died when the oxygen gave out. The avalanche, it was found, had come not just from Miner's Nose but from the slopes on the other side of the valley as well: a collision of walls of snow and ice.

Faith Nitz, Ballenger's girlfriend, was working for the Squaw Valley lodge at the time of the avalanche. It was a dreadful winter there, too. She had not been able to get in touch with Ballenger lately, and she worried. "I knew what kind of snow they would be getting down there," she told me. He phoned her from Three Rivers the morning the helicopter lifted him out. His first words to her were, "Let's get married." ("Not till he was threatened with death did he really think he ought to marry me," she said.) She met him at the Reno airport. His hair had turned gray. "He was pale and gray faced and gray haired and just so shaken," she said. Back in Squaw Valley, he paced frantically, unable to talk about what had happened. He spent a couple of days in a hospital at Truckee, sedated. Then they made wedding plans. "Now that I think he's going to be crazy for life," she told herself, "he wants to get married." They were married that April. He lost himself in the mountains again—"I always thought of the mountains as the other women in his life," Faith said. But he said in the *Quest* article that he was afraid of mountains for a long time: "My legs shook on avalanche routes and there were times when I could scarcely ski."

In the early summer after the avalanche, Jeff Ballenger, who was twelve, went with his father to retrieve his possessions from Mineral King. The snow was still deep. He saw groves of trees that had been snapped off cleanly, as if lumberjacks had sawed them. "The thing that really stands out," Jeff told me, "is these boxcar-size chunks of snow that had come to rest in the mountains and sat around among the cabins like stone statues on Easter Island." I asked if his father had shown how the return was affecting him. No, he said: "He never would have done that sort of thing in front of me. He was a Hemingway sort of person."

Ballenger died of lung cancer in 1984 at the age of fifty-eight. Jeff spread his ashes at the head of Seventy-five Chutes, a tough ski run and Ballenger's favorite, on a mountain named KT-22 at Squaw Valley. During his last illness, Ballenger had talked to Faith about Randy. He felt a survivor's guilt, she said: "He couldn't reach him, couldn't get him out." He had been fond of the young man. "I'll see Randy," he said when he was dying.

If Disney had developed the resort and then a winter like that of 1968–69 had hit, at least a murderous avalanche would not have been likely. Ballenger thought the danger could have been forestalled. Crews of experts like him would have been on duty; the road would have been open for reinforcements and equipment and, if necessary, evacuation. Nature wouldn't have kept Disney out; it took Congress and the law, and also public sentiment, or the vocal part of public sentiment. And of course the road. I left the Mineral King Valley that morning closer than before to agreeing with Hicks—the retired, cabin-owning Hicks—and the Sierra Club. After all, the road was there; the infirm and inexperienced could drive in and see the country if they wanted to do so enough to tackle the curves, though finding a parking place might be a different matter—every lot I saw that morning was packed with cars pulled over embedded boulders or with their wheels in holes between thick roots.

Still, on my way down the road that morning I met only twenty-five cars. At the one-every-six-seconds rate that Justice Blackmun had foreseen, I would have met nine hundred in that hour and a half. At that, the ranger at the exit gate told me it was an especially busy Saturday because of a homeowners' gathering in the valley. As I wound lower, haze began to dim the view of the tops of the timbered ridges where I had been. From State Highway 99, as I drove north to Fresno from Visalia, I could no longer see the mountains and could barely make out the silhouette of a single brown hill in their direction. (Mountain View Motel, a sign said.) I was back at the altitude of the kind of duty that produces filth. At least I would soon be out of it again. I was headed for the Cascades, the third of the four major ranges to visit in this refresher course in the impermanence, for me, of upward escapes.

Part III

The Cascades

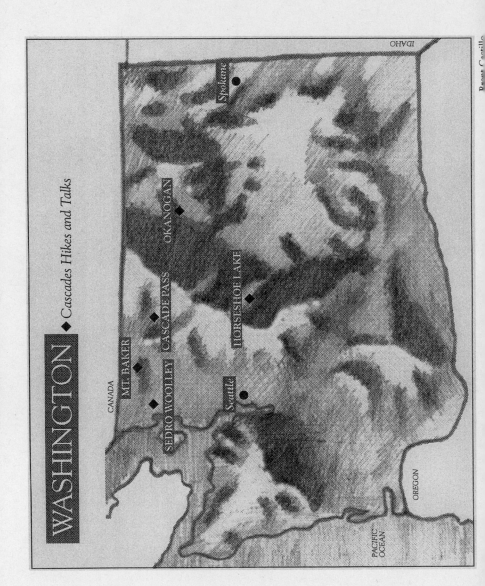

WASHINGTON

Cascades Hikes and Talks

CANADA

MT. BAKER

SEDRO WOOLLEY

CASCADE PASS

OKANOGAN

HORSESHOE LAKE

Seattle

Spokane

IDAHO

OREGON

PACIFIC OCEAN

CHAPTER NINE

Even a mere turboprop plane like the one I took for the thirty-minute flight from Fresno to San Jose seals you into a can of virtual reality, a world in which the same processed air that takes off with you lands with you, the attendant's speech on safety accents the prepositions like a voice out of an ill-programmed synthesizer, and the oxygen masks wait in their artificial wombs for a glitch in the artificial atmosphere to drop them into service. I sat in a row with an exit at the window end. A memorandum in the seat pocket in front of me said to ask for another seat if "you do not understand these instructions, or lack sufficient visual capacity (require aids beyond contact lenses or glasses) or aural capacity (require aids beyond a hearing aid) to understand these and crewmember instructions or to impart information orally to others." The elegance of those lines not engaging my attention for long, I observed that we were flying over a bank of clouds as level as an ocean. The tops of hills, covered with trees, stuck up like islands. If you lived on one of them, your world would be the bright sky, a floor of cloud, the occasional silver airplane, and the celestially illuminated, pointed islands on which neighbors were, like you, fugitives from that previous life. But people around me sat untransfigured, reading and talking and never glancing out the windows. We eased down, the propellers whirling up shreds of glitter at the first touch of the cloud. After a short passage through amniotic vapor, we emerged, not in entire forgetfulness, above San Jose. The air was as gray and dismal as if it had been High Technology that said, back then, "Let there be visual discernibility facilitation."

On the flight from San Jose to Seattle, we followed a long lake shaped like a salamander with many hands, the fingers highlighted in

143

reddish-yellow sand: Shasta Lake, I guessed, and low water. Soon we flew a little east of Mount Shasta, solitary and far above timberline; then east of Crater Lake, an enameled blue as striking as when I had seen it from the rim road forty years before; then hillside forests with square clear-cuts that hung from the horizontal logging roads like dirty sheets from clotheslines; then Mount Hood, off to the east, striking; later Mount Rainier in the distance, huge; then the Olympics to the west, disappointing because I had expected them to look as big as a segment of the Alps. As we landed, I saw Mount Baker, an otherworldly white, to the north. All this way my seatmate, a large, dark-haired man with a black mustache and dark glasses, wearing jeans with a big silver belt buckle, read a paperback of Louis L'Amour's *Mustang Man* without looking up.

We landed at the airport in the south part of Seattle, and I met my son, Andy, who had flown up from Houston to hike with me. He and I headed north on Interstate 5 in a rented car, from high points observing a city laid out like the slopes of different colors that came together in White Chief Canyon: a mass of black buildings, then a saddle to the north, then a smaller massif of white and gray. I had never seen Seattle, though when I was in my twenties I had worked for a newspaper in Spokane, over the mountains and east across the volcanic plains almost to Idaho. Our destination was Marblemount, a little town on the Skagit River near the road that led to the trail to Cascade Pass, which had been recommended to me as a nice day hike.

The Cascades, as we drove parallel to them in the late afternoon, rose in shapes like those of the Front Range in Colorado and had the same ballooning thunderclouds tethered to them. One large peak with a vein of snow down the middle thrust up into the thunderheads and vanished like Mount Evans or Longs Peak. The strange thing to me, brought up in the Great Plains perspective, was looking east instead of west to such mountains—that, and looking over my right shoulder at the snowy bulk of Mount Rainier, thinking at first that it was a cloud because no mountain 120 miles away could occupy that much sky. We turned east on State Highway 20 and followed the Skagit River between forested foothills to Marblemount. There we checked into a cabin and went to a restaurant up the road, sitting at an outdoor table in the chill and watching the sinking sun make fringed tops on the hills to our west.

The next morning, when we drove back to the cabin after break-fast down the road, thin clouds were streaming out of the ground like hatches of sheer-bodied insects; you could see ground below them, see into them, and see the sun shimmering behind them. They looked insubstantial and threatless, not clouds that would hang above the world and create gloom. The foothills that rose from the back ends of the farms were densely, uniformly forested except in the scabs of clear-cutting. At the upper edge of each naked square, the bare trunks of the forest reared up like a stockade. Forests in the Rockies, being sparser, would not have shown the violence so starkly.

Another strangeness was, as I kept reminding myself, that many of these hills rose to only 2,500 or 3,000 feet above sea level—a lower altitude than even exists in Colorado; if it did exist there, it would be far below the lower timberline, in the domain of sparse grass. And whereas farms in the valleys of the Rockies meet the slopes and forests in a cleanly marked edge, these little farms merged with nature in tol-erant, ragged ecotones. The thrifty farmhouses stood right against the road. On the other side of the road, very close, the Skagit flowed with a deceptive blandness; I watched it nearly repulsing a small motor launch that was struggling upstream. By Rocky Mountain standards, this was a gigantic watercourse.

Before we took the road to the trailhead, we stopped so I could talk with Robert R. Mierendorf, archaeologist for North Cascades National Park, who, before eight o'clock, was already in his office in a barrackslike building as he had said he would be. He told me about Chelan Indians who lived to the east of Cascade Pass and Skagit Indians who lived to the west. Both, in former times, had gone up to the pass for hunting and berrying. I wanted to know whether they also went for inspiration.

"A lot of times, they went to the mountains for the same reasons we do," he said, "for spiritual and ceremonial reasons, however we define that in our heads."

Did he mean whole tribes at once, or young men on vision quests, or what?

"*Individuals* on vision quests," he said. "I wouldn't specify. I wouldn't confine it to either gender."

Women may have gone by themselves on vision quests?

"Uh-huh."

Was that peculiar to this area?

"I think it's generally true of the Native American people and their ancestors throughout the mountains," he said. I must have looked skeptical or at least surprised. "Remember," he said,

> statements like that that I just made are based upon information that we get from interviewing Native American people, from informants, within the last couple of hundred years or the last hundred years. The last hundred years are not to be considered representative of the last ten thousand. A lot of people make this mistake. We don't know for sure what happened back then.

About hunting, he said no game chutes of the Front Range kind had been found. These Indians went on high-country hunts for deer, goats, marmots, and upland game such as ptarmigan. At lower elevations, they hunted elk. Salmon were a staple on the west side. On the east side, Lake Chelan was salmonless but had big trout. It was fruitful country.

As a veteran of the road to Mineral King, I am disinclined to make much of the road that leads to the Cascade Pass trailhead, which, in the same number of miles, couldn't have had more than a few dozen curves. In the lower reaches we drove through tunnels of trees that were nearly as dark as tunnels in rock. The trailhead was at 3,700 feet, behind a parking lot that looked across a narrow canyon toward steep stone mountains with glaciers hanging far down the sides. The mountains were craggy and, being so close, seemed tremendous, though, as the map showed, they were only in the 8,000-foot range. Several other cars were parked in the lot.

We started walking. It was almost too warm, but breezes cooled us. The trail went up easy grades in the shade. We took our time; Andy, who is taller than I and keeps in shape by jogging regularly and playing touch football on Sundays in the Houston heat, must have found the pace boring. The peninsulas between switchbacks were deep in ferns and berry vines. Mierendorf's young helper, a husky outdoor type, had told us not to cut across switchbacks. I supposed he meant because of erosion, but no—he meant because of danger; with so much greenery covering the slopes, you couldn't tell what was beneath; it might be a fifteen- or twenty-foot dropoff. We saw a small red doe browsing at the side of the trail. She lifted her pointed nose only when we came even with her, three or four feet away, and only for a moment. Then she went back to her browsing. We inferred that we were not the first human beings she had seen.

The Douglas firs rose to a hundred feet and more—fine trees, but this forest had nothing like the variety of the great western-slope forests in the Sierra Nevada. As we climbed, the woods grew cleaner, the ferns fewer and lower, the trees a little farther apart, the whole scene lighter. Though the trail book said there was always mud here, we hit only a few small patches. The footing was mostly needles. Across the way, also contrary to the trail book, we had frequent fine views of Mount Johannesburg and its mighty glaciers. It was good seeing such sights with Andy, who responds to them as I do. We kept hearing a creek but couldn't find it in the undergrowth. A bird sang a two-noted tune. At trailside, as in a tropical rain forest, water dripped down stair-step boulders covered with green lichens. We heard voices of a child and an adult and shortly met a heavy man and a girl of about ten coming down. He said they had not gone all the way to the pass. "We got pooped," he said. "It just keeps going and going." They talked with us for a minute and went on.

We sat on a rock, eating apples and drinking from our canteens, and after a while a man came bouncing down the trail and stopped to talk. He had a red face, a sizable nose, and bright blue eyes and was wearing jeans, a canvas cap, running shoes—one of them had a small hole in the toe—and a flowered pink polyester sport shirt with long sleeves. No pack, no canteen; he was not a modish hiker, nor of an age to be. He said he had been up to the pass, but just for the day: "My grandson, he's always saying, 'Well, why don't you go up there and stay overnight?' and everything, and I say, well, my ears aren't long enough. I can't pack anything on my back that will last me that long." He agreed when I remarked that another problem with staying overnight was that the ground got harder as the years passed. "I'm beginning to find out that the trail goes longer and steeper, too," he said.

He had a cackly, happy laugh and a vigorous voice, rather high pitched and with a bit of an edge, like that of a man tossing cheerful insults at his domino partners. He said he had been retired twenty years; he had worked in logging camps a long time and then had been with the Forest Service twenty-six years. "So after I retired," he said, "everybody says, 'Take it easy; oh, Christ, you can't do that. Got to take it easy.'" He laughed again. His name, he said, was Albert Frisell, and he lived in Burlington, west of us and near the coast.

Whump! "There goes a slide," he said. We all looked across the canyon at the glaciers. Not seeing anything, we decided the slide must be on the other side of the mountain. "Glad I wasn't under it," Albert Frisell said. Andy and I had heard the same sound once or twice earlier, also without locating the source. Frisell said he hiked a lot. He had made fourteen trips that summer, all of them day hikes. "I've covered about all the trails," he said, "but then I go and hike 'em again. It's something to do."

Andy said, "It's great to live up here and be able to do that."

"Well," Frisell said, "I want to do it as long as I can. My grandson, he's a computer guy that works for Boeing, you know, and I get him up here once in a while." He mimed a young man looking around at the scenery with an uncomprehending expression. "He says, 'Granddad, you're weird.'" (The cackle.)

Frisell said he was eighty years old, plus. That encouraged me, I said: "If you can hike like that when you're eighty years and some months . . ."

"Well, like I say, we lived on this stump ranch," he said, "and I've been in the woods as long as I could walk. Always been out in the woods. And I worked in the woods."

I asked about the pencil in his pocket. Did he keep a journal? No, he said, he wrote down the time when he left the car, to see what kind of pace he was setting. Usually he made about two miles an hour, he said, and that was what he had been doing that day; it was a good trail, so you didn't have to stop and rest. I said two miles an hour was moving right along. He went on, "Some trails, you stop every hundred feet and *hack-at-too,* and your old heart goes *uh-cup-poo, uh-cup-poo, uh-cup-poo.*" He laughed. "You wonder if you're gonna make it or not." He said he was living in logging camps when he was thirteen: "It's all I know. Too dumb to do anything else."

Andy offered him a drink from his canteen. "No, no," Frisell said. "I don't drink water. I don't drink anything when I'm hiking. I found out years ago that you can't drink water very often and work. You'll get sick." After a bit, I asked him about clear-cutting. "It's just stupid," he said—very poor management. "Course I'm too old to worry about it, but to me it's not right." He looked at Andy's new light-weight hiking boots. "You've got some pretty good-looking shoes there," he said. Andy said, well, he didn't get to use them very much. "Mine, looka there," Frisell said. "I got one that's got a hole, ha, ha, ha, I don't know if that's gonna last me this summer or not. I'm gonna have to start moaning and groaning when I see my grandson and tell him, 'Oh, gee, my *shoes* are wearing out.'"

The talk turned to bugs; I told him I had expected mosquitoes but hadn't seen any. Well, he said, usually you saw them in open places, not in the woods. "And the worst part isn't the mosquitoes; it's these little bitty old sweat flies and no-see-ums. Man, they'll—*ggrrzitt*—like that." A horsefly, now, "he'll buzz around you for two miles, see, but these other ones, they see you, *boom,* like that." Once he had met a bunch of young men hiking up a certain trail—he could tell that they were city dudes: "'Boy,' I says, 'you better watch those horseflies. Those horseflies up there are as big as butterflies.' They just look at you, you know. And another guy told him, well, 'Better watch out for old Bigfoot—I thought I heard him the other day.' But they don't believe me, you know?" He gave the laugh.

"Well, this is not getting home and doing somethin' to home, I guess. I get a lot of 'honey-do' jobs when I get home." He looked across the canyon. "I wish I'd see a great big old slide come off of there," he said, "but I guess they're hangin' tough." He told us, "Well, take care," and was off down the trail, standing straight and rocking a little from side to side.

Andy and I heard another rumble. We walked a hundred feet back down the trail to an opening in the forest to get a better view in case anything happened on our side. Across the way were three hanging glaciers. The one to our right was the biggest, with a deep swell near the bottom like rising bread. The edge nearest us looked sixty or eighty feet high—a precipice of snow, compacted into white ice by the years. Downslope from the glacier, a couple of long arroyos glinted with ice water. Now and then one of the brooks in them burst over a granite lip and took to the air like a spider's bungee thread. Those and other little cascades, all across the slope, filled the canyon with a practically visible stage whisper.

We had watched for only seconds when it happened. A huge chunk broke soundlessly off the near edge of the biggest glacier and, amid a cloud of snow dust and mist, toppled so gradually that if I had seen it on television I would have been sure the projectionist had slowed the machinery. It was as slow as a big Douglas fir coming down under the ax. After a few seconds, the sound reached us—a great clap, by far the loudest of the day, followed by the sustained roar of the river of ice slabs that we saw shuffling swiftly down a rock bed, shoving boulders ahead of it. The front of the flow poured down the open slope, swerved behind a crag, emerged accelerating, surged over a waterfall in foam like breakers, sped over open slopes again, and eventually, a thousand feet from the starting point and visibly attenuated by then, squeezed its remnants into the narrow bed of a brook and streamed over one more waterfall before playing out. We had stood still, watching it, for four minutes and forty seconds. "Well," Andy said, "if Frisell was watching, he got his wish." He could hardly have missed it, in fact. I wished his grandson could have seen it with him, but maybe even that would have bored him. Along with certain storms and sunsets in the Rockies, it was one of the most majestic shows I had ever seen in the mountains. Also one of the deadliest: a climber below the glacier would have had no chance of surviving. It was a reminder never to cross below a steep glacier during the warmth of a summer midmorning. We looked awhile longer. Andy saw a vertical edge of newly exposed ice, shiny and green, where the side of the glacier had pulled loose. I never found it. But what wonderful luck to have seen the slide together, to know that we could call up the memory during family Scrabble games for years.

As we started up the trail again, I asked Andy, "What did you do with your apple core?" Though he stays too busy lawyering in a city too far from mountains to spend as much time up high as I—his more sensible priorities not permitting that kind of escape as much as mine do, anyway—he is nonetheless of a generation much more sensitive to environmental protocol than mine. He answered, "Put it back in the sack. Why?" I had done the same with mine, but only because I had been debating for most of a year. We hiked on. Three men his age, in their early thirties, coming down, said they had spent the night on top; they hadn't seen the great snowslide. One said you could walk the glacier above the pass without crampons. Another made the Bunyanesque observation that from up high, you could look down into Doubtful Lake. We went our ways.

Before long we were in the beginnings of krummholz, though some fair-sized trees remained in view above us. Trickles kept coming over the trail; nearly every crack had water in it. Across the canyon, many tiny streams fell downslope amid the green patches of stunted trees, ending up in what must be the headwaters of the Cascade River, invisible in the narrows of its course. We heard another loud boom but couldn't find the source. Close by, purple thistles grew, and small pink heather blossoms on their woody stems, and columbines with yellow petals like the ones in the Sierra Nevada but with bright red spurs, not pink like those. The grass was knee high.

A green sign between wooden stakes less than a foot high said we were on Cascade Pass. It also forbade camping; extensive human impact had damaged vegetation, it said. As Andy observed, the sign was in a flat place, a perfect campsite. Our altitude was 5,393 feet—about the same as the top of the capitol dome in Denver. Two young men were crouched over a camp stove in the pass, one of them stirring eggs in a skillet. They were looking east, away from us, and seemed not to want to be disturbed; still, they answered questions civilly, showing us the trail to Stahale Arm. Like Kearsarge Pass, this pass apportioned its territories cleanly, east and west. Chelan Indians and Skagit Indians should have had no misunderstandings about territory. The wet-dry division wasn't as apparent here as in California, though; in either direction, we looked down on similar forests and low greenery.

We started upslope amid purple asters that were probably two inches across, with wide gold centers. The sun on the lush vegetation brought out an overripe smell. The trail steepened. Ahead, a red spike buck stepped out of krummholz and onto a hanging meadow, browsing. Two teenage boys above us stopped and talked to him. He kept on browsing. The trail, narrow and cut into the ground by years of obedient hikers, led through a steep, flowery meadow, the first I had seen in the West Coast ranges that reminded me of Colorado. Viewed from below, it seemed almost solid in flowers. Tall blue lupines predominated, with more of the purple asters, some small white blossoms growing with a flat head like salad herbs, here and there an antenna holding aloft a white shaving brush of mountain bistort or mountain dock, familiar also in the Rockies, and some little yellow flowers with an inlay of deeper gold on each of their five petals, probably cinquefoil. Above the way we had come, now that we had climbed a thousand feet above the pass, we saw summit ridges like the one near Mount Dana that I had declined to cross. It was forbidding high country, craggy and toothy and with much loose rock, too steep and rocky for ski touring and too unstable for hiking, not to mention the danger of snowslides.

A little farther along our way, we came to the overlook of a lake that was round, deep, and green, with an island on the north side: Doubtful Lake, no doubt. You could look down into it as the hikers had told us. Around the island, the shoal water was sallow. Farther out it turned to emerald, shading into dark-green depths. It must have been fifteen hundred feet below us. At least we were too high for Sloughs of Despond. We went on. The trail was moist and soft underfoot. We were beginning to feel the altitude, which must have been by then about 7,000 feet—the altitude at which you start the longest way up Pikes Peak, with seven thousand feet more to climb. Low as it seemed by those measures, we were high enough, or exposed enough, to have a respectable timberline breeze. We also had each his own horsefly, circling the head like a radio-controlled plane.

When we rounded hummocks, we got new views of jagged country with glaciers, and Andy, more wedded to cities than I, was reminded of the way you go around corners in San Francisco afoot and surprise new views of the city, the bay, and the bridges. Finally we were above the last of the krummholz, in true alpine terrain. Somebody had marked the trail with little cairns, though the way was perfectly clear. I see markers like that in all mountains and wonder who puts them there and why. I suspect that they are evidences of a species of creative anachronism, a way of playing Kit Carson with other members of your church youth group. The trail steepened, became shallow and rocky, and shortly led into a sparse rock slide.

We met a man and woman from Alaska who said they had been up to Stahale Glacier. They lived in Anchorage, where, he said, you saw a lot of the same plants as these. Soon we were at the base of the glacier, which was smaller and much gentler than the one that had calved. Two men were sitting on rocks at their campsite, one of them reading a paperback. Deciding against an unequipped try at the glacier and the steep pinnacle above it, we turned back, scrambling down the fall line of a rock slide to get back onto the trail.

Andy was hiking ahead of me, and when we came again to the part of the trail that was sunk into the soil and scarcely more than a boot wide, I somehow tripped. We were keeping to a fairly brisk pace now that our way was all downhill, and with no time to react, I found myself flying off to the right, approximately parallel to the ground and feet first. The landing spot could hardly have been better; it was on an easy slope amid grass and flowers. Also I managed—or, rather, happened, since there was no time to contrive anything—to land on my pack, which had no metal frame to dig into me but was only a sack containing mostly soft things such as a sweater, a parka, and a reflecting blanket (fortunately no overripe bananas).

I saw Andy hurrying my way, and I said, "I'm OK. Just tripped." He had heard me stumble and turned in time to see me in midflight. I did have a cramp just below the calf of my right leg, I found when I got up. I remembered that something had jammed my heel as if trying to jolt me onto tiptoes. The cramp smoothed itself out after I had hobbled a couple of hundred yards. But I reflected: what if the trail had been at the rim of a sheer drop? Or what if the cramp had been a fracture, or if my head had hit a rock when I came down? It is with reason that the books say not to hike alone.

I heard yells from the slopes south of the pass, which were steep and covered with loose rock. The cries sounded distressed at first, then took on a note of laughter. When we met a man and woman coming up, I asked if they had heard. Yes, the woman said with contempt, and earlier she had seen the people who were responsible. "They looked like the kind of guys who would yell when they weren't in trouble," she said. We reached the pass and swung down the much wider trail toward the parking lot. After a while Andy noticed the absence of something that had been with us on the tundra. "We seem to be below the horsefly line," he said. But not below the line of all nuisances; when we stopped to rest in the woods below the place where we had talked to Albert Frisell, the mosquitoes were waiting. So were some annoying small flies.

We went on, and before long we stepped onto the parking lot. It had been eight hours and thirty-two minutes since we had started walking. At the edge of Stahale Glacier, we must have been at 8,000 feet or higher; we had climbed at least 4,300 feet. Neither of us was very tired. When Andy goes to the mountains, he leaves sea level one day and usually hikes above 13,000 feet in New Mexico the next, and as he said, these comparatively low altitudes made a big difference.

Today, of course, he had hiked slower than usual, not wanting to wear me out. Possibly because of the companionship and possibly because the air lacked the unreal lightness of greater altitude, I had not felt the special serenity of certain moments on previous hikes. On the other hand, the companionship was unbeatable, and we had the snowslide to remember the rest of our lives.

CHAPTER TEN

Ｅast and west do contrast in the Cascades, though not as much as in the Sierra Nevada. We had driven only a half mile over Washington Pass, altitude 5,477 feet, when we noticed that the glaciers that plumped whole sides of peaks to the west had been replaced by room-sized chips of snow like those I had seen in the southern Sierra, except that these were five thousand feet lower. Several miles farther east and down, the timber became more like that of the Colorado foothills and less like that of the wet west side of the Cascades, which, except for the clear-cut patches, looks like a Weyerhaeuser ad. At the bottom of the pass, cattle grazed and sprinklers whirled in a broad irrigated valley along the Methow (pronounced METT-how) River. South slopes were given over to sagebrush and a few red-barked ponderosa pines. North slopes had alternating timber and park land. Now and then we saw a grove of white aspens. With the river below, this looked like the country in Wyoming where the Virginian and his bride set up their honeymoon camp. The stream was as clear as vodka, not a chewy green like the Skagit, and it had small white rocks sticking out of it— a dry-country stream.

We drove through Winthrop, which had grown false-fronted buildings with names like Jack's Saloon and the So-and-So Mercantile Company in the thirty-seven years since I had last driven there on the way to weekend hikes when I worked for *The Spokesman-Review* out of Spokane. In the country beyond, the trees formed dense stands on the tops of the hills but began to space out as they descended from those comparatively wet places, crowding into the arroyos for moisture just as they did in the foothills west of Denver. Turning off toward Okanogan, we left the Methow and, after a low pass, dropped into aspen country. The slender trunks of one young grove made a white wall at the far edge of a dwarf-apple orchard. After a while we could see the Okanogan Valley from above—orchards everywhere with round-crowned, uniformly spaced trees. We pulled into Okanogan. The downtown was drab like those of the 1940s but evidently not in need of any false-front hokum; I saw no boarded-up buildings. The Okanogan River, looking as if it had been strained through tea bags, ran parallel to the highway. We ate lunch and then went to meet the people we had come to see.

Alice and Howard Culp, in their mid-to-late seventies, had a rambling house on the outskirts of town. He was a big man, a little stooped, with blue eyes and thick, white, wavy hair. She had a shy, winsome smile and a barely audible voice that took on volume in little bursts of reminiscent enthusiasm. They told me about spending their honeymoon in 1936 on a Forest Service lookout above timberline, fifteen miles from a road. They walked to the lookout. Each month's supply of groceries was brought in by pack horses. The food held out fairly well, but for the last two days of the first month, Alice Culp told me, they had nothing left but oatmeal. "First we had oatmeal with milk and sugar," she said, "and then finally we ran out of milk and sugar and just had oatmeal."

Their lookout was on top of Diamond Point, fifty miles northwest of Okanogan, and it wasn't a tower but just a cabin on the edge of a cliff, with windows all around. "We could spit out our door a thousand feet down," she said. "We didn't have to be on a tower." These days, she said, she didn't even like to go up in her daughter's office building in Seattle, but back then living on a precipice didn't scare her: "You get used to it when you're young." The view was all peaks and ridges outward and upward and velvety green forests below. To eat, aside from oatmeal, she and her new husband had such as ham, raisins, canned milk, and the makings of biscuits and hotcakes. The altitude was 7,900 feet—too high to cook beans or potatoes satisfactorily.

Cooking was a problem in other ways, too. Once, the forest ranger, Frank Burge, and his wife came to visit, and Alice served them green biscuits—the effect of using too much baking powder for the altitude. The ranger and his wife asked how the Culps managed to keep themselves and the lookout so clean, living on a rock a quarter mile above the nearest spring. It wasn't hard. Howard packed water up on his back, and they bathed in a metal washtub. Then they washed their clothes with the same water. Then they scrubbed the floor with it.

They had few visitors, but they were on the telephone a lot—especially she, he said: "I think the other lookouts were kind of envious, having Alice up there, and they were all by themselves. And they talked to her half of the night. They were forever wanting a recipe for this or a recipe for that." If they got cabin fever, the two of them would start out on a night when the fire danger looked low, preferably after a light rain, and hike down their mountain, across valleys and up ridges to some other mountaintop for a visit with another lookout, violating regulations. They could do that in the dark because Howard was born with radar, and they weren't likely to be found out because they got back home before the morning checks. She told Andy about one of their trips while I talked with Howard. "She said they'd walk for three or four hours," Andy said later, "and one time she remembered that they got there and were just so hungry"—that sounded exactly like her, I thought—"and all the fellow there had was macaroni. He was a high-school-age kid, and he thought he was doing real well to have macaroni."

Sometimes, while her husband stayed and watched for fires, Alice walked down the long trail and over Billy Goat Pass to the road to go into town. There were always bears in the creek bottoms along the way, but they didn't bother her—"They would give a big woof, and away they'd go," she said. Since then she has heard about people being dragged off and never heard from again. "I'm deathly afraid of bears now," she said. "I don't want to go camping." The first time she hiked out, it was to see a dentist; she had a terrible toothache. She got in their Model A, which they had left at the end of the road, and drove twenty miles to Winthrop, then over a one-lane road without turnouts to Loup Loup Pass, then to Okanogan. The next day, less the tooth, she drove back to the trailhead and hiked home. Sometimes she walked out to get supplemental groceries. "When you grow up in the fruit country, you get so hungry for fresh fruit," she said. She would drive to Winthrop and, the next day, load up her pack and hike back to the lookout. She had placed her order by phone before leaving the lookout.

"Did you ever try ordering groceries over the telephone?" Howard asked. "I remember Alice ordered five pounds of cheese, and she got five pounds of split peas." (She must have said "Swiss cheese," it occurred to me later.) One thing they craved, like most people who spend time in the woods, was fresh tomatoes. She ordered some once, along with rice, ears of corn, and other groceries. She hiked in, picked up the order, and hauled it home on her back. "I'm sure the grocer thought he was doing the right thing," she said. "He packed fresh tomatoes in the rice, and when I got there, it was just all smashed into one big mush."

On their exposed site, up so high, the weather could be violent. If you saw an electrical storm coming, the rules said, you were supposed to sit on a glass-legged stool. "But there was only one," Alice said. Once, when a storm came in and Howard had disconnected the radio antenna as instructed, the Culps' cat grew playful. "He went over and made a bat at the antenna," Howard said. "The static electricity had built up on it, and it felt kind of a shock and jumped back into the middle of the floor, and then I started watching it. And it kind of went sneaking up on that antenna, and got about yay close to it, and a big old blue spark jumps from the antenna over to the cat's nose." The cat stayed under the bed the rest of the day.

One storm melted the phone lines for several hundred feet, and when the jolt hit the cabin, it knocked Howard cold. The Forest Service almost immediately sent someone up to investigate because he hadn't reported himself OK after the storm passed. Howard began stirring just as the man arrived. He had been unconscious two hours, but he was OK; he went right back to work. When he looked on the ground outside, he found the telephone wire melted into beads.

At the end of the summer, Alice and Howard hiked out in a hard rainstorm. "I had a new outfit on," she said. "I had green jodhpurs and a maroon wool shirt, and by the time I got out to stay at the hotel, I was maroon on the top half and green on the bottom half because the dyes just weren't that good." She turned to Howard. "And remember that wonderful meal?" She choked for a moment, as she often did when some warm memory was aroused, and she squeezed out, "It tasted so good."

They spent their first three married summers in the lookout. The rest of the year, Howard attended Whitworth College in Spokane. During the fall harvest, he worked as a fruit inspector and she sorted apples. When the second World War was on, they went back to the lookout business, this time not for fires but for enemy airplanes—as relief workers for the Air Warning Service—and once spent a winter above timberline on Buck Peak. He went on to a career with the Forest Service, retiring as a range technician. Then for several years he was a contractor to the Forest Service. One job of trail maintenance put him within a mile of Diamond Point, and he and the two youngest of their four sons, who were members of his trail crew, went up for a look. The lookout had burned down.

That reminiscence didn't visibly affect either of the Culps, but Alice's voice broke again when she told me, "My very fondest memory is how beautiful it was up there." I asked if it was a strain on a new marriage, being isolated together for so long. "Well," she said, "the banker had told us, 'If you two can make it up there all alone all summer, you'll make it your whole life.'" They were on their way to doing that when I saw them. Somehow the story of their honeymoon, unlike any experience of mine though it was, filled me with nostalgia. Their insouciance was characteristic of the Thirties, which I do remember, and it is a quality that I think the present decade may lack.

I had planned our trip to give us the dry-side perspective of the Cascades, just as I had wanted to see both sides of the Sierra Nevada. (The west-east difference in the Rockies is subtler than either. I think most Coloradoans, set down in mountains in their state, would be unable to look around and tell you which side of the Continental Divide they were on.) We drove along the Columbia River toward Lake Chelan through country with dark rock caps on the buttes and with summit fringes of evergreens. On the north slopes, where snow stayed longer in the spring, sparse pine timber came down almost to the river. Apple orchards climbed the hills like vineyards of the gentler slopes along the Rhine—and the Columbia is as great a river as the Rhine, though uncastled and un-Lorelei'd. Exactly at the top line of the orchards, the sagebrush began. Northwest of Wenatchee, on the way to Leavenworth, our next stopping place, the Wenatchee River valley was often one solid orchard.

Then came Leavenworth, which I remembered from 1954 for its famous ski jump and a small business section, including a meat market where the proprietor cut thick T-bones for me and six or seven friends who had rented a ski cabin twenty or thirty miles west of there, on the east side of Stevens Pass. Since then Leavenworth had decided to devote itself to catching tourists. The decision seemed to have been unanimous, and the outcome was uniformly pseudo-Teutonic. Places of business included Das Photo Haus, Die Musikbox, Der Markt Platz, Das Oak Haus and (not *und*) Gallerie, and Heidle Burger. A diner in a bus was called Der Kaffee Bus. A sign said, "Elect Dale Foreman state representative, GOP. Danke Schoen." A Safeway sign on a supermarket was in pseudo-Fraktur, its ornate reddish letters bordered in cream. Still, some of the atmosphere turned out to be either authentic or a conscientious fake: Andy and I had good spaetzle and German beer in a basement-level café—the beer not the best preparation for the next day's hike, but we didn't expect altitude to be a problem.

Having picked up permits from the Forest Service office in town, we started up the Lake Stuart trail at 9:30 the next morning to take our first close-up look at the east side of the mountains. This, we found, was drier than the Cascade Pass country but not as dry as the Okanogan country. The woods were rocky, fairly open, and, at that hour, cool, shady, and fragrant, especially when we passed a grove of nice cedars. The undergrowth reached the knees, not the waist or shoulders as on the west side; if we had cut across a switchback here, we wouldn't have had to worry about lurking cliffs. We walked an hour before the first fairly steep pitch, from the top of which we got a glimpse of a snowfield on a peak up the canyon. We crossed a small, brushy stream, very swift. The day turned warm. An invisible woodpecker tapped deliberately. When we stopped for apples, a fly stung me through the sweaty back of my shirt. Other bugs were a nuisance, too. We moved on quickly.

The going stayed easy; in two miles we climbed only a little more than five hundred feet. We had the trail almost to ourselves, too, meeting only a man and a boy, together, in that time, though there had been a dozen cars in the parking lot at the trailhead. We passed through meadows of paintbrushes, purple thistles, yellow flowers shaped like snapdragons, and purple twins of those—three petals below, two above, the paired ones like Mickey Mouse ears. At the edge of Lake Stuart, which we had reached with remarkably little effort, we stopped to look at a display of flowers that seemed downright planned, the variety was so great and the arrangement so harmonious. It grew in the shelter of a large boulder with a seep at its base, and as we stood, a pleasant whiff of cool moisture from the lake crossed us. Except for the bugs, it should have been a delightful walk, but somehow it wasn't starting that way. I was depressed by bad news from a publisher, and the three maximal beers each of us had drunk in the basement *Gemütlichkeit* of the night before were not adding spring to our steps. Possibly it was those predisposing influences that made the country, lovely though it was, seem characterless to me.

A woman in a group of five hikers coming down told us the trail ahead was bad—many fallen trees across it. We were at about 5,000 feet, quite a bit below timberline still, whereas on the wet west side, where snow lingers into what would be the growing season and summers are cool, we might already have been in krummholz at that altitude. Soon we saw what the woman meant, and after scrambling over or ducking under a half-dozen big fallen trees, we decided to cut straight uphill in the direction of Horseshoe Lake, our goal. Up we went, scrambling over stone outcrops. We ate lunch on one of them and then scrambled on, zigzagging to lessen the steep grade and picking our way among small fallen trees, which slanted unhelpfully downslope, and a lot of gooseberry and alder tangles, with small embedded rocks as an added nuisance. It was tough going, and it was hot and dry in spite of the altitude. The bugs were an increasing annoyance.

Finally we hit a small trail that did not vanish. Horseshoe Lake, which we reached a shade after two o'clock, was pretty enough, and its setting had a timberline look even though some fair-sized trees remained. The altitude was about 6,250 feet. We climbed slabs for two or three hundred feet above the lake and still saw trees, though most of them were dwarf. Dry and tired, we headed back to Horseshoe, got onto the little trail, took it steeply down to Lake Stuart, followed it through a bog that slurped at our boots, and crawled over and under a few logs. It was much better than the way we had gone up.

Shortly we came to a camp and asked a woman if she could spare a couple of water-purification tablets. Fortunately she could; we had taken only one canteen each and had emptied those. The medicinal water made us feel better, though we agreed that when we were back in Leavenworth we would each order a jeroboam of the undoctored kind. Like all trails, this one seemed longer going down than going up, but we finally came, heavy footed, to the parking area. "Here goes," Andy said from behind me and burst past, racing me to the car as he did when he was small. But I didn't race; walking was exertion enough, and he would have won by yards anyway. So ended the most disagree-able hike of my West Coast trip, not to characterize the whole east side of the Cascades by one bad experience that was more my fault than its. And so back to Leavenworth. And so, the next day, back to Seattle.

* * * * *

We went west over Stevens Pass and into the city, where I traded Andy, who wanted to visit his cousin and see the sights, for my brother, Bob, who was there to see his daughter. Bob and I drove back north on the interstate so I could talk with Saul Weisberg, director of the North Cascades Institute. His office was in a barracks at Sedro Woolley—all offices of people connected with the woods and moun-tains in Washington state seem to be in barracks.

The first thing I asked Weisberg was whether the country above timberline in the North Cascades was seriously threatened. In the pro-tected places, he said, it is threatened by just one thing: "people not knowing how fragile it is." The habitat is well designed to deal with wind and snow, he said, "but it's not designed to deal with Vibram soles." I told him I had hiked up to Cascade Pass. "You know where that little patio is, right when you come to the top?" he asked. I did remember a flat place. "And did you see that pipe that sticks up there, with the USGS marker on it?" No. He said it stood more than waist height off the ground now, but the top used to be at ground level. People had damaged the plants, and then the wind had swept away the exposed earth. "Those little meadows right by the path are all grasses," he said, "and normally they would all be huckleberry and lupine."

Weisberg had an air like missionaries I had met: devout, even zeal-ous, but also realistically aware of the existence of the unsaved—meaning people who walk on vegetation. He was wearing shorts, and he had hairy legs, a slight frame, and a small voice with the neutral tone of one giving nurses' aides a lecture on sexually transmitted dis-eases. Damage, he said, can happen quickly where people camp. "Obviously, if you put your camp in a meadow, the plants beneath your tent are flattened down," he said.

> But if you look, you see what the real damage has been. It's right in front of your tent where your boots sit when you put your boots on and off in the morning and at night, where your heels dig in. And right around wherever you're cooking—if you're

using a stove, right where your heels dig in around the cook site, and those areas—plant damage happens, you know, within a day or two of use. Somebody else comes up the next day, of course, and they see a nice flat spot. So they think, you know, it's a good idea, and they'll camp in the same spot, and within a short time you can get a permanent bare campsite established.

So the North Cascades National Park has prohibited camping in sub-alpine meadows since the early 1980s. Camping on snow or rock is fine. Weisberg said people used to camp on more than fifty sites on Stahale Arm, where Andy and I had gone—above Cascade Pass—until camping there was prohibited in 1979. (Hmm. We had seen two campers far up on the arm at the base of the glacier. Their site, as I recalled, was in a draw and invisible from below.) Then the park people began replacing the ruined plants, thousands of them every year. Some of the sites were coming back, he said, and some were not.

It was hard for me to connect this small, eastern-academic man with the rough mountains, and what he told me next made a closer connection than I would ever have imagined. "I was the back-country ranger up at Cascade Pass in 1979," he said. He had the job for seven years, in fact, in different parts of the park, shooing campers off the alpine meadows and rescuing fallen climbers. He would spend ten days in the high country, go out to civilization for four days, "buy food and take a shower, and then go back in." As a climbing ranger, he took part in all rescues. But mostly he went into remote areas and climbed peaks, learning routes, looking for plants that people had damaged. Those were the best trips, he said: the exploratory ones. Usually he went with another ranger. They hiked from lake to lake and from ridge to ridge. Camped on a ridge, they would look ahead to the next day's terrain and think: "Impossible." But amid the towers, spires, and glaciers, a way would always open up when the time came. It might not be an ideal way; ticklish situations were standard, as was bad weather. It snowed every month of the year.

He loved the work, but he told me he burned out on the job. It wasn't the hard going; it was the rescues. "A lot of the time when you get called in on a rescue, it's a body recovery," he said. On Mount Shuksan, he helped carry out a man who had fallen several hundred yards and broken both legs. A storm was coming in. Weisberg and the other rescuers rappelled down to him on the ice and carried him out by hand, not even using a stretcher much of the time because of the difficulty. The man was screaming with pain, but Weisberg said that kind of rescue didn't disturb him greatly: "You were helping somebody." Often climbers got into trouble because of their determination to reach the summit. A shame, Weisberg thought, and not just because of the danger. "People are often so focused on that goal," he said, "that they forget about the goal of just being out in a beautiful place, which to my mind is much more important." Hikers in the high country tend to abandon the trails and head straight across the tundra for their destination. Weisberg said, showing more moderation than I had expected, that this is not a major threat if people are few. But in popular areas such as Cascade Pass and around Mount Shuksan, he found that the impromptu trails were destructive and human wastes tainted the water.

People were usually good about carrying stoves and not making fires up high, Weisberg said. I had supposed that fires above timberline were forbidden because they might spread, smoldering, through the matted vegetation, but he said the reason was that the soil needed the decomposed wood. "Mountain soils are very, very poor," he said, "especially in the Northwest, where there's so much rain that leaches out nutrients anyway." Something else about the soil is the effect of dead heather. Because heather has woody stems, people think it is tough; but when walked on, its branches break. It takes hundreds of years for heather to reestablish itself in the bad conditions of timberline, Weisberg said. "One of the problems with heathers is that when they do die, the needles and the branches are so acidic that when they decompose, they keep other things from coming in," he said. "Which works real well when they're living and thriving—they stop other things from growing up through them." Grasses, sedges, and herbs, being more resilient, survive better than heather even though they are easier to mash, he said. Unless they're destroyed, they spring back the next year.

I asked Weisberg about procedures for walking in the high country. "I think one of the best things to do is try to not wear boots as much as possible," he said. "Usually what I would do when I was climbing was to carry my climbing boots on my pack and wear tennis shoes or, you know, low-topped smooth soles." He wore those even with seventy-pound packs. (That would be half his weight, I imagine.) They were more comfortable than heavy boots, he said, and a lot better for the vegetation. Aside from wearing soft soles, he said, "I would try to stick to snow as much as possible and either walk on rocks or pick a route that followed sedge meadows and grasses more than going through the big lupine meadows; and especially trying to walk around the heathers and huckleberries and other woody plants as much as possible." Sometimes that's impossible, he said; there may be only one way to go. A small group in that case should spread out, but a large group should go single file "so that you end up making a trail, but you make just one."

I asked him what he did with an apple core in the back country and was not surprised at his answer. "Take it out," he said. "I always talk to people about taking out everything, not so much because it won't biodegrade but because it's kind of like, you know, it would eventually degrade in your living room, too. You just wouldn't leave it there because it doesn't belong there."

Weisberg was in his late thirties. He was born in New York, grew up mostly in Ohio, began working in the Cascades, sometimes as a lookout, during the summers when he was in college, and took the job as a ranger when he was in his early twenties. A couple of years before he left that job, he married a young Seattle woman who was a ranger doing botanical work in the back country. They had been friends before, and they met again on a hike. In 1980 Weisberg started organizing the North Cascades Institute. It offered its first programs in 1986. The institute goes into classrooms to teach about mountains, watersheds, Indians, birds, butterflies, and geology. It takes whole classes of children into the mountains along with their teachers, sometimes backpacking.

One course for grown people is called The Poetics of Wild Places. Participants go into the mountains and read nature writers from Thoreau to John Muir to John McPhee. They also read poets— Weisberg likes Mary Oliver, Gary Snyder, Kenneth Rexroth, and Tim McNulty—and they sit around the campfire in the evening and write. Writing in such a setting is fine for the initial outburst, Weisberg said; the descriptive and reflective moods work well there. It's not good for revising, but he finds a lot of what he writes there to be salvageable later; his poems have been published in natural-history journals and the like. The teaching part of his job, he said, is "the art of helping people learn what they should be doing"—the words of a missionary and cop.

He was a surprising man. I envied him because he seemed to love his job wholeheartedly and because he had found a way to spend a lot of time in the mountains doing things that his conscience not only accepted but endorsed. He reminded me of the many passionate specialists in this or that aspect of the wild whom, as a reporter, I had interviewed and accompanied on their jobs: the helpers of beached sea animals, the range-management specialists, the archaeologists like Sonny Montague. I always admired their enthusiasm and knowledge.

One more little hike remained for me in the Cascades. I wanted just a taste of Mount Baker, whose form haunts all of coastal northwestern Washington. Though only 10,778 feet above sea level—a shade lower than Cameron Cone outside Colorado Springs, which ranks there as only a high foothill—Baker has ice and snow enough for a whole range of the Colorado Rockies, and it carries almost as heavy an accumulation of lore. Indians in the early days of European settlement refused to accompany white explorers to the top, saying Kulshan, the deity of the mountain, might become angry. When Kulshan became angry, he emitted fire, smoke, and lava. The unimaginative pioneers climbed the mountain anyway.

Their successors did more than that—they held races up it. The Mount Baker marathon had a three-year tenure, beginning in 1911. The run went up ninety-seven hundred feet in either fourteen or sixteen miles, depending on which of two trails the runners chose, and back down to the start. A contestant in a challenge race a few weeks after the third marathon made it on the shorter trail in six hours and two minutes—less than thirteen minutes a mile. But the courses froze, bruised, and fractured contestants. In the last marathon, one runner fell into a crevasse and, jogging in place to keep from freezing, held out for the five hours before he was rescued. Promoters thereupon gave up the race because of the danger, as John C. Miles relates in *Koma Kulshan*.

Bob and I had something less strenuous in mind, since he was more in shape for boating than hiking and my knees were hurting from my two-week series of hikes. At Saul Weisberg's suggestion, we drove to the top of the Mount Baker road and walked along the Ptarmigan Ridge Trail from the parking lot. Mount Baker rose in white symmetry close ahead, and when we turned around, Mount Shuksan (pronounced Shuck-s'n, not Shook-san, a woman in a store along the highway told me) stood jagged in snow and formal dark rock. The trail guide said Shuksan was one of the most beautiful mountains in the world, but possibly because I was still resenting the dryness and heat of the walk above Leavenworth, I was more impressed with Baker, which looked all snow from a little above our level to the top. I had never before thought snow-and-ice-climbing would interest me, but from this close to the glaciers, I wished I could go on up. The day's rest had renewed my enthusiasm. Besides, we were soft-shod and packless, and the trail was the mom-and-pop kind. We took it for maybe three-quarters of a mile and looked over the west side of the slope into a steep, forested gorge with water glinting through meadows in the lowering sun. Our altitude was less than 6,000 feet, I think, but we were well into the krummholz. A coney hunched on a rock, a dark animal with round ears. Bob, as always, saw it first. He studied it with binoculars; it had a little-old-man's face, he said.

We stood and looked at the country awhile, following the trail with our eyes across empty tundra slopes and up to glacier level—both of us speculating on routes and obstacles, no doubt, but no longer with the notion that we might go up there one day. Then we went back to the car, seeing three marmots on the way. They were dark tailed with badger-gray saddles and gray nose tips: hoary marmots, different from the yellow-bellied kind we knew in the Rockies. They and the coney delighted Bob, confirming for him more than the heather and the openness that we had really returned to timberline, no matter that it was a low one. We drove to the lowlands and onto roads that took us to pleasures of the urban and maritime kind. From the ferry far out among the San Juan Islands, later, Mount Baker looked like the only mountain of consequence in all the North Cascades, though when we had been on its slopes, its neighbors had seemed only lesser greats.

I flew home, still sore kneed. At least I had two weeks to rest my tendons, except for workouts on the stairs, before heading for the northern Appalachians and my last round of climbs. After hiking in three ranges on these two summers' worth of vacations, I looked forward to the leafier views and thicker air of the fourth range. And I felt no enthusiasm at all about the prospect of the two weeks of work in between.

PART IV

The Appalachians

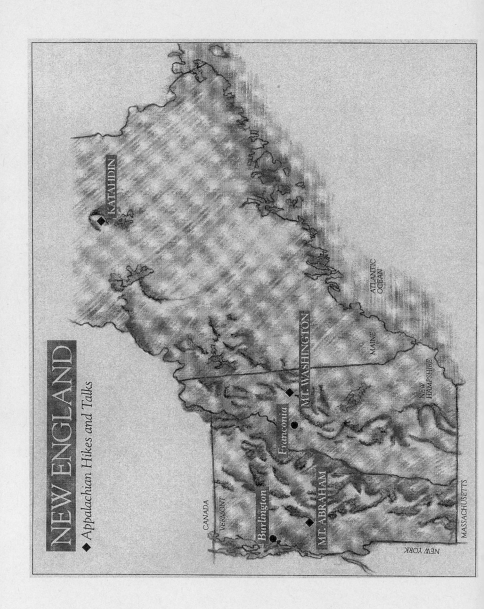

NEW ENGLAND

◆ Appalachian Hikes and Talks

KATAHDIN

ATLANTIC
OCEAN

MAINE

MT. WASHINGTON

Franconia

NEW
HAMPSHIRE

CANADA

VERMONT

Burlington

MT. ABRAHAM

MASSACHUSETTS

NEW YORK

CHAPTER ELEVEN

Having acted on my innocent western assumption that where there were highways there would be a motel room, I found myself driving north from Portsmouth, New Hampshire, heading for north-central Maine at 1:26 of a summer Sunday morning without a place to stay or much hope of getting one. I would find nothing along the coast, the man in a full motel at Portsmouth had told me, and I shouldn't head inland too soon, either, because that would take me to Sebago Lake, where everything would also be full. Go to Portland, he said, and turn inland. Even then he wasn't sure I would have any luck. I should have thought; of course there would be thousands here from New York and Boston and the unnumbered incorporations of smokestacks and houses sticking out of the forests between. Possibly I would have found something if I had been earlier, but my plane had been delayed five hours in Dallas by mechanical trouble. There I was, one of the homeless, and my priorities leapfrogged accordingly. The fabled mountain, Katahdin, ceased to be my goal. I lived for a bed.

Signs along the Maine Turnpike said, "Watch for Moose in Roadway." Other signs said to drive on the right except to pass. On the right, it occurred to me, a moose might burst from the woods into the path of a car in one jump. The worry helped keep me awake. It became 3:25. At Auburn, forty miles back, where I had last asked, a man at a motel said he doubted that I would find anything until the other side of Uh-GUS-tuh. Here was Augusta, and the night clerk sent me to Winthrop, where, he had heard an hour or two earlier, three rooms were available. I drove the ten miles, took a wrong turn, retreated, and found the motel. When I got out of my car, an elderly woman, nicely dressed, was walking from the office to her car, which was parked close to the door. I expected her to hurry into her car, eyes down, as our ways crossed. But she looked straight at me, smiled, and said, rhetorically, "What are we doing out at this hour of night?" Pleasant. It turned out that the motel operator had rented her his last room. There were several vacancies in Waterville, he said. Like the other night clerks, he was concerned about my situation and seemed happy to share the information that had crackled at him over the network. His tip was valid. I found a room on my second inquiry in Waterville and slept for five hours before checkout time.

On the road again late on a Sunday morning, I made a traffic count: eight cars going my way on the quarter mile of Interstate 95 that I could see. That wasn't the kind of congestion that the motel-room famine indicated, but it was considerably more than the night before, when I had been able to drive most of the time with my brights on. Along the highway, the cottage businesses reminded me of the Ozarks. Signs offered Jo's Jams and Jellies; Penobscot Paving—Driveways, Walkways; Honey, Fresh Eggs; Auto Electric; and, without explanation, Birch Bogg Guides. I had turned onto State Highway 16 above Orono. New hay lay in the fields. A light rain was falling, and it had stayed cool enough and dark enough that the orange squash blossoms in somebody's garden still flared gaudily at three in the afternoon. Now and then I saw a red maple branch, though it was only the middle of August. The country began to roll. I went around a turn and saw a considerable hill to the northwest, too rounded and in the wrong direction to be Katahdin. Hills soon began filling the frame of the highway cut, though the woods generally hid them otherwise. I crossed a lovely river that moved enough to swirl around the rocks, then deepened, broadened, and slowed darkly at the edge of Milo. There was no name on the bridge, a fine, big river being presumably unworthy of note in such a watery place. The highway map said it was the Sebec.

State Highway 11 led to Millinocket between lakes that the map showed but the woods usually hid, and then I was on the way to Baxter State Park and Katahdin. The name of Katahdin, the highest mountain in Maine, had connoted adventure and mystery for me since I was seven or eight and read a serial in a boys' magazine about an Indian who heroically saved his friend from an avalanche there. Possibly it was the Abol Slide, which in 1816 "tore off a wide swath of mountainside, leaving bare earth and rock from top to bottom of the giant slope," as Laura and Guy Waterman describe it in *Forest and Crag: A History of Hiking, Trail Blazing, and Adventure in the Northeast Mountains*. Now I was within twenty-six miles of the mountain, and every time I rounded a curve and saw it and its massif, my responses were an internal thump at its bulk and height, then the thought that no, that was a cloud, and then, instantly, the recognition that it was what it appeared to be. It was a real mountain, for all that its altitude, 5,267 feet, was only that of the highest plains at the base of the foothills in Colorado. A low, separate rise in the foreground emphasized the distance from base to summit, and a half girdle of clouds at about the midway contour of the peak pointed up that effect. The sky was light gray now, clearly outlining the long summit ridge.

At the check-in station for the state park, a signboard listed four classes of possible conditions on top of Katahdin. Number I meant open, II meant open but not recommended, III meant one or two trails closed, and IV meant mandatory closing of all trails: no hiking above timberline. The next day's predicted condition was II, with a 40 percent chance of showers. I would go, of course. I asked the ranger at the station, a chubby young woman, if there was drinking water at the Roaring Brook camp, where I had reserved a bunk. Yes, she said: a stream ran right past it. What, I said, you drink the water out of the stream untreated? "I lived there for two months and did," she said. After all, she said, the camp was at "quite a bit higher altitude." (One of my park booklets said the altitude at Roaring Brook was 1,489 feet. My house on the flat in Wichita is only a hundred feet lower.) Then lawsuit discretion took over and she said, "We do recommend that people treat it." I was surprised by all this. Even in the wildest parts of the Colorado Rockies, I would not drink water directly from a stream. Giardia must not have found its way to northern Maine.

After nearly eight miles over a rocky, pitted dirt road, I parked at the campground, dumped my pack on a lower bunk in a log shelter to stake my claim, and walked four-tenths of a mile to see Sandy Pond, on the way meeting twenty-two hikers in groups of two or three. At the pond, I saw many small trout rising. Also one moose rising. She was standing a couple of hundred yards from me across the pond, feeding, and I timed her submersions at nineteen to twenty-five seconds each from the going-under slosh to the coming-up one. After a while I walked back to the car and drove to the nearest town,

Millinocket, for supper—a Glorified Hamburger at the Trail's End Diner for $2.05, the altitude of the next day's hike being too little, in my judgment, to require avoidance of protein. Then I drove back to camp and lay down, instantly uncomfortable, in my mummy bag on the plywood bunk. The bed situation in Maine was really tough.

During the night, while I tried everything but yoga to find a position in which the plywood didn't chafe my knees or elbows, I kept hearing what I thought was a steady rain. The morning, though, when it finally came, was as much blue as white; I had been hearing the creek. More or less awake, I started walking from the ranger station at 6:45. Two parties had signed out before me, one of them at four o'clock—no doubt going up to see the first sunlight strike the United States. I took the Helon Taylor Trail (named for a former park supervisor) through woods that were pale from their plurality of birches, though with also some beeches and small evergreens. The trail was steep, rocky, and rooty; in many places, I stepped from one rock up to another. I was not as out of breath as I would have been at 8,000 feet, but I felt lethargic from the two bad nights. The other occupant of my half of the bunkhouse had been a young man going to college in Providence who, with some time off, had just finished conducting a six-week camp in northern Maine. In the dark, I never got a look at him. There were six bunks for the two of us, in case either had seen any point in repositioning his agony. Probably I had slept more than I thought; the sleep scientists say that is usually the way.

On the trail, I looked ahead through the treetops and saw a mountain above timberline: Pamola Peak, a shade less than 5,000 feet above sea level. It is named for its spirit, whereas Katahdin comes from an Indian name meaning "the greatest mountain," according to Stephen Clark's *Katahdin*. Pamola Peak was a long way above, and yet the trees around me were beginning to show signs of stunting. I had been on the trail only thirty-five minutes. I couldn't be higher than 2,500 feet above sea level.

Another difference from the Rockies was the humidity, which I remembered from hikes in New Hampshire a few years earlier when I was living on Long Island. Though I had considered putting on a sweater when I set out, I felt slick now with the sweat of walking and clambering. The trail was an occasional painted blue blaze on a boulder. Once, I grabbed a birch on either side of me and pulled myself up between; the trunks felt smooth and cool and as solid as mastodon bones set in concrete. Here, crossing the trail fifty-five minutes along the way, was a creek a yard wide and a hand deep, perfectly clear, with grains and chips of rock glittering on the bottom. I couldn't resist dipping my canteen into it for a refill and a drink. I walked on and immediately saw—downstream, thank God—what had to be toilet paper on the ground amid the trees.

The trail became more and more an unmodified arroyo, going straight upslope with never a switchback. I used both hands, picked my way, sometimes climbed seven or eight feet up handholds on a large rock. I tried to avoid putting my knee down because the sand-and-gravel-encrusted rocks hurt it. I was surprised that the trail guide in Clark's book said nothing about such conditions, though it did say the climb was difficult and steep. Easterners must take clambering and boulder scaling for granted. In the Rockies, this would not be called a trail.

Most of the trees had shrunk to head height now, and before long I broke into the open and felt a breeze. It wasn't timberline yet, but by standing on a boulder I could see what was around me: a cirque to the north and west, surely the big one at the base of Katahdin; and starting in the northwest, a high ridge above timberline that sloped east or northeast into timber and ended up at a rocky bluff maybe two hundred feet high—Hamlin Ridge, I think, the north part of the east-opening Katahdin horseshoe. I went on. The rock underfoot looked just like the gray rock of the Rockies, the Sierra Nevada, and parts of the Cascades. Soon the dwarf spruce and fir around me dropped off to matted krummholz. It was not quite 8:30, so I had walked less than two hours.

A junco flitted low amid the growth and disappeared behind a rock, showing the white bars of its tail as it spread its landing apparatus—the same bird, allowing for regional variations, that I had seen in all the other ranges, a real timberline fixture. The blueberries on bushes along the "trail" had gradually faded from dusty purple to lighter and lighter blue, and now I saw a cluster that was nearly all green; the altitude was at work. Here was pink heather, too, like that above Cascade Pass in Washington. Timberlines, like deserts or rain forests, show a clear kinship from place to place. I looked south from the open ridge and saw lakes, lakes, lakes, as on a Minnesota postcard. They stretched away into haze at the southern horizon, with woods and low hills between. It was a grand scene, and I had the looking to myself. So far I had not seen another person.

The trail went straight up the ridge line among boulders, dividing the north and south slopes like a Mohawk haircut. When I stepped to the scalp of the south side, I looked southwest and thought I could see the plateau to which Thoreau climbed. On a preliminary climb up a foothill, he said in his journal, he walked over the tops of "ancient black spruce-trees, (Abies nigra,) old as the flood, from two to ten or twelve feet in height, their tops flat and spreading." In that place, he said, "the principle of vegetation was hard put to it." He went on upward: "Having slumped, scrambled, rolled, bounced, and walked, by turns, over this scraggy country, I arrived upon a side-hill, or rather side-mountain, where rocks, gray silent rocks, were the flocks and herds that pastured, chewing a rocky cud at sunset."

A visit from Thoreau: that was something no western range could claim. Though Thoreau thought he had climbed Katahdin, William Howarth says in *Thoreau in the Mountains* that he made it only to about the 4,600-foot level on the western tableland of the massif or near the base of the south peak of Katahdin. Nonetheless, his delusion supplied him with impressions as well as the real thing would have. One impression was of a man on top of a mountain: "He is more lone than you can imagine. There is less of substantial thought and fair understanding in him, than in the plains where men inhabit. His reason is dispersed and shadowy, more thin and subtile like the air."

Men's habitations are still mainly on the plains, I could tell him. But men on their annual vacations flee into the subtile air, where duty can't find them and thoughts come out dispersed because of a synergistic relation between altitude and alcohol. The flanks of Katahdin seem not to have intoxicated Thoreau but to have filled him with austere thoughts. He said of the reception Nature gave to man in such a place: "She does not smile on him as in the plains. She seems to say sternly, why came ye here before your time? This ground is not prepared for you. Is it not enough that I smile in the valleys? I have never made this soil for thy feet, this air for thy breathing, these rocks for thy neighbors."

For my part, I did not find the Katahdin air too stern for breathing, though I was practically at the upper limit of the krummholz. The trail became easier, but there were still places where I reached for a handhold and pulled myself up. If I fell, I would be bruised, nothing worse. Two hundred feet ahead and above, an embryonic cloud, barely more a shape than the air around it, moved across the peak like a scrim in front of a stage backdrop, hiding nothing. Before long I was inside such a cloud, but I knew mainly because the air around me took on just a suggestion of glitter, as if the light were touching snow grains too small to see. Then I was upslope from the clouds, watching them move along with an occasional glint like a school of chub in a stream. A chipmunk chirped at me from among rocks, invisible. A mysterious domain, timberline, and not always stern.

I hurried, wanting to get across Pamola Peak and onto the Knife-Edge Trail to Katahdin before more clouds came up, but I pushed too hard and had to stop for rest, water, and apple newtons. It was all right, I saw. The clouds had scattered and diminished enough that there was no hurry. But as I chewed, here came a big one from nowhere, puffing into existence in midair downslope from me. It burst up the steep south slope as quickly as fire through gasoline vapor, and in a second it was all around me, though I could see the sun shining through it. A few seconds before, it had not existed, but now it stretched for a couple of miles eastward and downslope.

I grabbed my pack, hunched into the straps, turned, and hurried higher, hitting a pace I would never have tried at 12,000 feet. It was alarming to see how fast the cloud swirled past, to be shown weather of such power and speed. I rushed through the cloud and soon was on top of Pamola; the cookies had given me quite a boost. A sign pointing more or less south to the beginning of the knife edge said that Baxter Peak—the more recent, more political name for Katahdin—was 1.1 miles away. It warned against taking that route if the weather was bad. I walked to an edge a few feet west and looked far down into the cirque, hearing a rush of water from a source I couldn't find. It had taken me three hours to climb the 3 1/6 miles and 3,413 feet to Pamola.

The knife-edge ridge started from a level that looked a hundred feet or so lower, but I felt energetic enough not to regret the loss of altitude. To get to the ridge, I had to turn around and let myself down over a tall pink rock, hanging by my hands while my feet felt for a hold. I was again surprised that the guidebook did not mention such a place. The fall, if my hands had slipped on the lichens lining the rock, would have been only two or three feet, but not every woman, child, or old man would be able to get past the spot. After that the knife edge was easy; it was like walking a one-lane boulder field with a dropoff of several hundred feet on either side. Remembering the misstep that had launched me sideways off the trail above Cascade Pass, I lifted and planted my feet like a mechanical man. But there was scarcely a place where I found myself unavoidably poised above a drop; I could always move to one side or the other and get away from it. This was nothing like as tricky or steep as the ridge to Mount Dana; if I did fall, I would have a chance to grab something and slow myself.

I felt relaxed and confident. Clouds kept drifting around me; they filled my nostrils and lungs soothingly, like chilled steam. I could see far enough to pick my route by the painted blue dashes on the rocks, which went up the ridge one above the other like a fence line and disappeared into clouds. Three hikers met me—a man in his forties with two teenage boys, the first people I had seen since setting out. The man said they had left the main peak twelve minutes before. Don't go down by the Cathedral Trail, he said—too much hand-over-hand; take the Saddle Trail. We went our ways. I passed within sight of a cairn that must mark the South Peak, and shortly I was on top of Katahdin. The clouds still hung about me.

A tall woman in her thirties, wearing short shorts, was on the summit. I asked her if there was a register to sign. "No," she said, "you really just kind of have to leave your heart here, I guess." A man near us, older than I, said there used to be a scroll. He was also wearing shorts, and his legs were covered with scratches, some of them old, some new.

"Did you come up the St. John Trail?" he asked me. I said no, the HEE-lahn Taylor Trail.

"The HEE-l'n Taylor? Oh, yeah, that's the old St. John Trail."

The woman, Peggy Hamill, said, "I like that trail. That's a nice trail." I felt squelched—it had seemed to me like a tough trail. She said she was camping at Chimney Pond, down in the cirque, and had come up the Saddle Trail. She had two fourteen-year-olds with her who had talked of crossing the Knife-Edge Trail, but they changed their minds when the clouds came in. "They decided they'd rather go to camp and eat cookies," she said. "I think that's a good choice. I can't go across, 'cause I'm too scared." I felt better. I also felt better, in retrospect, about my defection on the ridge to Mount Dana.

The woman was a nurse from Union, near the coast. The man, Lawrence Hopper, lived in Millinocket. He told me he had come up that day by the Abol Trail, the shortest one, Thoreau's route; it had a lot of gravel on the rocks; you could easily slip. He liked to fill his canteen at Thoreau Spring, he said: "Not rate in the spring itself; but you goa baack probably fifty yahds, it's so cold you can't keep your hand in it." The three of us talked about the Colorado mountains and the easier trails there. "It's like walking on a meadow," he said. She agreed: "You just walk along on the ground." She wondered where all the climbers were today: "Usually it's a parade across here." He said it was the fewest people he had seen on top in the last two years. In the late thirties, he said, he would come up and find no one at all. He climbed the mountain two or three times a year. "My thing is really boycycling, though," he said. "I've boycycled across the United States." And that, he said, was since his retirement. He was sixty-eight and had worked at the post office for years. He was white haired and small and wiry, a good climbing and bicycling type. He said good-bye and started down.

Shortly people began arriving—some men and girls first. One of the men had the others of his party pose against the summit cairn while he took their picture. A weathered wooden sign, propped up on boulders, said, "Northern Terminus of the Appalachian Trail." It said it was 2,135 miles to Springer Mountain, Georgia. That was all. I would have expected a more festive sign if I had walked 2,135 miles. Two women I hadn't seen were sitting behind a boulder near the sign. Other hikers were approaching. There would be a fair crowd before long.

When I talked to Lawrence Hopper by phone after my trip, he told me he used to spend three or four days on Mount Katahdin and never see a person. Twelve years ago, he said, he climbed the mountain with his eleven-year-old granddaughter after several years' absence. He could hardly believe the increased crowds—"It was like a bunch of soldiers walking along there single file." But he had trouble with people when he spent a week in the Rockies, too. "Everywhere that we climbed there, we even had jeeps go by us," he said. I could pick more nearly solitary places in the Rockies for him. No doubt the same exist in Maine, but maybe not above timberline.

I walked west along the summit ridge, looking for the Saddle Trail, and met a man who was coming up from the Cathedral Trail. His wife was a couple of hundred feet behind him. She was a botanist, he said: "We'd have probably been up here an hour ago if we hadn't seen things." She came up, out of breath. They lived west of Denver, it developed; their names were Dick and Loraine Yeatts; they were in their fifties. Both had climbed "essentially" all the 14,000-foot peaks in Colorado. They agreed heartily that the flowers in the Rockies surpassed the scattered ones we had seen here, but then this was late in the season for northern New England, especially up so high.

When I talked with her later, she told me that they had gone down the way I had come up, across the Knife-Edge Trail and down the Helon Taylor Trail. They were surprised at how much work it took, how rough the country was. He grew up in Pennsylvania, she in Chicago, but it was their first time hiking in New England. They had both been in love with the Rockies for decades. They tried to get into the mountains every week, and in the winter they went ski touring at least one weekend; they had climbed a number of big mountains on skis. "One of the reasons," she said, "is that I'm so eager to be above timberline. That's one of my passions."

She said she worked for the Denver Botanic Gardens and was doing an extensive flower survey for Rocky Mountain National Park; she was finishing work on a book about alpine flowers. He taught physics at Colorado School of Mines in Golden. I asked him what his decision would have been if Harvard or Columbia had offered him a teaching job. "Probably no," he said, and she said, "We have given up a lot in the way of lifestyle and benefits in order to live a lifestyle that we find extremely enjoyable." Since she was a botanist, I asked about the harm in stepping on a tundra plant. Overstated, she said: "If a person steps on a plant once, it's not going to hurt it." And what do the Yeattses do with an apple core? They throw it away unless somebody is watching. "There's plenty of pikas up there that love those apple cores," she said.

Saying good-bye to the Yeattses, I walked on in search of the trail down. The clouds were still a nuisance because they shut out the view, but they kept the air cool and fresh. The footing was mostly fist-sized rocks that rolled. To the side of the trail and up the slope to the south as far as I could see in the cloud, the ground was covered with grass or sedge that had long green stems and tawny-red tassels, feathered at the ends. The tassels waved in the wind, which was increasing. Before long I was in the upper limit of krummholz. It was the same kind of mat that Thoreau had mentioned. I could see that a man might walk across the top of it, though he would need big feet.

Here were still more people: a man and three teenage girls on their way up and then two guys with big packs. No; one was a woman. "You must be hiking the Appalachian Trail," I said to the two, but she said no, they were just going in for a week. They had done the hardest part, too, he said—the rest was downhill or level. When I told them which way I had come, he said, "Wow. That's quite a hike." They said, as Peggy Hamill had said, that Mount Washington in New Hampshire, though higher, was an easier climb. I said the rock piles here did slow you down. "Trails out West aren't like this, as rocky, are they?" she said. No, I said. She said that they had met a fellow the previous year who was coming down Mount Washington, "and he was walking in such a way that I figured he had a handicap." She wondered if he was blind, and when she questioned him, she found he could barely talk. "Come to find out that he was just hurtin'," she said. "He was from out West and had done a lot of climbing out there, but, 'Son of a gun, over here they put up a pile of rocks and say, "See if you can make it to the top of that."'" But she said she could do without the rattlesnakes of the West. I said I had never seen one in the mountains; they seemed pleasantly surprised. The couple's names were Walter and Jo Ann Pyrzyk, and they lived eighty miles away. She took off her cap; her red-gold hair cut years off her. As we parted, she said she was grateful to Percival P. Baxter, a former governor, for having given the state the property for the park that included Katahdin, back when there was land, land, land.

The Saddle Trail, reputedly the easiest of the lot, dropped off the ridge so sharply that it took some resolve to step over the side and start down. It had loose sand and gravel on top of steep, outward-canted rocks, and a fall would have broken a bone. Now and then I put a hand down to steady myself. A pair of young women coming up stopped to talk, and one said when I told her about the ranges I had sampled in recent weeks, "I hope you're not doing all your hiking by yourself." I told her I usually went where there were other people to carry me down with my broken leg. But she was right. Though an immediately fatal fall is just as fatal in company as in solitude, company keeps you from suffering drawn-out cold, shock, thirst, and possibly death with a broken bone in some isolated arroyo. On western hikes, at least, I told myself, I must always take someone.

The trail dropped into the birches: so timberline had ended for another hike, and for me there was no more thrill in the leaving than there had been in the attaining or, for that matter, the staying—I had never quite felt above timberline. Maybe it was because the clouds had shut down my perspective much of the time and also because there were so many people on top that I couldn't lie back on a rock and shed my ties to time. The sparseness and dullness of the alpine vegetation and the lack of marmots and coneys were drawbacks, too. And there were no mule deer with great racks and no elk, no bighorn sheep, no goats. And no snow. I had to say it had been a disappointment.

Still, it was better than no timberline. If you lived in the Northeast, you would want to get up sometimes. The view, what I had seen before the clouds appeared, was enough to justify climbing to open country, even in the absence of other timberline attractions. In the fall, if you dared climb Katahdin then, the spread of color in the forests below must be spectacular.

A trickle of a spring ran close against the trail. I saw tall yellow flowers with mustard inside the cups and a black-and-yellow bumble-bee wallowing in them. Then came a glade, damp, with pretty flowers a half inch across, five-petaled, a pale pink with red pinstripes lengthwise of the petals. The leaves looked exactly like the tangy sheep sorrel I used to find in Texas lawns and eat when I was a kid. As I looked, a man, a woman, and two girls of ten or twelve came up and stopped to rest. They lived in Surrey and had started their hike at Roaring Brook. When I told them I lived in Kansas, they exclaimed, as people in Maine always did. "Some great mountain climbing there," the man said. "We were just talking about that. We're going to drive cross-country next year, and we say we're going to do our hikin' in Kansas." I asked how the girls were making it. "With the kids," he said, "it's more attitude than energy. And they've got the energy." Not the attitude, I judged. They stared into space in martyred boredom. I left the family to its good cheer. The spring became a creek running among rocks. I heard frogs and soon was at Chimney Pond, where a hand-lettered note on a piece of paper on a clipboard said, "Katahdin has the worst weather in Maine and conditions change quickly." A rather modest statement, in view of what I had heard about the power and suddenness of that weather.

The worst of the weather came on a late-October night in 1963. A state report on the incident gives the facts the way such reports do, telling in chronological fashion how a middle-aged woman and a park ranger who tried to save her died on the steep slopes beneath the knife edge. At the time the board of review met, fifteen days after the deaths, the bodies had not been found, and it was taken for granted that they would not be found until spring. It was a beautiful October 28, a Monday, when two Massachusetts women, Helen Mower and Margaret Ivusic, climbed the Cathedral Trail from Chimney Pond to the summit. They had lunch, rested, and set out onto the knife edge, expecting only to take a look and then return by way of the Saddle Trail. Margaret Ivusic, who was about fifty and had taken up hiking only two or three years before, walked ahead of her companion, and they were separated for a quarter of an hour. Then the other woman heard her calling from somewhere down the north side of the ridge. "Helen, this is a short cut," the voice said. "I think it is the best way to go."

But Helen Mower was afraid to leave the trail, and each went her way. "We are both determined women," the survivor told the board of review. She walked across, yelling at the other woman occasionally but getting no response. At the top of the Chimney Trail, against Pamola Peak, she finally got an answer: Her friend was stuck—unable to move up or down. She seemed not to be injured. Helen Mower told her friend she would go down Pamola Peak by the Dudley Trail and get help at Chimney Pond. It was past midafternoon. "I'll see you tomorrow, I hope," the stranded one called. When Helen Mower arrived at the pond at about 6:40 P.M., it was dark, and no one else was there. She walked to the edge of the pond and again—the weather was that still—was able to exchange shouted words with her friend. She built a fire and waited for someone to come.

At 8:15 Ralph Heath, a thirty-seven-year-old park ranger, arrived, dead tired after a hard day. He, too, stood by the pond and talked with the stranded woman, "apparently establishing that she was uninjured," according to the report. He told her he would try to rescue her as soon as there was light. He radioed word of the situation to Helon Taylor, his boss, and went to bed. Unable to sleep, he heard a door slamming in the wind and, worried about the change in the weather, got up, borrowed Helen Mower's rucksack, stocked it with food, an eighty-foot rope, and other emergency supplies, and set out. Returning at four that morning, he told her that he had gone off the knife edge using his rope and had come close enough to her friend to talk easily, though he couldn't get to her without more rope.

He had breakfast, asked Taylor to send help, and a little after six o'clock set out again, saying he would go around the pond and try to climb to the waterfall that he thought was near the other woman's position—the water I had heard from the top of Pamola Peak, I imagine. As he left, Helen Mower heard on the radio that another ranger was on the way, and she shouted that information to Ralph Heath. "Fine," he said. "Thank you." The report says, "That was the last known contact by sight or sound that anyone had with Ranger Heath." An icy rain was falling at the pond, and it was snowing higher up, but the wind, though noticeable, was still within a normal range. Help began arriving before eight o'clock.

By then the weather had turned vicious, and it kept getting worse. "Snow, blizzard all day" is the best the report can do to characterize the conditions, but one of the leaders of the search, Elmer Knowlton, a game and fish warden at the time, described them in terms of his own experience when we talked on the phone. It was the worst storm he had ever seen, he said, "absolutely horrendous," with trees toppling everywhere. "Of all the three days I was there," he said, "I never saw the mountain at all, and there was just a steady scream of wind. It was the only time in my life that I have seen the wind come down the chimney with such force that it made perfect circles of smoke come up around the covers of the ram-down stove." Knowlton set out for the ridge, taking a few steps, being knocked flat by the wind, getting up to stagger a few more steps, and so on. He passed a cow moose and her calf. "She was just standing there, covered with snow," he said, "and she let me walk right by her, within eight feet, and I was half by her before I even saw her."

This, remember, was below timberline and at a comparatively low altitude. The stranded woman and the ranger who had gone to help her were a thousand or more feet above and fully exposed. The wind up there would have been much stronger. Knowlton and a ranger made it to the foot of the ridge. Their shouts brought no response; they could hardly have been heard ten feet away. There was no possibility of climbing farther.

The next day, a Thursday, some climbers reached the top of Katahdin but, the vicious weather continuing, could not get onto the knife edge. On Friday a group climbed Pamola Peak but again was forced back. On Saturday William Putnam of Springfield,

Massachusetts, chairman of the Mountain Leadership Committee of the Appalachian Mountain Club, led a party up Pamola and down to the top of a ravine called the Chimney, climbing in weather that he still described as ferocious. He decided that "it would be foolhardy to try to proceed further west [along the Knife-Edge Trail] than the Chimney under existing wind and snow conditions," the report says. He and two others climbed part of the way down the Chimney and searched the face immediately west of it. Then Putnam radioed that the search might as well be called off. He said, according to the report, that the snow above timberline on Pamola

> was wet for the first two or three inches. He said this was the snow that was sliding a great deal but was not particularly dangerous. Below that he said the snow was hard, dry and wind packed . . . He said, "Those people were dead on Tuesday, there is no question in my mind." He said that no one would have lived under conditions of wind and temperature that must have existed to pack the snow in such a way.

On April 27, six months after the women had started their hike, Knowlton and another warden climbed Pamola Peak and sat on a sheltered ledge just below the summit, searching with binoculars. After more than three hours, Knowlton spotted a rope running down the face of a large rock and hanging below it. Two days later members of a search-and-rescue team roped themselves down to the rock and dug where the rope Knowlton had seen disappeared in the snow. Beneath the eighteen-inch cover of snow, they found the woman's body lying facedown, encased in ice and dressed in a warm jacket and a wool hood. It took the rest of that day and two more days to chop it free—they finally had to use ice-melting salt. The rope that led to the body was tied to the rock twenty-five feet above. The supplementary report to the board of review says an autopsy reportedly showed that Margaret Ivusic had died of injuries so severe that she could not have survived more than two hours after suffering them. When and where she had fallen was not known.

The searchers waited two weeks to look for Heath's body. They found it four hundred feet above the other body, according to the report (Knowlton says it was two hundred). Heath had on only "a summer shirt and trousers and a cruisers jacket." Knowlton is sure that Heath had reached the woman and attached the rope, probably hoping to anchor himself and let her down. Unable to do anything in the terrific wind (and perceiving, very probably, that it was too late to help in any case), he must have tried to climb to the ridge top to make his way down. The blizzard ended his climb. There was not even a bruise on his body.

I hiked the easy 3.3 miles from Chimney Pond down to my camp. The trail grew level and sandy, and it was a pleasure to be able to swing out. Later the rocks came back, but I made the distance in an hour and a half, stopping to talk briefly with several of the numerous hikers I met. The ranger at Roaring Brook, a tall, nice kid named Jeff Madore, showed me figures on the number who had climbed the various trails: in July, 1,578 had gone up the Helon Taylor Trail and 7,703 up all the others. That meant 9,281 had climbed Katahdin during that month, Madore said, but I think not. The figures came from the register, and the signatures were put on at the starts, not the ends, of hikes. A third of the people on the last segment of my hike back from Katahdin had told me they were going only as far as Chimney Pond. Even so, two-thirds of 9,281 is 200 people a day on top of that strenuous, potentially deadly, and, but for its isolation and reputation, rather dull mountain. Judging by the license plates I saw in the Roaring Brook lot, most were from Maine. So there were woods and waters around them wherever they worked. Maybe they could dispense with extremes of height and solitude—their daily lives satisfied some of that need.

I spent the night in an inn on the road to Millinocket, sleeping soundly and long. In town the next morning, I spoke with Joan King, reservation clerk for Baxter State Park. The trails in the park had no switchbacks, I observed: was that philosophy, or necessity? All she knew was what the trail builders had done. "Right from the beginning, that's the way they did it," she said, "right straight up." I thanked her and set out for New Hampshire and the highest mountain in the Northeast.

CHAPTER TWELVE

The first known climber of Mount Washington was Darby Field, who was thirty-two and lived around Durham in southern New Hampshire. He probably hoped to find valuable ore on top—the year was 1642, a century and a half and more before the day when Europeans and Americans, possibly because they needed mental and physical relief from the Industrial Revolution, would begin to think of mountain climbing as a sport. He was accompanied, according to Laura and Guy Waterman *(Forest and Crag)*, by at least one Indian from his part of the state. (Those from around the mountain did not dare invade the resident god's territory.) It is not known which route he took, but a magistrate from Maine, Thomas Gorges, said in a letter shortly afterward that Field had sat five hours on top in "terrible freezing weather." The month was probably June. Later that summer Field climbed the mountain again, this time "with other settlers," and still later Gorges and a companion climbed it. Since nobody found any treasure, that was the end of recorded climbs for a long time.

I think cities must have to grow up and begin to stifle people before climbing becomes attractive of itself, though William Prescott, in his *Conquest of Mexico*, ascribes pretty much modern motives to Cortez's men who in 1519 tried to climb Popocatepetl:

> The mysterious terrors which hung over the spot, and the wild love of adventure, made some of the Spanish cavaliers desirous to attempt the ascent, which the natives declared that no man could accomplish and live. Cortés encouraged them in the enterprise, willing to show the Indians that no achievement was above the dauntless daring of his followers.

(They failed because of volcanic activity, but two years later another party of Spaniards made it.)

In 1858, when climbing Mount Washington had become popular enough that the first two of what have been many deaths from bad weather on its slopes had occurred, Thoreau made his second ascent (his first was in 1839). He carried food including "a moist sweet plum cake very good and lasting," which Howarth *(Thoreau in the Mountains)* likens to gorp. His route was along what is now the highway, Howarth says, and in fact work toward making a carriage road of it had been in progress for three years and would be completed in three more. When Thoreau was on top with his companions, "a cloud invested us all, a cool driving mist." He advised other climbers, "It is unwise for one to ramble over these mountains at any time, unless he is prepared to move with as much certainty as if he were solving a geometrical problem. A cloud may at any moment settle around him, and unless he has a compass and knows which way to go, he will be lost at once." Some of his observations are fanciful: "An ordinary rock in a fog, being in the apparent horizon, is exaggerated to, perhaps, at least ten times its size and distance. You will think you have gone further than you have to get to it." Right—and I wonder if, in reading *Walden,* we shouldn't divide the number of bean rows by ten.

Though Mount Washington, more than a thousand feet higher than Katahdin, is said to be an easier climb, its god has caused many more deaths. Those of the park ranger and the Massachusetts woman on Katahdin in 1963 were the first after the creation of Baxter State Park in 1931, and Elmer Knowlton of Millinocket could tell me of only one since then; but in 143 years, 110 people died on or near Mount Washington—many of them as a direct result of the vicious weather. True, Mount Washington has attracted climbers for a long time; the first trail to the top was built in 1819, the first bridle path in 1840, the carriage road in 1861, the cog railway in 1869.

A community of buildings grew up on the summit after the cog railroad was finished. The buildings included a weather station, a telegraph office, barns, sheds, the office of a newspaper called *Among the Clouds,* and a large resort hotel with its own orchestra. By 1880 nearly twenty thousand people were visiting the summit every year (most of them arriving, I assume, by cog train or carriage). In 1908 a fire destroyed most of the development. Weather observers and television technicians are the only year-round residents now. The observers have plenty to observe: the mountain is famous as the measuring place of the strongest wind ever recorded—231 miles an hour in 1934. But in spite of its weather and really alpine look—so much of it being above timberline— and for all the stories about deaths of healthy and well-equipped climbers at all times of the year, Mount Washington, to my mind, lacks the mystique that invests Katahdin. This may be simply because it has a highway up it and some buildings and towers on top. Pikes Peak and Mount Evans have been translated into prose the same way.

I got to Mount Washington by way of a handful of pretty little towns in Maine that were too modest to put up signs at the outskirts with their names on them and then by way of New Hampshire roads that ran between hills with clouds on top. It was a Tuesday, the fourth day of the nine (including weekends) that I could be away from my job in Wichita, and I was looking forward to further experience of this third major range of the summer. But the clouds up high looked unpromising for the next day's climb. I flopped on the bed in my motel room in Gorham and slept much of what was left of the day.

The next morning I was the first customer at the Honey Bear café, where an elderly waitress shaped like the Venus of Willendorf served me a stack of hotcakes whose weight also evoked the Stone Age. After I had driven south to Pinkham Notch and started west up the trail to Mount Washington—the first part of it was an old logging road—I nonetheless felt fairly good. The sign at the start was more detailed than the note on the clipboard below Katahdin. "Try this trail," it said, "*only* if you are in top physical condition, well clothed and carrying extra clothing and food. Many have died above timberline from exposure. Turn back at first sign of bad weather." I turned off the logging road after a bit and took the Boott Spur Trail, earth floored and leaf covered. Before long the trail was blocked by a tall boulder, so that I had to haul myself up by roots and small trees. It was a harder obstacle than anything I had encountered on the trail up Katahdin, but it turned out to be the only one of consequence.

The sun was shining through a haze of humidity and possibly pollution. Not a cloud was in sight. As on the trail to Katahdin, I was cool but sweaty—a combination unknown in the West. The dominance of birches switched to that of evergreens as I climbed, and before long the evergreens began to shrink. I pulled out onto an overlook and gazed at

Tuckerman Ravine—a grand spectacle. I figured I was standing at about 4,300 feet, having started in the notch at 2,000. I could hear the stream in the bottom of the ravine. Back on the trail, I walked between stunted firs, sometimes reaching out to touch their springy boughs. Soon I emerged from the trees, breaking into knee-high krummholz as decisively as if I had stepped from a furnished room into a nearly empty one. The breeze, surprisingly, did not increase. The trail became steep, climbing fourteen hundred feet in the next three-quarters of a mile (according to a map in the AMC *White Mountain Guide,* put out by the Appalachian Mountain Club). Sometimes I used my hands for help.

At about 5,000 feet, I sat in a cooler breeze, had an apple, wrapped up the core and put it into my pack, smeared sunburn lotion onto my face and hands because the sun was fairly bright now, and hurried on. As on Katahdin, clouds kept skimming the summit; they enveloped the towers and summit house as they passed. I came to another sign—a more emphatic version of the first one: "STOP: THE AREA AHEAD HAS THE WORST WEATHER IN AMERICA. MANY HAVE DIED THERE FROM EXPOSURE, EVEN IN THE SUMMER. TURN BACK NOW IF THE WEATHER IS BAD." Around me the dwarf trees grew vertically for a few inches and then leaned sharply to the south; the north winds in winter must be something. A pamphlet put out by the Mount Washington Museum says that on top, "The wind exceeds hurricane force (75 mph) on an average of 104 days each year."

The trail topped out at the rocky southeast end of Boott Spur and joined the north-south and here nearly level Davis Path, which was marked by a jagged line of cairns. The grass alongside was green stemmed and red-tawny ended like that on Mount Katahdin, and when I looked closely at the ground, I saw the inescapable miniature white flowers that grew out of cushions. Over the sound of the wind, I heard the cog train hooting from behind the mountain: *HOOOO, HOO HOO HOO hoooo; woo woo woo ha-WOOOO.* The forecast had said afternoon thundershowers were likely, and it was already clouding up around me at a little before nine o'clock. The wind increased, rippling the heads of the grass. In a saddle—the western term for a feature that Yankee understatement has named a lawn, in this case Bigelow Lawn—the wind grew strong enough that I stopped to put on my windbreaker, sheltering behind a big cairn to do so.

Here came hikers: a woman and two teenage girls—her daughters, it developed. Her name was Lily Kosaka, she was forty-two years old, and she lived in Paramus, New Jersey. She said she had met a man the day before who had jogged from Pinkham Notch to the summit. He had inspired her. "This morning," she said, "I try. Only I jogged down from Hermit Shelter to Pinkham Notch and jogged up." Her times were thirty minutes down and forty-five minutes up, she said, and my AMC map says the distance is 2.4 miles each way, the difference in altitude eighteen hundred feet. She didn't look tired, I told her—she must be in very good shape. "Oh, yeah," she said. "I run the marathon a lot."

When she and her daughters had gone on, I had Bigelow Lawn to myself again, with nobody in sight, and I stopped to enjoy it. The wind ripped across the saddle as if it were a breezeway between the two rooms of a frontier cabin, making the grass buck and dance. Lawn, indeed. It was a desolate, thrilling place. With my jacket on and my hat straps tied down, I was comfortable, and for the time I was alone, I felt the timberline effect much as if I had been in Colorado, though without the added exclusiveness that the thin air of high altitude confers. To the west, I could see big mountains with ridges, saddles, and long swoops. To the east, the heights were less; over the profile of the saddle, I could see just the tops of those mountains sticking up. The view had what even my western sensibilities recognized as grandeur.

Wind or no wind, I might have surrendered to a weightless moment like those that had set my responsibilities afloat in other ranges; but those moments depend on solitude, which is hard to find in the East—here came another hiker. He was nineteen, his name was Tom Quinncy, he had driven over that morning from Wells, Maine, he needed to get home by about five that afternoon because it was his girlfriend's birthday, and he had climbed Mount Washington six times before, once in winter, when the ground blizzards were intense and scary. We hiked on together, picking our way among rocks, each of us often helping himself with his hands. By then our route had merged with the Crawford Path. We were in a cloud, and the wind had increased so much that I heard only a little of what he said over his shoulder. He was a biology major at American International College; his father, if I understood correctly, had once skied the headwall at

Tuckerman Ravine—a feat I had read about for years and now, having seen what looked like a sheer drop with water dripping from over-hangs here and there, could hardly believe.

We passed a wooden cross in the fog, the marker of some climber's death; I imagined that it and we and the fog looked like a frame from a British movie in which a stern aunt and a murderer were to play roles. Not long after that, we were on top. A sign said the alti-tude was 6,288 feet. The climb had taken me a shade more than three hours, and the gain in altitude had been more than that of the Mount Evans climb, the most tiring of all these two summers of hikes. I was not tired. Thick air makes the difference.

In the winter, the staffs of the Mount Washington Observatory and the television transmitting operation rotate—a week up, a week down. So I was told by a state park ranger named Ben Miller, work-ing the information counter in the summit house. People brushed past me, carrying sandwiches, soft drinks, children. The crush was about like that of the halls of a high school between classes, though the pace was slower. But Miller said this was a fairly light crowd. A husky fel-low in his late twenties with wavy, blondish hair, he said he stayed from mid-May till the end of the tourist season, three days and two nights in each shift; his wife and golden retriever lived in Jackson. Sometimes he saw furious weather on the summit, but then "there's spells in the summer when the wind won't blow over thirty miles an hour for a week." Thunderstorms were common: "If it's a busy day, it's very exciting because everyone that was outside runs into the building. It's very frightening to be outside up here in a thunder-storm." Now and then, Miller said, you saw a bolt run in a blue arc down the railroad tracks. He said about fifty thousand people a year hiked up the mountain (he may have said forty thousand a little later—the noise kept me from being sure.) About a thousand ran up. The distance was a little shy of eight miles, and the best time was just under an hour, he said. "Colorado runners do well," he said, "because they train at altitude."

The fog had packed the summit house in wool batting. I could see nothing past the window. Having asked permission, I went downstairs to the United States Weather Service observatory and talked with Joel White, a tall meteorologist with a neatly trimmed beard. On the bul-letin board in the observatory was a handwritten quatrain:

They that go up to the peak in ships,
That do business on Great Mountains:
These see the works of the Lord,
And His Wonders on the Height.

After "His" someone had penciled in "/Her." I suggest another change: make the first line end with "shifts." White, who was in his late forties and lived in Shelburne, said his shift began on a Wednesday and ended on the next Wednesday. He liked it, he said— "Every Wednesday is an adventure, either the adventure that you have planned for yourself when you're going down to the valley and you have six days to yourself, or the adventure of being on the summit for a week." He had a son and a daughter; I met the son, who was working in the summit house for the summer.

In the winter, White said, the meteorologists spend a lot of their time keeping ice off their instruments. On winter days as foggy as the day when we talked, everything gets coated with ice. Observers go out at least once an hour to climb the tower and clean off the instruments. It's the only way. "Obviously," White said, "you don't provide heat to your thermometer to keep it de-iced because you wouldn't have a realistic reading." So he and the others put on boots, sometimes with crampons, and as many layers of clothing as necessary—wool or some man-made material such as polypropylene—with a windbreaker on the outside. The layers include lots of overlapping to keep out the wind: gaiters between the boots and the bottom of the pants; gloves with gauntlets to fill the space between sleeves and the tops of gloves; balaclavas under the hoods to cover the neck above the zipper. Face masks and goggles are usually necessary. "It's quite an endeavor to get yourself dressed to go outside," White said.

Though he had a shy way of turning his head to the side and looking at me out of the corner of his eye as he talked, I had the feeling that he enjoyed telling about his work. It is adventurous work, and yet it has an element of scientific discovery. Every six hours, if it appears that there has been precipitation, somebody goes 150 feet from the building to fetch the precipitation can. But the rule isn't firm. "The objective of getting the precipitation can is to get it and you back here safely," White said, "and if you don't feel that that will happen, you postpone it six hours until hopefully the conditions are better." I asked if they used a rope or chain to find their way. "No," he said, "because that in itself is a problem, icing up and pulling away from you or tipping over or whatever." Anyway, he said, the problem isn't so much visibility as wind.

The wind must be a special hazard on the instrument tower, which is like a small lighthouse. The climber, though sheltered most of the way up, has to go out the last door onto the parapet. Then there's a three-rung ladder outside, up to the instruments. I asked White what he chipped the ice off the instruments with. "It's a very sophisticated blunt instrument," he said. "It's just a heavy piece of metal that fits nicely into the hand." When he bangs that against the support of the instrument, the rime ice shatters and falls.

I wanted to know about searches and rescues. Those are legally the responsibility of the Fish and Game Department, he said, and in the summer Mount Washington State Park personnel do them on the summit. When the park closes for the season,

> then we become the sole residents on the summit; we do what
> we can to help. Obviously if someone comes knocking on our
> door and is hypothermic, we'll bring them in and treat them. If
> someone has fallen and has hurt themselves badly skiing in the
> Great Gulf, we'll obviously turn out to help. But we cannot
> leave the station unmanned, and we cannot risk our staff by
> sending them out alone. So if we only have two people here,
> sometimes there's not much we can do other than check the
> immediate summit environs if they're looking for someone, and
> see if we can help them.

White had formerly been with the Appalachian Mountain Club, managing its system of huts, so he knew about mountain safety. He said most people who got into trouble in the White Mountains had misjudged themselves, the mountains, or the weather.

"The weather's pretty hard to judge, isn't it, because it's so very changeable?" I asked. That was just it, he said—the changeability. "And part of the judgment is to be prepared for the worst. There has been a weather station here for over sixty years, and the ruggedness of Mount Washington or above-timberline weather is well known, and it's posted on the bottom on all of the trails coming up to the summit."

He told me about an evacuation he had been involved in. Three young Coast Guardsmen had taken a winter hike through the Zealand Valley, west of Mount Washington, and one had gotten sick. The temperature was well below zero. The others left the sick one with his tent and cooking gear to set up camp and went to get help. "We responded, expecting to find a young person, a man sick to his stomach," White said. "Coming in on the trail—it was after dark by the time we got there—we found a partially clothed individual at the terminal stages of hypothermia—no gloves, no boots, no hat . . . who stopped respiration and breathing as we got there." The rescuers, unable to bring him around, packed his body out. "Here were three people trained by the Coast Guard to recognize hypothermia," White said,

> but their training was for hypothermia in the water. And they just did not make the transfer that that kind of thing could happen on land. And so what we learned from that is, number one, never leave a person until you are sure their camp is set up and they are comfortable and that they can take care of themselves; and when you go out on a rescue, you go out prepared for the worst. It's something that you have to adjust your mind to.

White hikes for pleasure. I asked if he had ever run into weather that made him feel endangered. "I've run into weather bad enough so that I've felt to turn back," he said, "and in fact I think that is one of the most difficult decisions that someone can make." He said there used to be a hut at Edmands Col, a pass between mountains in the Presidential Range to the north of Mount Washington. The Appalachian Mountain Club took it down as an attractive nuisance. "People strove to get to it if they were getting cold or felt that the conditions were getting worse," White said.

> And that would take them just beyond their abilities to cope. They'd get stuck there, they'd be overdue, and then we'd have to find someone, a trusty party to go find where they were. We usually found them at Edmands Col. They were OK. But if Edmands Col hadn't been there, they would not have gone that extra bit to get there, they would have turned around and got back down.

I wasn't sure that removing the shelter made perfect sense, but it is certainly true, and probably truest of all on Mount Washington, that the
way to relief from dangerous weather in the mountains is down, not
up. "There are very few true accidents that happen above timberline,"
White said. "They are mostly problems with judgment calls."

The deaths in the Presidential Range were listed in a display
upstairs. A young Englishman, Frederick Stickland, was the first, in
October 1849. He lost his way down the mountain in a storm. The second death was that of Lizzie Bourne, the twenty-three-year-old daughter of a Kennebunk, Maine, judge. Late in the afternoon of a
mid-September day in 1855, she started up the bridle path with her
uncle and his daughter. "They failed to heed advice to stay the night in
the Halfway House, were caught in high winds, wet clouds, and darkness, and finally sank exhausted and soaking wet not 200 yards from
the top, where unknowing guests were enjoying a cozy and convivial
dinner," the Watermans say in *Forest and Crag* (274). "Unable to rouse
the fallen girl, her uncle improvised a stone windbreak and kept himself
and his daughter alive through the night, but not, alas, poor Lizzie." A
young German, Ewald Weiss, left the summit house on a late-August
day in 1890 to walk to Mount Adams. His body has never been found.

On June 30, 1900, William Curtis and Allan Ormsbee set out to
climb the mountain and attend a field meeting of the Appalachian
Mountain Club on top. Curtis, sixty-two years old, was the founder
of the Fresh Air Club and was a nationally influential booster of ath-
letics. Ormsbee was twenty-eight and, like Curtis, a strong hiker. They
picked a bad day. "The mountain that day was wracked by ferocious
storm," the Watermans say (275-6), "with high winds, low visibility,
and driving rain at lower elevations, rain, sleet, and snow above tree-
line." They went up the Crawford Path, signing registers on peaks to
the south of Mount Washington: Clinton, Eisenhower (then Pleasant),
and Monroe. Just past Mount Pleasant, two descending hikers urged
them to turn back. "Neither of the ascending pair replied; perhaps
even then the storm had weakened their perceptions and responses,"
the Watermans say. Curtis made it a little past Mount Monroe and
died. Ormsbee made it to near the summit of Mount Washington.
Their bodies were found the next day.

"Two stronger hikers could scarcely have been named," Laura
and Guy Waterman say, "yet even they had been unable to survive a

walk up one of the standard hiking trails, in summer. Nothing could have more forcefully called attention to the seriousness of bad weather on Mount Washington." Two others, Paul Zanet and Judy March, died on July 19, 1958, of exposure on the Crawford Path a quarter mile below the summit. He was twenty-four, she seventeen. A pair of crosses marked the places where they died. I imagine that one of them was what I saw as Tom Quinney and I climbed the last pitch to the summit.

Not these, oh friends, but pleasanter tones and more joyful. When I started down, it was so foggy I could hardly see, and when I had gone a few steps down the rock pile, it began raining hard. With the wisdom gained from the drenchings above Diamond Lake and on Mount Evans, I was still wearing khaki pants made mostly of cotton. They immediately became soaked with chilly rain, but I was all right after the first jolt. The footing and the visibility were the problems. They made me nervous. Maybe I was stupid to try hiking under such conditions, I told myself. I walked carefully to keep from slipping, and, unable a lot of the time to see the next cairn, picked my way from rock to rock in what I hoped was the right direction. The tall cairns looked spectral when I found them. I peered at them and tried to decide whether they were really cairns, whether they were anything at all. Now and then hikers, coming up, popped out of the fog four or five steps in front of me. They always asked instantly how far it was to the summit. The last hikers, a couple, had a rather desperate sound, I thought.

But the trail went down, out of the wind, and although a few pellets of sleet had fallen when the rain started, it didn't seem dangerously cold. Shortly the fog began to thin. A young couple in shorts passed me, then slowed; the woman kept stopping and tugging at one of her white, midcalf socks. I lagged behind so as not to seem to intrude. The fog had lifted enough—or I had dropped far enough into its thinner skirts—that I again got a good view of the headwall of Tuckerman Ravine from above. Again I tried to imagine schussing that pitch. You don't ski; you fall; you die. I saw a boulder at the foot of the wall with a red cross painted on it and supposed it marked the site of a skier's death. But at the bottom, I passed a wooden box with emergency supplies inside and a red cross on top; so that must have been the message of the boulder. Then I came to a hut with a sign outside: "Spring skiers should be alert to falling ice in the 'Bowl.'"

In the hut, I talked with the assistant caretaker, Craig Collins, a tall, husky kid, twenty-four years old, wearing a cap with its bill backward. He sat at a desk by the window, which opened toward the headwall, up-slope from us. The couch I sat on was made of twisted wood like krummholz. Collins said skiers did schuss the headwall—he had done it himself—but not where the boulders were. They went down from the lip on the north or chutes on the south side of the cirque. I asked him for stories, and he told me appropriate ones for that mountain: ghost stories.

Years before, he said, the caretaker, Joe Gill, was looking out the window "and saw a guy—what he figured was a guy—halfway up the headwall." The wall at that point was sheer, and it attracted ice climbers. The caretaker didn't pay much attention at first, but when he looked an hour later, the climber hadn't moved. "So he took out his binoculars and looked up and saw him," Collins said, "and the guy, from what he could see, was just kind of kicking in midair. His legs were swinging, and his arms were swinging, but he didn't see any ropes or anything." Gill called Pinkham Notch and decided to go up and have a look. He put on crampons and hiked to where he had seen the climber. No climber was there. And though it was a calm day, no tracks were there, either—no sign that the climber had climbed out. End of story. That one had an honest ring; it did not end with the searcher finding some souvenir on the cliff face—say, a melted patch, still steaming, in the shape of a human being.

Collins told me another. Maybe eighty years before, a person had died about two hundred yards from the summit on the Crawford Path. Well, Joe Gill was walking past the cross (possibly this was the one I saw); it was a cloudy day, but the clouds seemed to pull back and leave a clear space around the cross. Gill used the word by which experienced mountain hands (I was told) refer to unprepared hikers: "He looked at the cross and said, 'Stupid goofer,'" Collins said, "and felt a hand come right up and push him from the front—knocked him on his butt." Thereafter, Collins said, when Gill walked past the cross, he laid off the insensitive remarks.

Then there was a woman named Margaret Thompson who worked a summer at the Lakes of the Clouds Hut on the upper slopes of Mount Washington. She was hiking to the summit to get supplies and, passing the same cross, made the same remark that Gill had made. Same response, only from behind. She landed on her face, getting scratched and bruised. "So now," Collins said, "every time she goes by, she goes under her breath, 'It could happen to anyone, it could happen to anyone.'"

The farther you go down from the top of Mount Washington, the less the habitat seems right for ghosts. On my way again, I fell in with a couple of young men from Berlin who had stopped for a moment. They were touring New England on the way to Montreal, where one was going to work for a while and the other would part ways with him and head back to Germany. After a little, I remarked that I didn't want to hold them up, and they gratefully shot on down the trail. A teenage girl carrying a daypack flitted past me, barely touching the basketball-sized rocks that by now made up most of the trail. I would have been afraid of slipping, though the rain had stopped some time before; I saw blue sky to the north.

My next companion was a small man I overtook; he was stumping down the trail and seemed glad to see someone his age. His name was Harvey Aronson—a retired civil engineer from Oceanside on Long Island. He had hiked out of Gorham for forty years, he said, and had climbed Mount Washington a number of times, though on that day he had stopped a little short of the summit because of the rain and fog. His wife, a botanist and biologist, wasn't a hiker, he said, and so they picked places where she could let him take the car and go climbing while she looked around town or stayed in the motel and read. Aronson gave me a tip about hiking in the fog: if there is more than one in your party, send one ahead to look for the next cairn ("carn," he called it). If he finds it, he calls to you. If he doesn't, you guide him back by voice. He told me about climbing the mountain with his ten-year-old daughter. "She complained continuously, 'Oh, it's boring, why are we going here, let's end it,'" he said. "Now I'll tell you, we got above Hermit Lake and we got to the beautiful, magnificent head-wall, and all of a sudden she loved it, she became a mountain goat."

Aronson and I talked for an hour and a quarter as we walked. We agreed to meet in town for supper later, along with his wife. When I walked across the parking lot to my car, the sun was shining brightly. Even the top of Mount Washington was free of clouds and sharply outlined in the newly washed air. It looked like an easy, inviting climb.

Thursday morning, August 20—the next to the last of my days off work, not counting the weekend. It was cold enough in Gorham that when I left the automatic laundry after washing and drying a load, I was glad to hug the warm clothes against me. Up high, clouds were already hanging over the mountains. I was headed for Vermont, which has few mountains above timberline, and those barely so; but first I had something to do back at Pinkham Notch, the starting and ending place for many east-side climbs of Mount Washington. I sat at an empty family-sized table in the eating area of the visitor center and talked with Tim Coffren, an Appalachian Mountain Club naturalist who has a degree in photography but says his main interest is ancient people. He is an interdisciplinary naturalist. "If you study primitive people," he said, "you have to study all nature sciences because what you're studying is how a person lives, what they talked about, what they did during daily life routines. You've got to know about plants, geology, animals, the environment itself, survival skills."

He was especially interested in the Abenaki, an Algonquin people who had moved from northern New Hampshire to Quebec when early European settlers in New England chased them out. No, he said, they probably hadn't ventured up to timberline, the realm of the gods. But their predecessors might have done so, nine to twelve thousand years ago when the continental glacier still blocked the valleys. The ridges would have been the easiest routes then, he said.

I asked what the weather up there must have been like, considering that it was terrible today and that everything below, back then, was ice. Worse, he said, but the people were used to it. Man, I thought: men, women, babies, old people, and bored ten-year-olds tramping ridges colder and more exposed than the ones that took the lives of Judy and Paul, of Curtis and Ormsbee, and of Lizzie Bourne, with nothing awaiting them below but still worse conditions. Coffren said those people had left hundreds of thousands of artifacts at a site called Square Ledge, forty miles to the north and about 2,000 feet above sea level. And he said charcoal deposits at the mouths of box canyons, along with projectile points embedded in the earth, suggested that the people had herded caribou into the canyons by means of fire and then thrown spears at them from the cliffs above. Nothing had been found in the valleys, under what had been deep ice. I asked if anything had been found in the high country. "Not in quantity," he said, "because we haven't looked up there. That's where we're at now." Coffren, as naturalist, worked with visitors, but he said he hadn't asked backpackers to be on the lookout for artifacts. "When you find a site," he said, striking the same note as the archaeologists in Colorado and California, "the first thing the treasure seekers want to do is raid the site, and we're trying to avoid that."

Before I left the visitor center at the notch, I examined the middens of a later mountain-centered culture. Bulletin boards reflected the passage of hikers, scientists, historians, romantics, and also a few of the disillusioned: I saw notices offering skis, a mountain bike, ski boots ("purple with fluorescent yellow buckles"), and a hardly used pack frame. Someone was looking for people to join in climbs of two or three Mexican volcanoes: "Anyone interested should be in good physical shape, experienced with crampons, mountaineering ax, rope travel and self-arrest." (Self-arrest with an ice ax was what failed to save Paul Fretwell and his friends from falling over the lip of the icy chute on South Arapaho Peak.)

There were ads for trail workers and for caretakers at back-country stations of the Appalachian Mountain Club. A typed notice asked for collaborators on a ski traverse in the St. Elias Mountain Range on the Alaska/Yukon border. Another said, "Appreciated: location of any presently used bat roosts . . . Information to be used as part of graduate thesis studying conservation of bats in New Hampshire." A notice from a masseuse said that massage "improves mobility of muscles and joints." And a hazy photograph looking south from Mount Washington showed "typical summertime photochemical smog." The message with it said that pollutants were carried into the White Mountains from industrial areas to the south and from emissions of automobile engines and coal-burning utilities. On a hazy summer day, it said, the view from the summit may be less than five miles, whereas you ought to be able to see a hundred. And so on—the thumbtacked evidence of a culture that sees nearly as much call to escape to the heights as a tougher people did when the valleys were full of ice, not industry.

CHAPTER THIRTEEN

The Mount Washington hike seemed to have ended my two summers'
vacation-time visits and revisits to timberline. I had set foot on more
or less the tops of all four major ranges, as planned, and now was going
on only to Vermont to interview a noted high-altitude physiologist and
climber in Burlington. (I say "only to Vermont" because Stephen F.
Arno, in his comprehensive *Timberline: Mountain and Arctic Forest
Frontiers,* allows the state no more than "a few acres of timberline vegetation," all of those in the Green Mountains.) But an interim purpose
developed on the road from Mount Washington when I saw that my
route would take me through Franconia, New Hampshire. That was
one of the places where Robert Frost had lived, and his house and
acreage were open to visitors. So I drove in anticipation of that visit,
tapering down from a month spent on, or preparing to be on, or just
having been on, some height too great to encourage bucolic or literary
thoughts. From my car windows, I saw life zones displayed on the
slopes like a retrospective of the country I had hiked through: the light
green of deciduous trees down low, then the more and more apparent
presence of evergreens until the dark predominated, then the visibly
smaller evergreens, then suddenly the lighter shades of the krummholz,
and finally the grays and burnt umbers of the alpine country.

Soon I was in Franconia, where a building designated Old Meeting
House looked so much like itself that I wondered if the name was
ironic, and many of the houses looked as if Manhattan lawyers had
spent fortunes fixing them up to be genuinely rustic. But Frost's house,
on a slope across a valley from ski slopes that had not been developed
when Frost was there, looked exactly like a farmhouse. Behind it was
a poetry trail blazed with poems nailed to trees here and there, a couple

of them presented as written on the spot, which was certainly not the case. Clouds covered the tops of the mountains across the way before I finished the little trail. The view would otherwise have been splendid, but of course Frost wasn't a writer about splendid views. His views, when he looked higher than the treetops, focused on individual mountains, such as the one that he knew was there, though it was night, because of the absence of stars, or the cone-shaped one to which the moon sent down caliperlike rays as if to measure it. Frost enjoyed mountains. He hiked part of the Long Trail through the Green Mountains when it was new, according to Lawrance Thompson's *Robert Frost: The Years of Triumph*. But mountains seldom appear in his poems as inspirational objects. They may serve a particular mood, as in "Were I in Trouble," in which the speaker sees car lights at night coming down a distant mountain where no road should be and feels unaccountably comforted. Otherwise, the reader has to supply any mountainous background he feels necessary behind the white spiders and pasture springs of Frost's close-ups.

I took a quick look at the only room of the Frost house that was open (the others were occupied by the current Frost poet-in-residence), got no particular impression from it except an old-house smell—didn't feel that I was in a shrine—and drove on toward Vermont. Though the creeks in both New Hampshire and Vermont looked like New England trails with water in them, I was surprised at the difference in the landscape otherwise after I crossed the border. (I had until then been only in a corner of Vermont, and that briefly.) Vermont looked more like Frost country than Franconia did (Frost lived in both states at various times). The mountains were gentler than those of New Hampshire. The soft forests along the ridges gave the landscape a strokable look. A mile from the Montpelier exit from Interstate 89, I saw a cone-shaped mountain to the west, and sure enough, a masked sun sent down rays to it in the afternoon haze.

In Burlington the next day, I talked with a man who had known the grandest and harshest of mountains: Dr. Charles S. Houston, the same who had brought Alexander Drummond down from the mountains above Aspen on a toboggan and made in him the first modern diagnosis of high-altitude pulmonary edema. As late as the early 1950s, Houston had been credited with more Asian climbing experience than any other American. He led the first American expedition to

K2 in the Himalayas in 1938 and helped organize an American-British expedition up Nanda Devi, which at 25,600 feet was, he told me, the highest mountain that had then been climbed. In 1953 he, with five other climbers, trying K2 again and failing again, spent a harrowing ten days on a ledge above 25,000 feet, confined to tiny tents by an unceasing blizzard that must have been as severe as any that ever occurred on Mount Washington, at least after the days of the glaciers. During that time, one of the party, Art Gilkey, developed blood clots in both legs, which migrated to his lungs and threatened to kill him. The party, giving up its climb, tried to carry him down the mountain. On a nearly sheer pitch, all five of the comparatively sound climbers fell. Their intertangled ropes saved them. But while treating the injured and trying to set up a new bivouac, they anchored Gilkey to the slope with two ice axes, and he died when the axes tore loose—possibly because of an ice or snowslide, Houston says in his *K2: The Savage Mountain*.

Sitting in Houston's living room, which looks across Lake Champlain to the alpine peaks of the northern Adirondacks in New York, I asked him if he and the others had possessed unusual powers of adjustment to altitude since they spent so much time so high and still were able to plan rationally and make a difficult technical climb down ice and sheer cliffs, part of the time carrying the impossible burden of a stricken companion. Houston must have been a powerful and elastic climber in his youth. He was close to eighty when we talked, a square, compact figure like a blocking back of the single-wing days, and when he wanted to show me a book, he rose from his deep chair and immediately strode across the room for it, rather than standing for a few seconds first to let his leg muscles unstiffen as I, sixteen years younger, had been doing for a decade. He said, well, they were all pretty worn out—they had gone ten days with almost no food and also with very little water because the stoves wouldn't stay lighted. Also, he said, they had been confined to their sleeping bags in the tents all that time, an experience that would weaken anyone, anywhere. He thought their minds must have been affected by the altitude, and yet they read poetry aloud, and they did make rational decisions, specifically about Gilkey and the summit. "We never considered leaving him and going down," he said. "We never thought of going down and coming back to get him. We—the decisions were either [that] one person, notably me, the doctor, would stay with him until he died or until they came back, or we'd all stay with him, or we'd all go down. As time passed, it was quite clear that we were going to all go down."

I'm sure their decision was helped by the reasonable attitude with which they had started the expedition. Houston touched on that attitude after telling me he had just finished, for a British book, two chapters describing his Nanda Devi and K2 expeditions.

It's quite clear from reading the diaries of the other members of the parties, which I have done, that these were adventures for us—they were exciting adventures, they were new, they were fresh, they were exploring—and that the summit would be very nice, and you tried very hard, but it was not what they say today—"Winning isn't everything, it's the only thing"; that wasn't true then.

He said he had tackled that subject in 1990 when he was on an expedition near Nanga Parbat with a British camera crew that was making a film to be called *The Climbers*. "But we were up at 14,000, and I wasn't expressing it very well," he said. "It doesn't look very good on the video, anyway."

Houston knows as well as anyone on earth, I imagine, just how altitude affects people's minds. In World War II, as a young physician with Himalayan climbing experience, he was put in charge of altitude-training units for naval fliers, his work culminating after the war in an experiment called Operation Everest, during which, over a period of four weeks, four men were taken in a pressure chamber to the equivalent of the top of Mount Everest. One could say that the experiment demonstrated that a man could survive on the summit of Everest without supplementary oxygen, he said. The experiment also demonstrated to the observers, who were in effect standing at sea level and talking to men 29,000 feet up, the extent to which the mind and body are affected by altitude. "It's impressive how impaired they are, although they're not aware of it," Houston said.

I remembered that in *K2: The Savage Mountain*, he had said (page 24) that pleasure in being in high places arose from the beauty of the air, the lure of discovery, the physical challenge, the danger, and, more important than any of those, the chance to break free of everyday concerns and confront the basics of existence. Had he felt the same way even on the 1953 expedition, when he had had to make decisions and take responsibility? No question, he said. True, on the 1938 expedition it had taken thirty-three days of walking to get to the mountain, and the only access to the outside world was by runner. In 1953 the isolation still existed, though the party had a radio on which it could occasionally hear news from outside. "But I think it's more refined than just being away from things," Houston said. "It's what Tillman [Bill Tillman, the British mountaineer] said: we were united by a common purpose and joined by a single hope. And it's—you're able to focus on one goal, one point in space and time that you want to achieve."

I asked if the physiological effects of altitude had a part in the exhilaration that some of us felt up high. He wasn't sure he could answer that, he said; lack of oxygen was like drinking,

> and when you're up there for a long time, there's certainly no question but, until you get up above twenty or twenty-two thousand feet, there are moments of such extraordinary beauty and clarity, and you feel so great. Yes, there is a tremendous exhilaration. Once you get above twenty-two thousand feet, though, it is a chore. Everything is hard. And the moments of beauty and joy are few and short. On a summit, yes, there is great exhilaration. [But] I've always suspected that people who are on top of Everest and K2 and tell you how wonderful they felt are probably wishfully thinking.

The last time he had climbed, he said, was on that 1990 expedition to Nanga Parbat with the BBC. It was, he said,

> a pretty rough trip. I flew over to Rawalpindi and flew up to Gilgit and took a bus to the roadhead, and then we walked for a week—I guess it was only five days, but it was steep, it was long, it was hard; the road was rough, and it was hotter than hell. We had a terrible trekking company; we had very poor food, very little food, bad water; we pushed hard—the whole trekking arrangement was, I thought, outrageous . . . But we finally got to 14,000 feet, where we stayed for a couple of days while they did the filming and the interviews. A beautiful, beautiful place. And then we came home. For me it was a rough trip. I had my seventy-seventh birthday there. It was pushing it for me.

I asked if, in spite of the hardships, he had still appreciated the beauty. Yes, he said:

> We did walk for eight, nine hours a day without enough food or water, and I still got enormous excitement of being back in that wild and wonderful country. Most of the day I spent just putting one foot in front of the other and just getting there, but whenever I could stop and look around, I loved it. When you got to base camp, it was difficult for two reasons. First, this beautiful meadow was strewn with the garbage of twenty expeditions, acres and acres of trash, and we spent a lot of time picking that up and swearing about it. And the other reason—two other reasons were—everybody came down with diarrhea at some point, and I got mine at base camp. It turned out to be giardia. And the third reason was that as we approached base camp, I realized I was beginning to get pulmonary edema. And so I thought, here we are at thirteen, fourteen thousand feet, I know I've got pulmonary edema, what am I gonna do, blah-blah-blah-blah-blah, I can't very well go down; have come here to do a job. So I stayed, but I didn't feel very good while I was there.

I asked if he had used oxygen. There wasn't any, he said, though he did take some Diamox, which helped a little. He would have known when his condition became dangerous enough that he had to go back down, he said. So he stayed. "Then on the way down," he said, "when I was going downhill and feeling better—lost ten pounds from diarrhea and all that—it still was enormously exhilarating, enormously exhilarating."

It encouraged as well as awed me that he had been able to take a Teddy Rooseveltian delight in his surroundings under those conditions at that age. He told me about an experiment he was about to conduct at Vail, Colorado, altitude 8,300 feet, with a group of 250 people between the ages of sixty-five and eighty-three, to determine whether old people, as he suspected, tolerate altitude better than young ones. Twenty-three of the group were being studied in Dallas at the time I interviewed him. They would be tested again after going to Vail. "That will give us the first-ever comparison of a carefully studied group of older people at sea level and at altitude," he said.

A few months later, after the experiment at Vail was over, he gave me the general conclusions by phone: whereas after going to that altitude from sea level more than 20 percent of the population of all ages would develop the symptoms of acute mountain sickness—headache, shortness of breath, nausea, weakness—only about 10 percent of the group of old people had done so. He said he didn't know what accounted for the difference. The people tested, he said, were in slightly better condition than the average older American but otherwise similar. Twenty-seven percent had a history of heart disease, 37 percent had high blood pressure, and 16 percent (this figure was below the national average) smoked.

I told him about observing a VO_2 max, the test given to the young men on top of Pikes Peak. The test measures the greatest amount of work you can do—the point at which you can't absorb any more oxygen. "It's a measure of acute exertion," Houston said, "and some of us challenge its applicability because it has nothing to do with the way a person climbs, which is, you *never* go to your max."

"If you were going to determine what a person could normally do," I said, "you'd have to figure out what kind of guts he had, isn't that right?"

He replied,

Now you've put your finger on the very nub of it, and that is that—as Hornbein [T. R. Hornbein, a high-altitude physiologist] has said repeatedly, and I couldn't agree more—in the last analysis, the body may reach a point where it can go no further, but the brain drives it on, the spirit drives it on. And some of the people who have done extraordinary climbs have gone beyond human capability because they have the heart and spirit to try, or you can call it "the insanity." And some of the things that people have done at very great altitude come very close to insane. There are several people, I know, who have just blindly kept going when they couldn't and have died.

I had stayed too long, and I got up to leave. When Houston opened the door for me, he looked out at the blue sky and the lake with the Adirondacks behind. "Wow!" he said. "Beautiful!"

I was on the way to Boston and the airport and home, but first there was Vermont to go through and part of New Hampshire. I headed south on State Highway 100 at the foot of mountains as caressable as stuffed toys. The valley farms had an unkempt, lived-in look. They tempted me to stop and wander through the weeds and grass and get lost in the woods. But I drove till I found a big barn of a motel in Waitsfield, where I asked, checking in, if there was a small mountain that I could climb in what was left of the afternoon.

That was how I found myself on the trail to Mount Abraham, altitude 4,052 feet. My starting point was Lincoln Gap, altitude 2,424 feet, and the distance to the summit, according to a sign, was 2.6 miles. I was setting out at 3:23 P.M.—an unthinkable hour, in most mountains, to be heading up a trail to a summit above timberline. But in the first ten minutes, I met at least ten hikers of various ages and styles coming down and, a little later, a party of fourteen, half of them children, plus three dogs. It was a sunny day with speckled shade on the trail. People expressed enthusiasm about conditions on top. "Beautiful view," a couple of them said. The trail had steps cut into it, with log reinforcements. In between rocks and logs, the earth was soggy. Sometimes the rocks were stratified, the damp ridges pointing almost straight downtrail—a little slippery. Sometimes there was a wet log to step on, and to minimize slips I put my foot flat and kept my ankle stiff like a knuckle-baller's wrist. It was a trail that fit the New England mode enough that it would have caused dismay in Colorado, but it was not nearly as hard as those on Katahdin or Mount Washington. The woods gradually became mostly evergreen. Already most of the trees were small. I could hardly believe that the little bit of altitude was throttling down the greenery so soon. This was just, as it were, a before-dinner walk.

Another walker appeared from a trail coming up on my right. He looked exactly in place—a farmer if I ever saw one. One of Frost's farmers, in fact. He was portly, gray haired and blue eyed, older than I, and wearing a long-sleeved work shirt like mine and farm pants, not hiking ones. He stopped, and I stopped. He wasn't going to the top, he said— "That's for another day." He lived in North Carolina, was an old Vermont hand, and had taught French and Spanish at Mississippi University for Women. His name was Blair Latshaw. He liked Frost, but it was too bad, wasn't it, those revelations about his character? (He meant the ones in the Thompson biography.) He used to hike in the Presidential Range in New Hampshire, carrying cornmeal, oatmeal, flour, and the like in a pack weighing fifty-five or sixty pounds. "When I see some of these guys hiking nowadays, carrying twenty, twenty-five pounds, you know, I figure 'Judas priest,'" he said. He had just returned from a five-day course in conversational Scottish Gaelic in Nova Scotia. He owned a self-instruction book on Welsh. He would not tell me how old he was or how long ago he had retired. We had a good talk, most of it not about mountains, and then we went our ways, the Literate Farmer and I. It was fitting that a character out of a Frost poem had walked up from the valley and turned onto that highland trail.

The trees began to look distinctly stunted. The woods were floored with green cushiony growth that covered the ground, rocks, logs, everything, in a way I had never before seen in the mountains, as if this were a rain forest—a dwarf rain forest. Two family groups with small children met me, one of them with a young German shepherd. I climbed on, and my right ear, surprisingly, crackled from the altitude. The trail became an arroyo with a nearly solid bed of pink stone. Over the tops of the increasingly shrunken evergreens I saw valleys and ridges, with cloud shadows on the timbered slopes just across the way.

On the last fairly steep pitch, the plane of the treetops zoomed downward like a hairline tapered with a razor. The tops were five feet high, then four, then three, and suddenly I was out of the trees and right there was the summit, a low rock dome. I stepped out on it, scarcely climbing anymore, and saw that I had it all to myself, though I had met thirty or more hikers on my way up. It was two minutes after five o'clock. My climb to timberline had taken an hour and thirty-nine minutes.

I stood at the edge of the flattened dome and saw a remarkable sight below, considering that I was above timberline. It was not crags and couloirs and sweeps of empty tundra. It was people's rural lives: green land cut into homey plots amid the trees, with white houses on the plots and a silo sticking up in the distance. There were mountains on the western, eastern, southern, and southeastern horizons, but my view up close was all farms and pastures and woods. It was a kind of merging I had never before observed from above: of timberline country with farms on which Frost's neighbors might have lived. In fact, Frost had had a cottage for years near Ripton, twelve miles south down the chain of the Green Mountains. His hike on the Long Trail had taken him as far north as Lincoln Gap, where I had parked and started my hike north. I stood in a light breeze and wondered at the harmony of a summit above timberline with a display of farms so close I could almost have seen a man or woman walking between the house and the barn to do the milking (true, some of those being milked down there were not cows but tourists) or heading out to the pasture to clean the spring.

The little summit was like a modest pink ring stone barely rising out of the filigree setting of the krummholz. No doubt it had less domestic moods—it was close enough to Mount Washington to suffer some of the same assaults of wind and fog, I felt sure—but it was hard to imagine them just then. And though I was alone for the moment, I felt none of the slipping away from duty, the canceling of time, that had come over me elsewhere. You couldn't stand on Mount Abraham on that clear day and unbuckle yourself from the world; the world was right at your feet, getting ready to do the evening chores. It was a delightful meeting of high and low, a place where it would be possible to live an honest life in the valley, sometimes too honest for comfort, and also to climb away from that life at clearly earned intervals and in scarcely any time be standing amid a plot of timberline country no bigger than a back pasture. Why hadn't I been born a Vermonter?—But if I had, and had grown up in the rocky tradition of those farms, the chances are that I would no more have thought of climbing a mountain for the sake of climbing it than Frost's farmer in "The Mountain": it wouldn't have seemed real. Certainly I couldn't have thrown over the chores and lost myself amid the heights like a Green Mountain Muir, even if I had wanted to do so. There were too few heights and too many hikers.

At almost 5:30, a man came up with two little boys. He put down his pack and got out jackets for them. The wind had risen and was hissing through the krummholz. I talked with the man for a couple of minutes and started down. In about a minute, I was below timberline. It was 6:47 when I clumped across the road to my car. I had been gone less than three and a half hours.

On the road to Boston the next day, and on the plane to Wichita, I reflected on Katahdin, Mount Washington, and Mount Abraham and on the climbs in the Sierra Nevada and the Cascades. I had been on top of three great ranges in a month, and except for a thirsty day in the eastern Cascades and the burning in my kneecaps from jouncing down those ranges, it had been a worthwhile revival, with the inevitable changes, of my more youthful experiences. Now I was feeling the glumness that had invaded my stomach ever since childhood when I had to come down from the mountains and head home. There was no question about the returning, though. My hiking vacations had not modified my going-to-work gene.

A few weeks later, I went to the mountains again. My wife and I took a long weekend and drove to Colorado. At the top of the Trail Ridge Road in Rocky Mountain National Park, I parked and walked a half mile or so on a paved trail across the tundra in a chilly, exhilarating gale just so I could say I had walked above the timberlines of all four ranges in the same year. The next day was a Sunday, and since both of us had to be at work Monday morning, we drove down the mountains and across the plains, a ten-hour trip home, much of it again through a dust storm. But when we pulled into Wichita and saw the haze around the downtown buildings, I was several hours past the glum stage and felt almost content as I contemplated the next day's schedule.

GLOSSARY

Alpenglow: Properly, sunlight that glows on mountains before sunrise or after sunset.

Alpenstock: A staff or stick (or dead tree branch) used as a help in walking.

Alpine tundra: The treeless land above the krummholz line.

Arroyo: A dry streambed; a gully.

Cairn: A guidepost or marker made of piled-up rocks.

Coney: A small animal that inhabits rock slides near timberline. It has round ears and no tail. Also called a *pika*.

Couloir: A steep, narrow gash on a mountainside.

Crampons: Long spikes buckled onto boots for ice climbing.

Escarpment: A steep and usually extensive slope.

Gendarme: An exposed pinnacle of rock.

Graupel: White ice particles that look like snow and are softer than hail.

High-altitude pulmonary edema (HAPE): A serious altitude illness affecting some people who go above 9,000 feet, especially if the climb is rapid. Symptoms may include shortness of breath, an often-bubbly cough, weakness, headache, and stupor. Some people die of HAPE.

Hypoxia: The effect on the body of getting too little oxygen.

Krummholz: Literally, "crooked wood." The gnarled, stunted trees that grow between the upper limit of forests and the alpine tundra.

Krummholz line: The level above which krummholz cannot grow.

Marmot: A mountain woodchuck, with regional variations.

Mountain sickness: A condition that affects some people above the 7,000-foot level. The symptoms are headache, nausea, troubled sleep, and shortness of breath.

Ouzel: A "dipper"—a bird that forages in mountain streams. Hikers see ouzels standing on rocks and doing knee bends. John Muir wrote an essay about ouzels (reprinted in *South of Yosemite*).

Pika: See *coney.*

Piton: A spike that a mountain climber drives into a wedge in a rocky face. It has a metal ring (a carabiner) into which a rope can be snapped.

Ringtail: A cacomistle. Also called a ring-tailed cat. It looks like a small, big-eared, big-eyed, long-tailed raccoon and likes dry, rough, southwestern country.

Switchback: The apex of a hairpin turn on a trail.

Timberline: The level above which forests do not grow. In this book, the term is often used loosely to include not just that level but everything above it.

Wrist-Rocket: A powerful commercial slingshot.

BIBLIOGRAPHY

Appalachian Mountain Club. *AMC White Mountain Guide*. 24th ed. Boston: Appalachian Mountain Club, 1987.

Arno, Stephen F. *Timberline: Mountain and Arctic Forest Frontiers*. Seattle: The Mountaineers, 1984.

Ballenger, Walter. "Avalanche! A Memoir of Survival in Mineral King, California." *Quest 79*, February–March 1979, 49.

Benedict, James B. "Footprints in the Snow: High-Altitude Cultural Ecology of the Colorado Front Range, U.S.A." *Arctic and Alpine Research* 24, no. 1 (1992):1–16.

Bettinger, Robert L. "Aboriginal Occupation at High Altitude: Alpine Villages in the White Mountains of Eastern California." *American Anthropologist* 93 (1991): 656–79.

Brown, Bolton Coit. "Wanderings in the High Sierra between Mt. King and Mt. Williamson." Part 1. *Sierra Club Bulletin* 2 (1897–99): 17–28.

Browning, Peter. "Mickey Mouse in the Mountains." *Harper's Magazine* 244, no. 1462 (March 1972): 65–71.

Cassells, E. Steve. *The Archaeology of Colorado*. Boulder: Johnson Publishing Co., 1983.

Chapman, Joseph A., and George A. Feldhamer, eds. *Wild Mammals of North America: Biology, Management, and Economics*. Baltimore: The Johns Hopkins University Press, 1982.

Clark, Stephen. *Katahdin*. Unity, Maine: North Country Press, 1985.

Craighead, John J.; Frank C. Craighead, Jr.; and Ray J. Davis, eds. *A Field Guide to Rocky Mountain Wildflowers*. Cambridge, Mass.: The Riverside Press, 1963.

Echevarría, Evelio. "The Inca Mountaineers: 1400–1800." In *The Mountain Spirit*, edited by Michael Charles Tobias and Harold Drasdo, 115–24. Woodstock, N. Y.: The Overlook Press, 1979.

Farquahr, Francis. "Sierra Club Then and Now." In *Voices for the Earth: A Treasury of the Sierra Club Bulletin, 1893–1977*, edited by Ann Gilliam, 48–53. San Francisco: Sierra Club Books, 1979.

Folsom, Franklin, and Mary Elting Folsom. *America's Ancient Treasures: A Guide to Archeological Sites and Museums in the United States and Canada*. 3rd ed. Albuquerque: University of New Mexico Press, 1983.

Ford, Herbert A. Extracts from diary, 23 October 1879–January 1882. Department of Western History, Denver Public Library.

Gibson, Bill. "History of the Great Sierra Consolidated Silver Company." Manuscript, 17 January 1964, Yosemite Museum Research Library, Yosemite National Park.

Gilliam, Harold. "Norman Clyde: Old Man of the Mountains." In *Voices for the Earth: A Treasury of the Sierra Club Bulletin, 1893–1977,* edited by Ann Gilliam, 74–77. San Francisco, Sierra Club Books, 1979.

Hano, Arnold. "Protectionists vs. Recreationists—The Battle of Mineral King." *The New York Times Magazine*, 17 August 1969, 24–66.

Houston, Charles S. "Acclimatization." In *Hypoxia: Man at Altitude*, by John R. Sutton, Norman L. Jones, and Charles S. Houston, 158–60. New York: Thieme-Stratton, 1982.

———. "Acute Pulmonary Edema of High Altitude." *The New England Journal of Medicine* 263, no. 10 (8 September 1960): 478–80.

———. "Oxygen Lack at High Altitude: A Mountaineer's Problem." In *Hypoxia: Man at Altitude*, by John R. Sutton, Norman L. Jones, and Charles S. Houston, 156–57. New York: Thieme-Stratton, 1982.

Houston, Charles S., and Robert H. Bates. *K2: The Savage Mountain*. New York: McGraw-Hill, 1954.

Houston, Charles S., R.C. Roach, B. Honigman, R.A. Nicholas, M. Yaron, C.K. Grissom, J.K. Alexander, and H.N. Hultgren. "How Well Do Older Persons Tolerate Moderate Altitude?" *Western Journal of Medicine* 162, no. 1 (January 1995): 32–36.

King, Clarence. *Mountaineering in the Sierra Nevada*. New York: 1871. Reprint, W. W. Norton and Company, 1935.

Miles, John C. *Koma Kulshan*. Seattle: The Mountaineers, 1984.

Muir, John. *The Mountains of California*. New York: The American Museum of Natural History and Anchor Books, 1961.

———. *South of Yosemite: Selected Writings of John Muir*. Edited by Frederic R. Gunsky. Garden City, N.Y.: The Natural History Press, 1968.

Ormes, Robert M. *Guide to the Colorado Mountains*. 8th ed. Denver: Mountain West Printing and Publishing, 1986.

Prescott, William Hickling. *The History of the Conquest of Mexico*. The Modern Library. New York: Random House, n.d.

Reinhard, Johan. "Sacred Peaks of the Andes." *National Geographic* 181, no. 3 (March 1992), 84–111.

Rhoda, Franklin. "Report on the Topography of the San Juan Country." In *Annual Report of the United States Geological and Geographical Survey of the Territories, Embracing Colorado and Parts of Adjacent Territories: Being a Report of the Progress of the Exploration for the year 1874*, 451–96. Washington, D.C.: Government Printing Office, 1876.

Sierra Club v. Morton, 92 S. Ct. 1361 (1972).

Smith, Dwight. *Above Timberline: A Wildlife Biologist's Rocky Mountain Journal*. Edited by Alan Anderson, Jr. New York: Alfred A. Knopf, 1981.

Storer, Tracy I., and Robert L. Usinger. *Sierra Nevada Natural History: An Illustrated Handbook*. Berkeley and Los Angeles: University of California Press, 1964.

Sutton, J. R., Norman L. Jones, and Charles S. Houston. *Hypoxia: Man at Altitude*. New York: Thieme-Stratton, 1982.

Thompson, Lawrance. *Robert Frost: The Years of Triumph, 1915–1938*. New York: Holt, Rinehart and Winston, 1970.

Thoreau, Henry David. *Thoreau in the Mountains: Writings by Henry David Thoreau*. Commentary by William Howarth. New York: Farrar, Straus and Giroux, 1982.

Tobias, Michael Charles, and Harold Drasdo, eds. *The Mountain Spirit*. Woodstock, N.Y.: The Overlook Press, 1979.

Turner, Tom. *Sierra Club: 100 Years of Protecting Nature*. New York: Harry N. Abrams, 1991.

Waring, James J. "High Altitudes: Effects and After-Effects of Residence at Moderate and Great Heights." *Journal of the Outdoor Life* 29, no. 6 (June 1932): 342.

Waterman, Laura, and Guy Waterman. *Forest and Crag: A History of Hiking, Trail Blazing, and Adventure in the Northeast Mountains*. Boston: Appalachian Mountain Club, 1989.

West, John B. *Everest: The Testing Place*. New York: McGraw-Hill, 1985.

Whitney, Stephen. *A Sierra Club Naturalist's Guide to the Sierra Nevada*. San Francisco: Sierra Club Books, 1979.

Wickstrom, C. Kristina Roper. "Spatial and Temporal Characteristics of High Altitude Site Patterning in the Southern Sierra Nevada." In *There Grows a Green Tree: Papers in Honor of David A. Fredrickson*, edited by G. White, P. Mikkelsen, W.R. Hildebrandt, and M.E. Basgall, 285–302. Davis, Calif.: Center for Archaeological Research, 1993.

INDEX

218

Skagit tribe. *See under* Indians
Skiing (*see also* Mineral King Valley,
    Disney proposal), 41–44, 48, 49,
    118, 119, 120, 130, 180
Smith, Dwight, 26
smog, 128, 129–30, 132, 201
snowslides (*see also* Mineral King
    Valley, snowslides in), 148,
    149–50
South Lake, 99
Spokane, Wash., 144, 155
Spokesman-Review, The, 155
spruce, Engelmann, 16, 80
Squaw Valley, Calif., 135, 137, 138
Stahale Arm, 151, 163
Stahale Glacier, 152, 153
stairs, training on, 4, 69, 126
Stanford, Mount, 89
Stanford University, 100
Stevens Pass, 159, 162
Stickland, Frederick, 196
Summit Lake, 64
switchbacks, cutting across, 76; lack
    of on Katahdin trails, 186

Taylor, Helon, 183
Testerman, Mort, 88
Testerman, Sandy, 88
Texas Panhandle, 123
Thompson, Margaret, 198–99
Thoreau, Henry David, 44, 176,
    179, 180, 188
Three Rivers, Calif., 117, 137
timberline (*see also* altitude, high;
    Indians; krummholz; Vermont):
    altitudes of, 6, 7, 37, 209; appeal
    of, 5, 15, 84, 180; in Cascades,
    156, 161; cause of, 3; characteris-
    tics of, 3; in contiguous forty-eight
    states, 5; lower, 145; in northern
    Appalachians, 174, 184, 185, 211;
    on peace march, 58; serenity above,
    24–25, 105, 131–32, 154, 191,
    211; in Sierra Nevada, 70, 99, 103,

104, 127; skiing above, 48, 128;
    wind above, 6, 111, 112, 115
Tioga Lake, 105, 107, 108, 116
Tioga Pass, 73, 101, 107, 112
Torreys Peak, 59
treasure hunters and vandals, 54, 77,
    201
Triple Falls, 95
trout, 39–40, 73, 75–76, 78, 91, 108,
    114, 115, 116
Truckee, Calif., 138
tundra, alpine. *See* altitude, high;
    timberline
Tuolumne Meadows, 103
Tweed, William, 119, 122, 135
Tyndall, Mount, 97

U. S. Forest Service, 55, 56, 84, 107,
    116, 119, 121, 136, 147, 156,
    159
U. S. Geological Survey, 100; maps,
    10, 112; marker, 162

Vaughan, Tyson, 33, 35
vegetation, alpine (*see also* flowers,
    mountain): damage by hikers,
    25–26, 60, 77, 82, 126–27,
    162–63, 164–65, 180; damage by
    mining, 61; damage by oil
    drilling, 61; footgear to avoid
    harming, 164–65; sparseness on
    Katahdin, 182
Vermont, 202, 203, 208–12
Vidette Meadows, 91
Visalia, Calif., 117, 139
Vittands, John, 102–3
VO$_2$ max, 33, 34, 208

Waitsfield, Vt., 209
Wallowa Mountains, 5
Ward, Colo., 46, 47–48, 52
Washington, Mount, 187–200; alti-
    tude of, 192; Bigelow Lawn on,
    190, 191; Boott Spur Trail to,